Surviving the Special Educational Needs System

of related interest

Asperger's Syndrome
A Guide for Parents and Professionals
Tony Attwood
Foreword by Lorna Wing
ISBN 1 85302 577 1

Parent to Parent
Information and Inspiration for Parents Dealing with Autism
or Asperger's Syndrome
Ann Boushéy
ISBN 1 84310 774 0

Understanding Autism Spectrum Disorders
Frequently Asked Questions
Diane Yapko
ISBN 1 84310 756 2

Getting Services for your Child on the Autism Spectrum
DeAnn Hyatt-Foley and Matthew G. Foley
ISBN 1 85302 914 9

Dyslexia
How Would I Cope? 3rd edition
Michael Ryden
ISBN 1 85302 385 X

Practical Strategies for Living with Dyslexia
Maria Chivers
ISBN 1 85302 905 X

Surviving the Special Educational Needs System
How to be a 'Velvet Bulldozer'

Sandy Row

Jessica Kingsley Publishers
London and Philadelphia

First published in 2005
by Jessica Kingsley Publishers
116 Pentonville Road
London N1 9JB, UK
and
400 Market Street, Suite 400
Philadelphia, PA 19106, USA
www.jkp.com

Copyright © Sandy Row 2005

Library of Congress Cataloging in Publication Data
Row, Sandy.
    Surviving the special educational needs system : how to be a "velvet bulldozer" / Sandy Row.
        p. cm.
    Includes bibliographical references.
    ISBN 1-84310-262-5 (pbk.)
    1. Children with disabilities--Great Britain. 2. Children with disabilities--Great Britain--Identification. 3. Special education--Great Britain . I. Title.
        LC4706.G7R69 2004
        371.9'0941--dc22

                                                            2004013633

British Library Cataloguing in Publication Data
A CIP catalogue record for this book is available from the British Library

ISBN-13: 978 1 84310 262 5
ISBN-10: 1 84310 262 5

Printed and Bound in Great Britain by
Athenaeum Press, Gateshead, Tyne and Wear

This book is dedicated to my wonderful
and very long-suffering husband who sometimes 'didn't recognize'
me but somehow, incredibly and against the odds, through it all
kept on loving me – thanks for the neck massages, IT help,
and toasted cheese sandwiches too!

It is also dedicated to my exceptional children with love from their
Mummy. Knowing you all has changed my life in many ways.

Also to the memory of my late parents, John and Vera,
who passed on to me a desire for justice, an ingrained distaste for
bullies and a tenacity that has astonished many,
including, and especially, myself!

Many of life's failures are people who did not realize how close they were to success when they gave up.

Thomas A. Edison

Contents

Acknowledgements

My thanks go to all those who have unfailingly supported us through the most difficult of times; to our wonderful families (you all know who you are and I love you all) without whose love and concern I think we'd have sunk long ago and to our loyal friends who've shared laughter, tears, triumphs and disasters.

I want to convey my thanks and respect to that remarkable band of people, parents and unpaid carers, who've given me everything they could spare in terms of time, encouragement and love, as it was all they were able to give. It was the 'widow's might' (all they could give they gave) and very much appreciated.

We are privileged, however, to have met some amazing people who went the 'extra mile' for our family and who showed faith in us when things were so bleak: Paul Mayhew (and all the Cruckton team), Claire Franklin, Debbie Halder, Isobel Brookfield, Dame Steve Shirley, Professor Colin Terrell, our 'angel' Chris, Dr Richard Cook, supporters and volunteers at the NAS, Autism West Midlands, Peter Hoskin, Mick Bates, A.M. Bryn and Julie, Sandra, Felix, Beverly, and all the house parents and co-workers at Coleg Elidyr, Mr and Mrs Kendall (and staff) at Derwen College, and Mr Seymour and the staff at St David's College, helpful friends from Swanwick, dear brave Gizzie who christened me the 'velvet bulldozer', the AWF, Adoption UK, Jessica Kingsley and all at JKP for believing in me, Mike Cromei, Eagle House and all in the RNA. Our faithful dogs and cats for late night cuddles at the computer.

You were all wonderful, thank you, and if I've forgotten to mention you by name please forgive me as you know I'm a bit of a basket case now.

God bless all the above and all 'carers' everywhere.

Introduction

Why you need to read this book

Does your child have:

- dyslexia?
- dyspraxia?
- ADHD?
- ADD?
- autism (ASD)?
- Asperger's syndrome?
- Fragile X or other chromosomal disorder?
- hearing problems?
- sight problems?
- physical problems?
- learning problems?

or is in some other way disadvantaged so he or she needs extra help to cope with mainstream schooling?

If so, you will need to plot a course through the special educational needs system. This is often very tricky indeed and can be very isolating. There is a legal process that *must* be followed if you want to try to achieve your aims. We learned this piece of wisdom very late and to our cost.

We want to enlighten you as to your legal rights in all this. Sometimes those in authority will 'forget' to tell you about your rights and you and your child are then at a huge disadvantage.

Definition of special educational needs

Children have special educational needs if they have a learning difficulty which calls for special educational provision to be made for them.

Children have a learning difficulty if they:

(a)   have a significantly greater difficulty in learning than the majority of children of the same age

(b)   have a disability which prevents or hinders them from making use of educational facilities of a kind generally provided for children of the same age in schools within the area of the local education authority

(c)   are under compulsory school age and fall within the definition at (a) or (b) above or would so do if special educational provision was not made for them.

Special educational provision means:

(a)   for children of two or over, educational provision which is additional to, or otherwise different from, the educational provision made generally for children of their age in schools maintained by the LEA, other than special schools, in the area

(b)   for children under two educational provision of any kind.

(Section 312, Education Act 1996)

I was asked the other day what would be on my 'wish list'. I wished that I could have been given a book thirteen years ago (that was when we adopted and unwittingly entered the twilight zone of special educational needs) that contained the knowledge that I have now. It would have saved our children, and us, years of difficulty and heartache. I genuinely hope that this book realizes one of your wishes too and helps you to avoid some of the elephant pits into which we fell.

This practical survival guide, written with genuine empathy and warmth with a dash of humour, will, I hope, help you through the quagmire of jargon and personalities you will encounter on your journey through the parallel world of special educational needs to a successful and happy outcome for your child.

You may think you haven't the time to read yet another book when all you want is to *get help*. But I urge you to read on so that you can learn from our mistakes. You should be able to achieve far more, and in a much shorter time, than us, as we stumbled around the system trying desperately to get assistance and being thwarted.

I have tried to write this book in the order I think would be most helpful. I might have got this wrong, however: it might be helpful if you start off by reading what happened to our children (Chapters 8 to 13).

For ease of reference – I know how busy you are with your children – I have tried to break the book down into manageable chunks so that you can dip in to find the piece of information that is relevant to where you are right now on your particular journey. I've waded through so much legal stuff that sometimes I've forgotten what I was looking for in the first place! The chapters which are specifically about my children are long but I hope you'll forgive me. There was a lot to tell!

There are other books out there. They will tell you what *should* happen under the rules of the system. The difference with this book is that it tells you what *really* happens.

Maybe something we say might 'ring a bell' with you. You may recognize certain behaviours or problems. I want to inspire you because I am so pleased to tell you that as I write this book our older children are doing really well now. After all their traumas they are experiencing some happiness and success. Now that they are receiving the correct help they are busy and productive in their own ways.

My daughter Alice is now nearly twenty and, although still emotionally wobbly, is doing so well. The older boys are happily working their socks off in their various colleges and schools. We are still investigating the extent of our youngest son Jack's difficulties but it is likely that he will have to move to a more supported educational placement. All this hard work was worthwhile and I do so hope that my advice will help you and your children.

We had such a miserable time. I want to show you what is possible, against all the odds.

The stress of the continual fight with authority, added to the strain of actually caring for your special needs child, is enormous and should not be overlooked.

Realizing you need help is a hard step to take, as it involves an element of admission of failure on your part (although in reality you have certainly not failed!). However, *getting* help is often much harder.

The divorce rate for couples with special needs children is allegedly twice the national average. This is a tragic and alarming statistic, but

Jargon busting and understanding short forms

I'm not including this in an index at the back. You need this information before you start this book. People in the SEN world use a bewildering range of language and short forms so it needs to be at the front where you will notice it. See, I've just done it. SEN = special educational needs.

You have to get used to this as you will no doubt have to go to meetings and enter into correspondence. I hope that this section de- mystifies the language for you so that you no longer feel at a disadvantage.

One of our friends went to a council meeting where the 'Ed Psych' was mentioned throughout. At the end one of the councillors asked: 'Which one was Ed Sike?'

For example:

LEA	local education authority
SEN	special educational needs
ASD	autistic spectrum disorder
LD	learning difficulties
SENDIST	special educational needs and disability tribunal
SN	special needs
NAS	National Autistic Society.

When you enter the world of SEN, you will suddenly be introduced to a huge range of characters who are vitally important in your child's life and they will usually be referred to in some shortened form.

For example:

SENCO	special educational needs coordinator
EP	educational psychologist (sometimes 'Ed Psych')
PEP	principal educational psychologist
SALT	speech and language therapist
SS	Social Services
CDT	Children with Disabilities Team, part of Social Services

ADT   Adults with Disabilities Team, part of Social Services

Natspec   the Association of National Specialist Colleges.

Important 'buzz words' to remember: 'appropriate' and 'best value'. 'Multi-agency' may also be mentioned. This refers to occasions, for example, when representatives of Health, Education and Social Services (or some of these three) may come together to discuss your child, or act on your child's behalf.

So there we are, and if I slip into short forms just think of my tired little fingers typing this and please forgive me.

hardly surprising. Our experiences took us 'to the brink' as a couple. Somehow we have clawed our way back into our relationship but the strain has taken its toll. It surely needn't be like this.

Legislation has to be changed so that the parents and carers of children with special needs can work *with* those in authority instead of the people in authority spending huge amounts of precious resources fighting the parents who are only trying to get help for their children.

Our LEA engaged a barrister on two occasions to fight us. Talk about a tank against a pea shooter!

It is difficult to marshall a united front of parents and carers, as they are generally so exhausted they don't have time to attend meetings and canvass MPs, etc. Their voice and therefore their concerns continue to go unheard.

If you have a child who has special needs there would appear to be legislation in place to allow you to access help for them. So on paper this is seemingly simple – maybe because the piece of paper has been written by a professional who goes home in the evening to a peaceful environment and isn't up half the night either worrying about her child or trying to stop him running off into the night. Perhaps that professional won't have nightmare Christmas experiences, disastrous holidays, a house that is being broken up around her, a child who may be very violent or suicidal (because he is so confused, frightened by life and unhappy), a lifestyle that is so complicated (because where *do* you find a 'babysitter' for a sixteen- and seventeen-year-old who can't be left on their own?) that going out becomes a distant memory and friends who don't understand what is going on in her life disappear over the horizon, leaving her lonelier and more isolated than ever.

We fervently believe that life shouldn't be like this. Life as a carer for children with special needs can be extremely rewarding, as well as extremely exhausting. There is supposed to be a system in place which will help you to establish the most appropriate lifestyle for your child, but at the moment there is inequality as to who can access it.

For example, I trained and worked as a secretary. Whilst I am not brilliantly computer literate I can at least type very fast and string a sentence or two together. This has been invaluable in our fight. However, if you are outside the circle of those in the know and have few skills you are immediately disadvantaged. Whilst it is not impossible to succeed you could have a very hard time. It really is like trying to find your way through the Hampton Court maze – without any of the fun!

You will see that we not only waded through the Statementing procedure for Richard, but then had to fight two tribunals on his behalf to achieve a Statement that accurately reflected his difficulties and put in place appropriate help for him.

We hope this guide will provide you with a map to negotiate the twists and turns, avoid the blind alleys and achieve your goal of appropriate help for your children, whatever their age, so that they may live safe, fulfilling and happy lives.

I'm not trying to be controversial or frightening but we were naïve and our children have suffered hugely because of our ignorance. This book shows you what we did wrong, and the consequences. Then what we did right, and the consequences. It is an honest appraisal of our experiences from which I hope you will draw something useful for your particular circumstances.

In our experience, those in authority will sometimes actually mislead, or cover up information.

After ten years (yes, I *did* say ten years!) of trying to get our eldest child assessed and 'digging' uselessly for information we requested early years medical files for another of our children and found in that file the proof that Alice should have been Statemented when she was six years old. Sadly, she was *sixteen* by then. We have therefore learned to rely on nobody but ourselves. We found that there may be social workers and people in the education system but they all had a different agenda to us.

We are the parents of four adopted children: Alice, Alex, Richard and Jack. All of them, it transpired eventually, had special educational needs. The older three have now been diagnosed as being on the autistic spectrum (Asperger's syndrome – or so near on the spectrum as to make no difference) and Jack, the youngest, is dyslexic. Unfortunately we know that he is not just dyslexic but also has other problems. All have challenging learning difficulties.

We have now been through the Statementing procedure more than once and have learned a lot from our mistakes. Let me help you to avoid the snares that await you if you are not careful.

Although it can be a long and difficult process, knowing what you're doing helps enormously. There are people and organizations out there who can help you – if you know where to find them.

We became swamped with paperwork. Boxes and boxes of the stuff. It took us a long while to get organized as we had no idea of what we were getting into. I hope that we can give you some helpful suggestions there too.

We have spent long years wrapped in red tape. Let us help you cut through some of it and spare you some pain.

Entering the world of special educational needs

If your child has problems then he needs and deserves appropriate help. It is his *right*. He will probably require a 'Statement of Special Educational Needs'.

'What's this?' you ask.

If we had properly understood the significance of the power that a Statement of Special Educational Needs wields, our lives could have been very different.

The Statement is the passport you require to access the extra provision for your child. Without a Statement your child won't get the support he needs; a situation serious enough at school, but with grave implications for the future.

A Statement of Special Educational Needs is a document drawn up by the local education authority of what the child's requirements are and how they plan to implement a strategy to address those needs. You will find a breakdown of Richard's original Statement in Chapter 2.

Now read on, intrepid and courageous traveller, and we will endeavour to guide and help you. Learn how to change from a mild-mannered Clark Kent to a 'velvet bulldozer' instead and, most importantly, *survive the experience!*

Chapter 1

Starting out: Don't be daunted

13 January 2003 marked an extraordinary day in our lives. I drove my son through the frosty morning to his first day at a residential college for young people with special educational needs (SEN) and learning difficulties (LD). It was the culmination of thirteen years of blood, sweat, toil and tears and an incredible journey.

As I drove away I started to shake and wept uncontrollably. I had to stop the car at the side of the road as all the emotion, exhaustion, anger and frustration poured out of me in a healing stream. Then I felt a sense of peace wash over me.

At last, after all the years of battling, all four of our children (a sibling group we had adopted nearly thirteen years previously) were in the appropriate placements. Two of them were now in special needs colleges: one at a school for autistic boys and one at a school for dyslexics. Having fought the authorities for years, firstly for accurate diagnosis and secondly for funding for the appropriate help and placements for them all, at last we could feel hopeful about their future.

But it wasn't always like this. Let me rewind a little…

'Perhaps if you'd been a little more encouraging to her she wouldn't be like this!'

Wallop! The sentiments of the LEA's educational psychologist sandbagged me in the guts – hard. I sat, shaken and slack-jawed. Aghast. Dejected.

It had taken me years to even get the LEA to agree to assess our daughter Alice, the eldest of our four adopted children, all siblings. We had lived with ten years of tantrums and difficulties – they had been with her for an hour, when she was on best behaviour – and *this* was their assessment. Still shaking I rushed to the nearest chemist for a bottle of

'Rescue Remedy' and took a large slug from the bottle. This was in the autumn of 1999. Our adopted family was collapsing about our ears and we seemed powerless to stop it.

However, in January 2000 Alice, who was sixteen by then, was finally diagnosed as being on the autistic spectrum. By March 2000 our middle son Richard, thirteen years old, was also confirmed as having an ASD. We only found this out after we paid for an independent psychologist to assess him. The LEA educational psychologist had told us that Richard was just of 'below average intelligence'. When we voiced our concern regarding a possible ASD diagnosis, as his behaviour was very similar to that of his now diagnosed sister, he then said: 'Oh, but you don't want him to have an ASD diagnosis!'

Maybe not, but we all needed to know what we were dealing with so that we could find the best way to help him and, equally important, access the appropriate support for him not just during his years in the education system but also for the rest of his life.

Our children who, it transpired, all had special educational needs did not get to the appropriate placements until they were sixteen, seventeen, fifteen and fourteen years old! All were misdiagnosed or undiagnosed for years.

We must seem very stupid parents as it has taken so long to machete our way through the system and finally access the right help for our children but I can assure you we tried very hard for a long time. I feel very sad knowing that had we been able to get help earlier, the lives of our children, and our lives, would have been very much easier and very much happier.

However, I think there are a lot of parents out there who are just like us. They simply don't have the experience, can't get advice easily and therefore don't know what they are dealing with and how to ask for help – and get it.

There are other books on the market written to tell you what your rights are. The difference is that, because we've had to do it for so many children, we have learned the hard way that sometimes things are not what they seem. This is why I've felt compelled to write this book.

So, how do you go about avoiding taking the same rutted track as us?

First, do not be intimidated by the 'experts'. Nobody else knows your child like you do. If you have a 'gut' feeling that there is something wrong, do not be deterred. A lovely 'tree feller' once corrected me when I called him an 'expert'. 'I don't like that,' he said. '"Ex" means a has-been and "spurt" implies something wet!'

Having met some of the so-called 'experts' in SEN I'm inclined to agree with him. To be fair, though, we have also met some excellent and committed people. Finding these people is sometimes very difficult, however.

We've also met professionals in the field of SEN who have been complicit in the act of trying to discredit us as parents. They have been unwilling to discredit us but cannot do anything about it as they 'need their jobs', which would clearly have been on the line if they had dared to stand up to those in higher positions. I feel very sorry for them. Some of them have been genuinely nice people faced with a terrible dilemma.

Unfortunately, as we all know, standing on principles doesn't pay the mortgage.

Second, throw dignity and pride out of the window. You won't be needing them any more. I know parents who have had to resort to begging or threatening. (I'm one of the former. I'm not proud of it and it didn't get me anywhere – knowledge was the thing that changed the situation. Standing five foot one and a half in stockinged feet I don't cut much of a threatening figure!)

I know I became a royal pain in the bum to the LEA. I *would not* go away. What they didn't realize was I *could not.* I had no choice other than to keep coming back for more, but I know I was very unpopular!

On one occasion I received a particularly unpleasant letter from the Statementing Officer threatening me and telling me I was *not* to repeat something. It was such an awful letter that my first reaction was to laugh. My husband did not share this view and nearly 'bust his buttons'. He was incandescent that these cowardly bullies had written to me clearly wishing to intimidate me.

I told my husband I would not dignify this with a response but that night dreamed that the Principal Educational Psychologist was strangling me. The dream was so vivid that I woke up shouting and sweating and turned on the light to look under the bed. It was very real and very frightening!

I decided my subconscious mind was trying to tell me something so I wrote a reply: a very reasonable letter telling them all about my late mother. She was widowed at a very early age and had been bullied, while in a very vulnerable state, by the local authority who were trying to compulsorily purchase our house. She was grieving, she was ill, she had no money, she had three young children to somehow raise alone, but she recognized injustice and she recognized the bullies for what they were.

So, God bless her, she fought back.

I don't know how she did it, how she found the strength to do it but she managed to get legal aid and a barrister was involved and she won! She managed to get compensation for the compulsory purchase, not a huge amount, but a lot more than they had offered in the first place.

So I told the LEA about my mother! I told them I loved her, admired her and revered her memory. I pointed out that I was raised by her standards and had watched her stand up to bullies. I told them I felt bullied by their authority and I wasn't going to give in to bullying either. I slept after that.

Third, get yourself a copy of the Code of Practice and some small 'stickit' pads. These will be extremely useful. You will find yourself quoting parts of the *Code of Practice* (COP) at dinner parties, if you have time to attend any. I've heard of people who have gone on to practise law having been through this procedure. We will tell you where to access these important tomes (see Appendix 1). They are slightly different in Scotland and Wales following devolution.

You have rights in law, as does your child, but don't expect anyone to point these rights out to you.

You need to be prepared or have people on your side who can be prepared for you.

Fourth, do not rely on any professional to give you the full picture. We have met some wonderful people – social workers, independent psychologists and doctors, etc. – in the SEN field. However, they actually only plough their own rather narrow furrow. Nobody will have the same 'overview' as you.

Also, they are all overworked and in understaffed departments. It is not unknown for someone to wait weeks or months for an answer to a question.

What we hadn't bargained on was the shocking fact that sometimes those who have the power to help simply don't. In fact, sometimes they actively *block* you accessing help.

Unfortunately, everyone these days is so busy protecting their budgets that it is often a real battle to get them to do something. It was a long time before we learned what was going on. So be warned – please. You just have to get out there and find the information for yourselves. Get yourself a 'virtual' deerstalker hat, magnifying glass and meerschaum pipe as you'll feel like Sherlock Holmes after a while.

Keep asking questions. This can be daunting but take a look at Appendix 1. Even if you don't see exactly what you need just try contacting some of them. Phone them *all* if necessary, as often one thing will lead on to another. I received advice and help from some very unlikely quarters sometimes.

Fifth, do not be daunted. Trust your judgement, have faith. There are people out there who can help you and we will assist your search.

God bless *all* parents, but especially those whose children have extra needs, 'special needs'. They really need Him.

Chapter 2

So how do you know when your child has special educational needs?

Are you wondering if your child's behaviour needs further investigation? Presumably you must have some doubts or fears, otherwise why did you buy this book?

You don't want to be labelled as a fussy or hysterical parent – I didn't. I certainly don't want to spread alarm but we were ill-informed and frankly downright ignorant in the area of SEN. If you are in the same situation then maybe this information might help you.

Unless your child has very obvious needs – is blind or deaf or has a physically evident problem – it may not be as easy as one might think to detect that there is something wrong that warrants serious investigation. Even then, if you feel sure that there is a problem you may well have a battle to persuade those in authority to investigate.

When should you be concerned?

The following pointers were relevant to us as the parents of children who turned out to be autistic. This chapter may be less directly useful to parents of children with other special needs. I will confess we knew nothing about autism until about four years ago, when our daughter's Steiner school mentioned that they thought that she displayed 'autistic tendencies'.

Like many people, we perceived a person with autism as being someone at the more extreme end of the autistic spectrum. We thought of the character in *Rain Man* or someone totally cut off from the rest of the world. We thought of children who don't display any tactile characteristics. We therefore thought it couldn't possibly apply to our children. *However, we were wrong.*

Professionals thought there was nothing the matter with our children. *However, they were wrong.*

The difference between ourselves and the professionals was that when we realized we were wrong – based on our investigations and assessments made by independent diagnosticians – we tried to put the situation right. Some of the professionals appeared to fight us all the way, either to save face or to save money.

If you begin to investigate autism spectrum disorders (ASD) you will probably hear the phrase 'triad of impairments' used and this is the bottom-line diagnostic tool. The triad consists of 'impairments in social interaction', 'impairments of communication' and 'impairments of imagination'.

Does your child display:

- violent mood swings?
- 'bad', 'naughty' or 'disruptive' behaviour particularly on re-turning from school?
- headaches, tummy aches, extreme exhaustion?
- self-harming?
- obsessive behaviour?
- destructive behaviour (cutting or tearing clothes)?
- age-inappropriate soiling of underpants?
- lack of imagination?
- problems with social interaction?

If any of these traits are shown, then read on...

Diagnosis of autism can sometimes be difficult as autists, although all somewhere on the autistic spectrum, may display different symptoms. We know a special needs co-ordinator in a mainstream school who is tearing his hair out as he has six high functioning autistic boys at his school who all behave very differently to his perception of autistic children!

However, there are some large pointers (our children did display them but we didn't realize what we were witnessing).

Does your child lack imagination?

'It's strange our children don't have any imaginative play,' I said several times. Unfortunately, I must have said it to the wrong people as nobody picked up on it: 'lack of imaginative play' is a classic sign of autistic tendencies.

I would build 'dens' for them in the garden and they simply wouldn't know what to do. They'd look blankly at me if I tried to make 'mud stew' on our pretend campfire. As I'd spent most of my childhood trawling the Mid-West in my imagination, pretending to be Laura from *Little House on the Prairie*, this was a mystery to me.

A large box remained a large box and didn't become a train, a car or a spaceship however hard we tried.

Imagination is also the tool we all use to work out what might happen next. Life can be very frightening if you do not have this skill.

Is social interaction difficult for your child?

Our autistic children simply didn't know what to do with a friend and have no empathy. Most autists find it hard to understand that other people have needs too. The fact that you are feeling sad or tired will just pass them by. Because they find interpreting body language so difficult the normal ebb and flow of conversation is very hard work for autists.

One of our children, when aged fourteen, was desperate to join in a conversation with a bunch of his peers we were ferrying in the car. He suddenly shouted 'sixpence' at them and started giggling hysterically as though he had made some hilarious joke. There was a puzzled pause from the other children as they tried to work out the relevance of this before they resumed their conversation and our son sat concentrating hard desperately trying to think of something funny to say.

When in his more manic phase he would constantly search for puns in conversation so that he would have something to say.

Is your child's language very delayed?

The triad of impairments covers speech and language difficulties. In our family's case language was the bigger problem of the two, although diagnosis was 'muddied' by speech impediments, some of which are physiological in origin.

All of our autistic children had great difficulty getting sentence structure right and tense was a nightmare. Their diction was also very poor which was put down to their early years' lack of stimulation.

Now, as young adults, their understanding of language is assessed to be approximately half that of children their chronological age. We had trained them in the basics of opening conversational gambits and because we worked so hard on their speech and spelling when they were younger their vocabularies seem quite good, but this has sadly confused the issue. Had we not worked so hard on helping them with the social aspects of speech and vocabulary, their difficulties in this area might have been picked up earlier. Had we been disinclined or not able to help them with their speech it might have meant that they would have been diagnosed and helped earlier.

Alex 'reports' the news to us even though we might have been sitting next to him and listening at the same time and often uses very odd phraseology. In his latest assessment his language was classed as 'severely delayed'.

Can they read but seem unable to understand what they are reading?

This applies to all our autists. This was one of the reasons why it took so long to get them diagnosed.

With great perseverance and patience, we taught them to read so in reading tests at primary school they did quite well. Sadly, the fact that they didn't understand a lot of what they were reading did not become apparent until later. They cannot follow the less obvious plots of television shows either. Anything not 'spelled out' is lost on them.

Can your child only cope with one instruction at a time?

I cannot ask the children to get their scarves, hats and gloves from upstairs. They would have to make a separate journey to retrieve each item of clothing – I found this very frustrating if we were in a hurry.

Is your child obsessive in some way?

On one of our first outings with our middle son, Richard, who was three at the time, he had a tantrum that lasted for an hour as he wanted to go to the loo but could not cope as the offered potty was green and his usual potty white.

Of course, we didn't realize what we were involved in then.

Richard would not get into bed if his pillow was the 'wrong way round'. This same boy is obsessed with football and, when at his most distressed, would sit for hours (and come down in the middle of the night as well if we didn't curb him) literally six inches away from the screen so he was virtually inside the television, totally lost in the world of little men chasing a ball.

Some children are obsessed by *Thomas the Tank Engine* and will watch the same video literally hundreds of times.

Does your child become distressed if his or her routine is disturbed?

With our autistic children things have to be 'just so' and our lives are run now to a routine. They would become very distressed if a routine was changed or if plans made could not be fulfilled. I am talking about much more than just simple childhood disappointment. We witnessed total inflexibility to the concept of change.

Is your child 'funny' about time?

You cannot say 'I'll be back in a moment' to our children (as they take it literally and having counted out the moments of your absence will then berate you on your return). I was cooking supper one night and my fifteen-year-old son came into the kitchen to ask what time the meal would be ready.

'Soon,' I replied.

'You know I can't cope with "soon"!' he shouted, then stamped his foot.

'OK, it'll be ready in six minutes,' I said.

He visibly relaxed, said 'thank you' and left.

Does your child simply behave 'oddly'?

Our children began school life behaving 'badly' at school but quite well at home, then (after a period of home schooling) some were quite passive (as long as they were not challenged) at school, but were like wild animals when we met them from the school bus.

The independent educational psychologist told us about 'learned passivity'. One of our sons learned to be very quiet and restrained during lessons but children can sustain this for just so long. By the time their confusing and stressful school day finishes their tolerance is exhausted. So their behaviour wasn't 'personal'.

This is just a small crumb of comfort to remember while you are trying to calm your child and stop her breaking up the home!

Is your child displaying signs of internalized distress?

Because of their impaired communication skills our children could not say 'Mum, I'm scared', or 'Dad, I'm unhappy'. Because they could not verbalize their fears they flagged up these symptoms in different ways which are simply seen as 'bad' behaviour. We now know that this was very distressed behaviour. We endured:

- stealing
- tantrums
- cutting holes in/shredding clothes
- soiling and urinating in clothes
- self-harming.

These are as upsetting for you, the parents, as you try to find your way to the source of the angst as it is for your children. For us it was like trying to help a baby who has tummy ache – but cannot tell you!

Does your child watch television with you but fail to understand the plot?

Alex was watching the video of *Titanic* for the umpteenth time. We had explained to him that it was based on a true and rather sad story.

He turned to me and said: 'So Jack and Rose are actors and the rest are real?'

He thought he was *really* watching the Titanic sink each time he saw the film with all the victims of the disaster.

Similarly, Richard was watching a community message about car crime which portrayed a young man stealing a car.

'I've seen him before!' he suddenly shouted, pointing at the screen. 'They should stop him. And,' he continued indignantly, 'I've seen him actually taking things out of cars.'

Clearly he hadn't grasped that these were advertisements, not real happenings. These are 'semantic pragmatic' problems.

Our older three children displayed all of the behaviours mentioned above at different stages in their mainstream school career and our youngest son would often come home from school with a blinding headache and such exhaustion that he would go straight to bed at 4.30pm and, worryingly, sleep until the following breakfast time.

We now know that our children cannot communicate their anxieties and distress in what might be considered the usual way. Whenever we witness 'bizarre' behaviour we now realize that it is our children's way of trying to highlight the fact that they are out of their depth and cannot cope with a situation.

Mainstream schooling can be tiring for any child. For a child with special needs it is ten times worse, although mainstream schooling can work for some children with SEN if they are lucky.

Sprechen Sie Deutsch?

We asked the independent educational psychologist why Richard was so out of control when I picked him up from the school bus. The psychologist told us that Richard's experience of school was like ours might be if we had to go to a school where all the lessons were conducted in German, all the other pupils and teachers spoke German to each other – in class, in the corridors and in the playground – only we were unable to speak German.

Richard spent the whole day trying to make sense of everything around him. By the time he had endured the stress of the school bus and arrived back with us his tolerance had been exhausted and he simply had to explode. This made our lives very difficult as it meant that we were constantly having to deal with violent outbursts and the real issue was buried whilst we were sidetracked by the bad behaviour.

Remember it is not 'just puberty', 'terrible twos' or 'oiky adolescence'. If your child is suffering from a problem, particularly if that problem is undiagnosed, he or she can display extremely strange behaviour. This is not normal and is not nice for your child or you. There is help out there. Do not give up the struggle to access it.

This chapter has listed some of the problem behaviours children may exhibit and the reasons for them.

Learn to 'read' your child. Look beyond the behaviour that is driving you around the bend. Why is he or she doing it? Will a proper diagnosis and different provision relieve some/all of it?

Chapter 3

So what does a Statement of Special Educational Needs look like?

We had no idea what a Statement of Special Educational Needs looked like, and I think if you conducted a straw poll in the street you'd find that 99 per cent of the public don't know either. Maybe one day when I've sorted out the red tape I'll be able to show you the Statement on the website (www.special-educational-needs.co.uk).

Statements can be truly dreadful, woolly and unclear. I will do my best to try to help you understand them and try to point you in the right direction of getting a better, more incisive Statement for your child.

The Statement is the blueprint, or recipe, for the help that your child should be receiving and has a basis in law. As we all know, if a recipe isn't clear then the cake will be leaden, and inedible. Statements are similar. If the Statement is unclear then very little will happen and all your hard work will be wasted.

The first Statement we saw, eleven years ago, I now read and weep over. It was pathetic. It concentrated very much on Alex's speech and was designed to be withdrawn, if his speech improved to a certain extent. Because we worked so hard with Alex on his speech – singing with him, talking with him, doing exercises with him – this is what happened and his Statement was withdrawn, which was a great shame as Alex still needed a lot of help. We were completely naïve and wet behind the ears and when we received notification of Alex's 'unStatementing' we said, 'Congratulations, haven't you done well!'

Looking back our son was completely hung out to dry and because of our total ignorance we didn't realize the following fundamental points:

- the legal implications of a Statement

- the Statement that he'd been given was inadequate

- we should have objected to his unStatementing. UnStatementing follows a similar pattern to Statementing and anyone looking at Alex would have known that this child definitely still needed help – not just with his speech. If we had objected Alex would have been reviewed, each year, by psychologists, speech therapists, physiotherapists, etc. and would have received extra help in school. It might not have taken until he was seventeen to have his autistic diagnosis confirmed.

If you look it up in the *Code of Practice* (COP) it will tell you that the Statement contains a number of different sections.

Part 1: Introduction

Section 1 of Part 1 quotes the appropriate Education Act and SEN Regulations. It should set out:

- the name and address of the child

- date of birth

- sex

- home language

- current school

- parent or person responsible for child

- telephone numbers of the above.

Section 2 of Part 1 sets out the Advice the Authority has taken into consideration when preparing the Statement.

This Advice could be in the form of reports from physiotherapists and speech and language therapists (SALT), reports from the present school, a report from the LEA educational psychologist (LEA EP), clinical medical officer (CMO) and parental advice (PA). You will notice that I put parents at the bottom of the list and this is because of the fact that your comments may well be considered at the bottom of the list. Bitter? *Moi?!*

A word of warning regarding 'Parental Advice'

At first glance this looks like an innocuous piece of paper with a few fairly generalized questions. It isn't. I was fortunate as just at the time we were supposed to be writing the PA I was given a copy of the guidelines from the COP published in 1994 (paragraph 3:100). I didn't have my own COP at that point. These guidelines were extremely helpful as they gave me specific questions to answer. My PA was certainly a much better document for this information as I was able to paint a much better picture of my child, putting 'flesh on the bones' following these questions point by point.

Oddly, I cannot find this information in the COP for Wales which was published in 2002. I feel certain that the guidelines will be of help to you so I am including them here. The COP states 'your written contribution can be as short or long as you wish'.

A – The early years
1. What do you remember about the early years that might help?
2. What was he like as a young baby?
3. Were you happy about progress at the time?
4. When did you first feel things were not right?
5. What happened?
6. What advice or help did you receive – from whom?

B – What is your child like now?
1. *General health*: Eating and sleeping habits: general fitness, absences from school, minor ailments – coughs and colds. Serious illnesses/accidents – periods in hospital. Any medicine or special diet? General alertness – tiredness, signs of use of drugs, smoking, drinking, glue sniffing.

2. *Physical skills*: Walking, running, climbing – riding a bike, football or other games, drawing pictures, writing, doing jigsaws; using construction kits, household gadgets, tools; sewing.

3. *Self-help*: Level of personal independence – dressing, etc: making bed, washing clothes, keeping room tidy, coping with day-to-day routine; budgeting pocket money, general independence – getting out and about.

4. *Communication*: Level of speech, explains, describes events, people, conveys information (e.g. messages to and from school), joins in conversation, uses telephone.

5. *Playing and learning at home*: How he spends time, watching TV, reading for pleasure and information, hobbies, concentration, sharing.

6. *Activities outside*: Belonging to clubs, sporting activities, happy to go alone.

7. *Relationships*: With parents, brothers and sisters; with friends; with other adults (friends and relations) at home generally, 'outside' generally. Is he a loner?

8. *Behaviour at home*: Co-operates, shares, listens to and carries out requests, helps in the house, offers help, fits in with family routines and 'rules'. Moods good and bad, sulking – temper tantrums, demonstrative, affectionate.

9. *At school*: Relationships with other children and teachers; progress with reading, writing, number, other subjects and activities at school. How the school has helped/not helped with your child. Have you been asked to help with school work – hearing child read – with what result? Does he enjoy school? What does he find easy or difficult?

C – *Your general views*

1. What do you think your child's special educational needs are?

2. How do you think these can be best provided for?

3. How do you compare your child with others of the same age?

4. What is your child good at or what does he enjoy doing?

5.   What does he worry about – is he aware of difficulties?

6.   What are your worries, concerns?

7.   Is there any other information you would like to give?

   (a)   about the family – major events that might have affected your child?

   (b)   reports from other people?

8.   With whom would you like more contact?

9.   How do you think your child's needs affect the needs of the family as a whole?

(Code of Practice on the Identification and Assessment of Special Educational Needs, 1994, pp.72–3)

Part 2: Special educational needs

This part is very important. 'Needs' is the vital word in this heading. In this section the LEA should state *very precisely* what 'needs' your child has. However, many are not precise. Many are actually very imprecise. (*Author's note.* If one were being cynical one might think that they were imprecise deliberately. This can make you feel as if you are fighting your way out of a bag of cotton wool without anything to fight against. It may, however, be that they are imprecise for different reasons. I can't think of a good one at present – but I'll let you know!)

For example, in the Final Statement for Richard the LEA used information from the SALT report that:

> Richard's language profile is uneven. Areas of most difficulty for Richard are those of a pragmatic nature, that is use of language, high level of semantic information and formulating expressive language to put his ideas across. As Richard gets older these high level difficulties will become more apparent. He will have problems with humour and sarcasm, which is more complex and subtle.

This is good, precise detail. However, we did not get such a Statement immediately: this was the *sixth* attempt to get this Statement accurate and this is why we have been to two SENDIST tribunals.

Part 3: Special educational provision

This is divided into three sections:

A Objectives

B Educational provision to meet needs and objectives

C Monitoring.

Part 4: Placement

This is the school which has been considered appropriate for your child. It may be you wish your child to continue at the school he is already at or you may wish to see a different school named in the placement.

Parts 5 and 6: Non-educational needs and non-educational provision

This concentrates on less specific needs, comments from medical advices, etc., and *is not enforceable by law.*

Points to remember

You may find that the Statement that is eventually sent to you is a very different kettle of fish! Bear in mind these points:

- By law the LEA have to send you a draft Statement and you only have a certain time in which to comment upon it.

- There are time constraints that surround the preparation of a Statement. These rules do change so check in your COP and get advice. In our case it was:

  Where an LEA serve notice on the child's parent informing him that they propose to make an assessment under section 167, or receive a request for such an assessment by the parent, the LEA shall within *six weeks* of the date of service of the notice, or of receipt of the request, give notice to the parent of their decision whether or not to make an assessment.

  So six weeks...

> Where under 167(4) an LEA have given notice to the parent
> of their decision to make an assessment they shall complete
> that assessment with ten weeks of the date on which such
> notice was given.

plus ten weeks…

> Where an LEA have made an assessment of the child's
> educational needs under section 167 they shall within two
> weeks of the date on which the assessment is completed
> either serve a copy of a proposed Statement on the parent or
> give notice of their decision not to make a Statement.

plus two weeks…

> Where an LEA have served a copy of a proposed Statement
> on the parent they shall within eight weeks of the date on
> which the proposed Statement is served serve a copy of the
> completed Statement.

> *(Special Educational Needs Code of Practice 1994, Section 3.94)*

plus another eight weeks, making twenty-six weeks (six months) in total.

- *Beware* – it has been known for LEAs to try to get away with
  flouting these time constraints – because, of course, the longer they take the more money they save. You know, sometimes I really yearn for those halcyon days when I trusted
  everyone. Somehow life was so much less complicated
  before we were dragged into the world of SEN. Ho hum!

You should also be aware that at the draft or proposed Statement stage,
you have the right to ask for a meeting with an officer of the LEA. If you
are happy with the proposed Statement then skip over this next bit.
However, if you have concerns regarding the content of the Statement or
the reports attached then you should ask for a meeting.

*You must ask, in writing, for the meeting within fifteen days of receiving your
copy of the proposed statement.* This doesn't mean that you will get, or have
to have, the meeting within that fifteen-day period. You just have to
request it within that time.

To request a meeting

I'm hoping that by this stage you will be receiving support and help from one of the bodies mentioned in Appendix 1. I would advise you to check the up-to-date position (with IPSEA, for example) but you should write something like the following to the Statementing Officer or DOE of the LEA (don't forget it is much better to write to them by name):

[*Your address*]

[*Their address*]

[*Date*]

Dear

Re My child and DOB Request for a meeting to discuss a proposed Statement

I am writing as the parent of... I acknowledge receipt of the proposed Statement of Special Educational Needs and to ask for a meeting with the Responsible Officer to discuss it.

Please note that the school we wish to be named on the Statement when it is finalized is...School. [*This last sentence of course only applies if you wish a different school to be named and is not necessary if you just want the needs or provision changed.*]

Yours sincerely

[*your name*]

cc [*your child's school*]

You should have a reply from the LEA within a week or two. Remember there is a legal time-frame surrounding the preparation of the Statement.

You do not have to give details of what you are not happy about at this stage but you should start preparing a document detailing your concerns. I found it helpful to go through the Statement point by point, numbering the points so that I could refer to 'number so and so' when I was discussing it with them.

The LEA have to agree to this meeting – the law says that they must do so after they have sent a parent a proposed statement.

Try not to attend this meeting (or any meeting) alone

This may sound a little paranoid but I found to my cost that some people rescinded later what they had said in meetings and as I had been on my own (my husband having had to go to work to support us all) there were often no witnesses. I later wished that I had recorded some of these meetings (I admit that I don't know what the legal position is regarding this so for goodness sake get up-to-date advice). Instead, after someone denied saying something I was reduced to bleating pitifully in frustration: 'But I didn't make it up – he *did* say that!'

This was a horrible situation. Particularly since I think, for a while, when the situation was so bizarre, my husband may have suspected that I *was* 'making it up'! I felt very alone and it was damaging for our marriage.

If you do not have a husband/partner to take with you try to find a sympathetic friend or ask for advice from IPSEA, ACE or NAS. I really would not wish to attend meetings like this again alone. It makes you vulnerable in more ways than one.

The first Statement arrives

We requested our first Statement in January 2000 and this Final Statement document is dated November 2000. We had received the draft at the end of September 2000. It isn't supposed to take any longer than six months from request to draft!

We felt this original Statement was totally ridiculous. I had made notes and I remember well my feelings of anger and despair as I went through this document. Having waited so long and worked so hard to achieve any Statement at all, frankly I wept. There were so many things wrong with it.

Amongst the Advices that were attached to this document was a double-sided sheet which was the offering from the social worker we had finally been allocated. It was suggesting that our son's difficulties only really presented themselves at home and that they were considering 'alternative parenting' (foster care) for our child. This was all fascinating stuff – particularly so when one bore in mind the fact that this man had *never even met our son*!!

We protested vehemently against this report at draft Statement stage but it went on to be included in two more Statements – including the *final* Final Statement, by which stage this comment was so preposterous we just laughed!

The draft Statement arrived with gaps in the numbered points and pages missing. There were also duplicates. I distinctly remember refuting in writing the points made in 'the second number 33'!!!! It felt like a conspiracy.

When I first spoke to a representative who was the first point of contact at the wonderful organization who helped us fight our case, she asked me to read her Part 2 of the Statement.

'What a load of b******s!' was her refreshing response.

In short it was a mess. I may be wrong, but it felt as though someone had been handed the file, told to make something of it, and had almost randomly extracted information from the Advices even when he didn't understand it sufficiently to *précis* accurately.

While what information *must* be contained in each part of the Statement is prescribed by regulation – there is nothing that says *how* it should be written. Therefore a Statement from one LEA is likely to look very different from that of another (i.e. just like percentages of children with Statements vary from one LEA to another).

What the first Statement said

Part 1

Well, to be fair they managed to get most of this right but then it was only our name and address, etc.

Part 2

This is very difficult to write about without actually quoting. However, the first point is that this was far too long – 7½ pages (our first tribunal Panel said it was the longest Part 2 they'd ever seen!) – and far too vague. The second point is that the information contained was not accurate and in places simply not true.

I took issue even with the first paragraph which implied that this was an impartial view! Also the information was cobbled together from earlier Advices and reports and a lot of information noted here was no longer relevant. It gave a bit of family history, then a few paragraphs regarding early concerns – medical conditions, speech and language, general ability and education.

It then went on to discuss Richard as he was at that time: physical activities, medical, general ability, self-help, speech language and communication skills, comprehension skills. The penultimate paragraph on this page took our breath away as they declared that Richard's liking for quiz books had just lately encompassed crosswords. My scribble reads 'not true'. I had said in the parents' Advice that he would be 'incapable of doing crosswords'. The LEA had completely misrepresented this piece of information.

There was an interesting comment about Richard not being much of a nuisance in school. We were told about 'learned passivity' where our son would sit very quietly in the hope that nobody would notice him. The teachers by this stage had learned not to give him challenges and avoided giving him homework as, if they did, it generally resulted in an explosion from Richard who couldn't cope; this disrupted the class.

The school naturally wanted to keep things on an even keel and therefore were able to report as above that Richard was not a nuisance. So that was all right then, wasn't it! He was by this stage heading down the slippery slope into clinical depression and self-harming.

The next outraged exclamation of 'not true' comes after a comment about Richard only being noticed by the SENCO after a problem on a school trip – he wouldn't change seats, had a huge tantrum and was very upset. Bit of a 'de-exaggeration' this. We had been discussing his problems and asking for something to be done since the first term of Year Seven.

Under 'diagnosis' the Statement said that there had been some confusion regarding this on our part! I don't think so. The LEA seemed confused over diagnosis, not us. When this first Statement was prepared the LEA were refusing to acknowledge that our son was autistic and therefore it seemed as if they did everything when writing the Statement to imply his problems stemmed from other causes: food colourings – which are mentioned three times – and, of course, us, his parents!

The next two pages were poor and woolly. It then went on to the LEA Psychological Advice – which was all extremely odd. As mentioned earlier, we trusted the skill and judgement of the LEA principal educational psychologist (PEP). I urge you to gather information from other sources so that you have a balanced view. The PEP either misdiagnosed or wouldn't diagnose our children and his assessment of Richard was particularly strange as the findings varied sometimes wildly. (OK, maybe he was just unlucky, but we and our children were the losers in this situation.) For example, we were told that Richard scored at 'less than 0.1 centile', on one assessment, then that he had the 'oral expression of a seventeen-year-old' when he was fourteen! Bizarre, and we were very puzzled by this, but the PEP has a lot of power so you need to have good evidence to refute anything you find not to be an accurate picture of your child.

If in doubt move heaven and earth to get an independent psychologist to assess your child so that you have an unbiased view (see Appendix 1 for contact details of the British Psychological Society). Please be aware that generally speaking the diagnosis of autism is regarded as a *medical* matter. At the time of writing the NAS regard only three professionals as able to diagnose:

- consultant psychiatrist
- consultant paediatrician
- consultant psychologist.

Most NHS regions now have 'assessment teams' often centred around Children's Development Centres, also some Centres of Excellence – for example, The Maudsley Hospital, The Newcomen Centre at Guy's Hospital (both in London) and Professor Elizabeth Newsom's team at the Early Years Centre in Nottingham.

The first three paragraphs of the next page of Richard's Statement paint such a muddled picture of our son. The LEA really didn't know what to make of Richard. Because of his autistic difficulties, coupled with some learning difficulties, he really does have a peculiar educational 'profile'. Some things he appears to grasp quite well and in other areas it is as though there is a black hole! However, this is a very Asperger's trait and bells should have been ringing loud and clear so that he could access appropriate help.

My copy of the document is covered in my scribbles. The forty-eight points noted here were a real hodge podge. (I counted these because I couldn't quite believe that having identified forty-eight points of need there are only five Objectives mentioned in Part 3 to cover them.) I hope that I have conveyed in Chapter 4 that Richard's Final Statement is expressed infinitely better.

Point 24 of the Needs listed in this Statement was particularly heart-rending. They pointed out Richard's obsession with sport and the fact that he is very active. But because of his problems he was unable to access many of the sports facilities at his old school which made him very sad and frustrated. You'll see in Chapter 11 what happened to Richard after he left mainstream, and that once he had started to recover he played masses of sport and this really helped restore his equilibrium.

At his old school he was only once picked for the house football team and then he asked that he be substituted and taken off as he was so distressed that he kept being told off by the referee. He knows the rules but applying them when under pressure from the rest of the team was horrendous. In contrast, when he was in Year Seven a group of sixth formers allowed him to be 'goalie' for their playtime game of football. Bearing in mind social interaction can be excruciating for Richard I could see that this would be a fairly safe option. The older boys expected nothing further from him than keeping goal. He could understand that social situation. Once those boys left he stopped going out into the playground altogether.

The discrepancy between Richard's chronological age and his actual reading comprehension was recorded in this section of the Statement – it was 50 months below his chronological age. No wonder he struggled!

Part 3: Special educational provision
A. OBJECTIVES

These set down areas to be developed. We didn't believe that these five objectives went far enough and in the Final Statement they were extended to ten much clearer and stronger points.

B. EDUCATIONAL PROVISION TO MEET NEEDS AND OBJECTIVES

I see that I scribbled the word 'same' at the end of most of the provisions when I first read this. This is because we had been fighting to get these changed at draft Statement stage to no avail. Many of these provisions were useless because they did not take into account the complexity of Richard's problems. One fairly simple point really didn't work at all. This was regarding the school's anti-bullying policy. I go into this in more detail in Chapter 11, which outlines the experiences Richard endured before he moved to a special needs school.

I suppose, to sum up, the 'provision' looked good to anyone at first glance. However, a lot of the points were out of date by the time it was produced as Richard had slipped further into his abyss. Also, in a busy mainstream school they were unrealistic expectations.

C. MONITORING

There were ten points in this section which relied on the SENCO being able to work twenty-four hours a day, I think. Richard's SENCO was a very nice man doing a very difficult job with insufficient resources. I believe he was genuinely fond of our son. He did his best to convey Richard's problems to the rest of the teachers. An Independent Education Plan (IEP) was presumably sent around to all the teachers. However, the school was quite large and some of the staff definitely did not understand Richard's problems. While these were laudable targets things definitely got a lot worse after this Statement was in place.

Part 4: Placement

This still named Richard's mainstream high school, much to our disappointment and his distress.

Parts 5 and 6: Non-educational needs and non-educational provision

Remember that nothing in Parts 5 and 6 is enforceable by law so don't allow anything vital to be mentioned in this part of your child's Statement.

One point in this section was a real red herring. Richard kept having his hearing tested as it was felt that this could be a problem and the fact that when assessed it was normal is mentioned here. Some time before this Statement was prepared Richard's auditory processing had been privately tested and found to be very strange. Basically it seems his brain 'scrambles' messages coming from the ears. I could not seem to put this across, even though I had submitted the results of the auditory processing test to the LEA. It wasn't his 'hearing' that needed looking at – it was his auditory processing!

Also Richard's vision varied from test to test. He has just been tested again, aged seventeen, and it has been suggested now that it might be an idea to try glasses. Up until now opticians didn't think it necessary. I wonder if this is also something to do with the Asperger's mind and we'll see what difference it makes, if any.

This section was still quoting from the Social Services Advice to which we had taken exception at the proposed Statement stage. Remember that the social worker had never met Richard when he wrote his Advice! His Advice was that Social Services should help to support us for a short while. This was a bit of a smoke screen. The social worker would visit us, waste a lot of our time chuntering on about nothing, then leave with the problem unchanged. He was another person who definitely didn't 'get' Richard and his problems at all. No practical support was offered at that time at all. No respite. No family aide. Zilch!

In this section the possibility of looking into foster care for Richard was also raised. This took our breath away and was very upsetting, as you can imagine. Our son was mentally ill when this Statement was prepared. He was extremely troubled and it seemed to us that the Statement implied this was our fault. We, my husband and I, were Richard's rock and refuge. We didn't give in to his tantrums but we didn't give up on him either. He clearly felt safe here: safe enough to let all his frustrations and anxiety out, safe enough to hide away. We now know that it is quite common to undermine parents. At the time it was very painful on a daily basis – made more so by the spectre of 'alternative parenting'.

Thank God that Social Services now seem to understand the vulnerable, complex and fragile nature of our children.

Is the Statement signed?
This Statement was actually signed and dated. Make sure that this happens as it has been reported that LEAs have 'forgotten' to do this, causing problems if you wish to appeal against the Statement – as you can imagine.

General points about the Statement
You will see in later chapters that we appealed against this Statement, which meant we had to go to a Special Educational and Disability Tribunal to argue the case. The LEA managed to convince the tribunal that Richard was *not* ASD. They also tried to convince us. The Statement said:

1. that we suggested that being ASD would have provided an explanation for Richard's language problems

2.   that we were confused over the diagnosis of SEN

3.   that the professor who had been involved did not feel that Richard met ICD-10 or DSM-IV diagnostic criteria for Asperger's or autism.

My response to the above would be

1.   Richard had been tested on 'speech' and, yes, he can speak. He found getting the order of words in sentences incredibly difficult especially when he was younger, and tense was a nightmare for a long time and required loads of input and effort from us over a wide time span. The breakthrough came when he was tested not just for 'speech' but for 'language'. They sound the same but are quite different. 'Language' assessments concentrate on the actual 'understanding' of language not just the ability to speak. For people with ASD there is often a very big discrepancy.

2.   We almost choked on our own bile when we read this sentence originally! We most certainly weren't 'confused' over our son's diagnosis by that stage. The LEA did their best to discredit the independent psychologist who had first diagnosed Richard – even going to the extent of reporting him to the British Psychological Society. Fortunately, the BPS found absolutely no case to answer and threw out the claim.

3.   This relates to an 'assessment' by a professor. I write 'assessment' in inverted commas because I think something went wrong or wires got crossed as none of the usual diagnostic assessments were carried out at this time. The 'assessment' consisted of a bit of a chat with us and Richard and some tests done on the back of an envelope! This professor has since agreed that, following further in-depth assessments, Richard is ASD. However, his earlier opinion did make the first tribunal very difficult.

Another professor from the same department confirmed, in 2001, that Richard *does* meet ICD-10 and DSM-IV criteria. (ICD-10 and DSM-IV are the two principal frameworks which are used in diagnosis of special needs, among others.) The reason I think something went wrong with the first procedure was that for the second assessment we were asked to complete forms and submit reports, undergo an hour-long telephone interview and then a face-to-face meeting before Richard endured an assessment, including blood tests, that stretched over a five-hour period. It was *completely* different to the first assessment and I guess the conclusion that can be drawn is that sometimes *anyone* can make a mistake. The original professor was extremely helpful subsequently but found himself in a peculiar situation. On the one hand he was being quoted as if he were the oracle in Richard's case when the LEA wanted it to look as though Richard wasn't ASD. On the other hand he was being completely ignored when he wrote a report and subsequent letters supporting Alice: she was in danger of being thrown out of her special needs college by Social Services, who said she didn't meet criteria for adult services!

I hope that I have conveyed the 'flavour' of the Statement, and that you are able to somehow compare it with anything that you are offered and also with the Final Statement, Richard's current document. This Final Statement is a much more concise document (for the very good reason that a lot of it was not written by the LEA but by our representative who helped us with the tribunal). It pretty accurately reflects our son's needs and what provision should be in place to help him. It has been a good 'recipe' and the cake is turning out well.

Chapter 4

The Final Statement

In this chapter I'm showing you the outline of the Final Statement that we received after we won the second tribunal (see Chapter 12). Sadly, I cannot show you the actual anonymous copy (which is a pity as it was a fine document) since there have been some legal wrangles regarding ownership of said Statement. But I hope that this chapter will still help you to have a clearer idea in your head as to what your Final Statement should say.

I cannot adequately express the joy and relief we felt when we received this document. It meant that the LEA had to take over the responsibility for financing Richard's education. Also, and in some ways just as important, it firmly established Richard's 'need'. This will be very important when we are trying to secure funding for a special needs college place (which we will be doing in the next few months).

We hope and pray that we won't have the same sort of problems with Social Services when it comes to accessing support and funding for later in Richard's life.

We had to battle ferociously to have Alice accepted into the Adults with Disabilities Team so that she could continue at her special needs college and then literally had to bang on doors in desperation to get Alex funded at his special needs college. We now know, from experience, that without a proper diagnostic label tied tightly to their toes it is all too easy for those in authority to turn their backs on even the most vulnerable people.

We are not taking Richard's college funding for granted but we are hoping that it might be slightly easier this time as it is actually recorded on his Statement that he requires a 'waking-hour curriculum using a consistency of approach throughout the day'.

'Waking-hour curriculum' is the new term for what used to be, and sometimes still is, called a '24-hour curriculum'. If you feel that your child needs a residential placement it is *vital* that you manage to get this phrase inserted into his or her Statement.

It's sad, but probably true, that you stand a much greater chance of success if you get assistance in your battle. Thank God there are now people out there you can turn to who can help you to fight. If you turn to Appendix 1 you will find the names and addresses of quite a few.

As three of our children are autistic, we found the National Autistic Society's educational advocacy service extremely valuable. For the first tribunal we did take advantage of a solicitor assigned to us through the NAS on a 'pro bono' arrangement. We were very grateful to the NAS for this help as we would have been totally alone otherwise. Sadly, we didn't win.

We probably would have lost whatever, but the solicitor assigned to us, while obviously very bright, had never actually handled a tribunal (the advocacy service relationship with the firm of solicitors was in its infancy). So when we walked into that hearing nobody on our side of the table had done this before. We were all tribunal 'virgins', one might say! Our solicitor handled herself well but their barrister had all the answers and was able to undermine our most important evidence and our expert witness (who was unable to attend on the day of the hearing – in retrospect I realize that we should have asked for an adjournment).

We now know that there are specialist solicitors who handle nothing else but these sort of cases because they form a specialist subject which seems to be quite unlike anything else.

For the second tribunal fight we were lucky enough to secure the advices of a wonderful representative from Resources for Autism. I have to admit I only found out about this organization when I received a very encouraging reply from Dame Steve Shirley following a letter to her foundation begging for advice and support. I shall remain eternally grateful for the fact that this busy woman took the time to write a very personal letter to me. She stated that her foundation could not help individuals but pointed me towards Resources for Autism who, when they took our case on, battled with all their might to help us succeed.

Our wonderful representative, Janet, had fought more than one hundred tribunals. This was one of the main differences with the second tribunal as Janet was able to interpret what was going on and help steer our battered little ship through very stormy waters, through dangerously rocky passages and home at last to safe harbour.

This is one of the inbuilt problems in the tribunal system.

Your LEA will have fought many tribunals, often with an experienced barrister who will him- or herself have been involved with and fought many tribunals.

The Chair of the tribunal panel is *always* legally qualified – and is either a solicitor or a barrister – and therefore well-versed in law and the tribunal system. The two lay people must have experience of special educational needs and may well have attended several tribunals.

This is just another day in their jobs, for which they are qualified and paid.

However well prepared you are, it will probably be your first or, if you are very unlucky, your second tribunal. You will be very emotionally involved, stressed and exhausted. You will know that this is an extremely important day for you and your child. You will have been putting in all the hours God sends to prepare your case, usually doing so around the constraints of your job plus your family commitments.

Tribunal day for you therefore is not the same thing at all.

This is why you really do *need* an advocate who can stand back a little from the problem and lend you the benefit of his or her experience, and who can help interpret what is going on.

We felt like we were in the middle of a Brian Rix farce towards the climax of our battle (only it wasn't in the slightest bit funny). Each postal delivery seemed to bring more and more ludicrous situations for us to deal with. By the time we arrived at the tribunal I was so stressed out I was unable to read! This was ironic as we were there to fight for our son who has great difficulty extracting meaning from the written word!

Fortunately, our case was so fully structured and we were so well-prepared by RFA that we were able to win this second tribunal *in spite* of my mental state. As a result, the LEA were *ordered* by SENDIST to amend the original Statement (which we discussed in Chapter 3) and to alter Part 4 to name the special needs residential school. All the waffle and padding were gone. This Final Statement was based on the document prepared by our great representative from Resources for Autism, Janet.

Part 1

Section 1, which sets out the factual stuff – name, address, etc. – remained the same, except that the 'current school' had by that time changed to the wonderful special needs establishment which a miracle had wrought earlier that year (see Chapter 11).

Section 2, the Advices, is a concise *précis* of the reports considered by the LEA; the original Statement, the physiotherapist's report, the second professor's report (although the LEA did manage to miss out all reference here to the latest report from the professor we had engaged privately two months prior to the tribunal, even though they do quote from his report in the Statement), the SALT report, and the annual review.

Part 2: Special educational needs

It is very important that the Needs are clearly and concisely stated. If not the Provision cannot follow correctly as one should dovetail into the other.

This is a huge improvement over the last Statement. It mentions that Richard was referred to a child and adolescent psychiatrist who diagnosed him as having an ASD. In the previous Statement the only mention of ASD had been very dismissive; all other mention had been removed, which was dangerous and damaging as teachers and others were not aware of his diagnosis, and therefore his difficulties, when they were dealing with him on a daily basis.

The previous Part 2 was 7 ½ pages long and identified forty-eight 'needs' – yet it was totally inadequate in content. This Part 2 was approximately 1 ¾ pages long. It was very tightly written (largely by Janet) quoting specific information, relevant to Richard, from the evidence in the Advices, such as Richard being described as a pupil of average verbal reasoning and low non-verbal reasoning. This was extracted from the independent psychologist's report. He had identified that this would give Richard particular difficulties in the more practical subjects: art, design, practical sciences and handwriting. Well, we could certainly identify with that.

Richard's difficult early years' history was condensed into one sentence. Then followed a comment (quoting from the Advices) about Richard's difficulties with socially interacting and how difficult this would continue to be.

The SALT report discussed Richard's strange language profile. The LEA included in the Statement details garnered from the SALT (speech and language therapy) report. It confirmed that Richard seems to have problems with pragmatics (that is, use of language, both understanding and understood), especially as he grows older. The report mentioned that emotions and humour, particulary subtle humour, are areas of difficulty for him. All of the above are factors which would make Richard's life unbearable if he didn't receive any help to make sense of the large amount of unspoken information that we all receive from the often confusing world around us.

It was pointed out that Richard's difficult start in life wouldn't have helped him, bearing in mind his inherited problems; but the evidence showed that he had continued to have social and communication problems showing that his difficulties were not down to early years' neglect alone – again this was taken from the Advices. This was a great relief as some people had tried to blame all his difficulties on this – perhaps in the hope that then they wouldn't have to do anything.

This is the sort of thing which is essential in a Statement so that the Provision can be tailored accordingly. The first Statement left this out.

One paragraph covers a condensed version of the very important physiotherapist's Advice (which also linked in to our Advice about how long it took Richard to learn to ride a bike).

The last paragraph of this section was sad but strong as it talked about Richard's oddness and vulnerability. Although he is much calmer when receiving the support of his SN school Richard can still be an anxious young man when he feels confused by situations which you or I would take in our stride. This is a lifelong problem.

We had engaged the independent psychologist to assess Richard two months before the tribunal hearing in the SN school so that he could really judge the appropriateness of the placement. This professor also appeared for us at the second tribunal, gave vital evidence and asked probing questions of the LEA. As well as obviously being someone who was highly qualified and experienced in this field he was also a very decent man and I would recommend him to anyone.

It was a huge relief to see these problems acknowledged in print as they were some of the points which we had worked so hard to get the LEA to understand.

So there we were, with an accurate summation of Richard's Needs at last.

Part 3: Special educational provision

A. Objectives

The ten objectives were clear, concise and precise. Each was just one pithy sentence (that spoke volumes), quite different to those in the previous Statement.

B. Educational provision to meet needs and objectives

'Richard will require placement in a small residential school for pupils with autistic spectrum disorders and related disorders, which can make the following provision:' This was a very definite statement from Janet who insisted that this vital sentence was in the Final Statement. This is another quote from the independent psychologist's report and it obviously stands alone as it is such a powerful sentence.

Points one to twelve were written specifically for Richard. Not a scrap of waffle or piffle or padding was allowed to creep in.

1. A structured and safe learning environment with clearly recognizable routines and procedures.

2. A waking-hour curriculum using a consistency of approach throughout the day.

3. A broad and balanced curriculum, with a high level of physical activity, which is suitably modified to suit Richard's needs.

4. Teaching in small groups with high staff:student ratio by teachers who have specialist training and are experienced in teaching pupils with ASD.

5. An appropriate peer group who are working at a similar level to himself to support his confidence and emerging self-advocacy skills.

6. All staff, including care staff, to be trained and experienced in teaching and/or supporting pupils with a diagnosis of ASD.

7. Input from a speech and language therapist to further assess and target his specific semantic and pragmatic difficulties, recognition and interpretation of more complex emotions, reasoning and inferencing skills.

8. A social skills/self-advocacy programme adapted to meet his needs.

9. A handwriting programme.

10. A life skills programme to develop his personal independence and the ability to make decisions.

11. A whole school ethos of high expectations.

12. Close liaison between home and school to encourage consistency of approach as well as the generalization of his learned skills.

All these points are an accurate summation of what Richard really does need to prepare him in any way for life. Looking through this document and observing Richard, eighteen months later, it is clear to me that these provisions have proved to be effective in helping Richard to sort himself out. That is the bottom line, I suppose: did the Statement work? Did it achieve the most appropriate outcome for your child?

C. Monitoring

These went down from the ten points proposed by the LEA in the original Statement to four clear, concise, precise sentences as follows:

1. The school will draw up an Individual Education Plan, with attainment targets linked to the Objectives detailed in 3A. The IEP will be reviewed termly.

2. The Annual Review will also report any modification to the National Curriculum, together with a report on the alternative provision being made.

3. These measures and attainments will be reported at the Annual Review.

4. Richard's parents to be invited to attend all IEP meetings, as well as Richard.

Part 4: Placement

I'm not ashamed to say that my husband and I both wept when we read that the residential special needs school had at last been named in Part 4.

Parts 5 and 6: Non-educational needs and Non-educational provision

Points 1–4 were fine; the odd hearing and vision comments were still there, but it'll do.

Point 5 (a) still mentioned that blasted report from the original social worker (who hadn't met Richard if you remember). However, by this stage (and another two social workers down the line) we *were* actually receiving some 'support' in the form of two hours a week from a family aide during holiday time which was increased to five hours per week (if there is anyone available!). This doesn't sound like much but it is better than nothing and is a help to give Richard something to look forward to.

Point 5(b) still mentioned the idea that Richard should possibly have alternative parenting methods. Yes, I know, but I sincerely hoped that this had been well and truly laid to rest and couldn't be bothered to nitpick.

Point 6 was important as it talked about Richard's social 'education' and, as mentioned earlier, *nothing* that appears in Parts 5 and 6 is enforceable by law. Therefore, may I remind you again to fight on if anything crucial is mentioned here but nowhere else in the Statement. In this case this had been highlighted and covered in the Provision that Janet insisted upon. Looking back I get an even better appreciation of how hard she worked to get this right. God bless you Janet – you're a star!

The not-Final Statement

I'll tell you a funny little story now. There was actually another Final Statement between the one featured in Chapter 3 and this one. It came after the tribunal decision arrived.

We speed read it, as you can imagine, with tears pouring down our cheeks. I was poleaxed by 'flu within a matter of hours and it wasn't until I managed to crawl back to my desk that I discovered (having read the document again more carefully) that the LEA had 'forgotten' three of the most vital points that had been stated in the decision from SENDIST!:

1. 'The LEA accepted that Richard required waking-hours provision which we found they were not able to provide themselves. Such provision is made at…School.'

2. 'Richard's intellectual profile and his autistic spectrum difficulties lead us to conclude that he requires teaching by specialist, experienced teachers and support staff.'

3. 'Richard will require placement in a small residential school for pupils with autistic spectrum disorders and related disorders, which can make the following provision…'

These had all been left out and yet are at the very heart of the Statement. There was a discrepancy because of the way the LEA's barrister had marked up the Statement prior to the hearing: he had noted that the LEA would not agree to the need for a residential specialist school which could provide a waking-hour curriculum, nor to the other two points. The tribunal ruled in our favour and the LEA then omitted the parts they had not initially agreed!

I was back on the telephone to Janet, our representative from the charity, and SENDIST immediately. Whilst Janet was checking her facts I spoke to the very helpful clerk at SENDIST.

They assured me that the LEA *must* comply with the SENDIST decision and suggested I send a polite letter to the LEA pointing out their oversight and copying in SENDIST, who had sent out the decision.

With Janet's help I wrote a letter to the director of education and urgently faxed over the letter to the LEA. The points were inserted in full. A new copy of the Statement was drawn up and was sent to us and the *final* Final Statement was at last in place.

Chapter 5

So how do you go about getting a Statement?

When we applied, a relatively short time ago, for the children to receive extra help at school it was usual for the child then to be placed somewhere on the Special Needs Register. Or if the school identified a need they would ask you if the child could be placed at a certain stage on the register. However, schools apparently no longer have to keep a register of children with special needs (although apparently many still do).

Please look in your COP – you have got a COP by now haven't you? You really do need it – it doesn't cost anything. It is possible that the wording or even principles in the COP will have changed since I wrote this book. It sometimes feels as though the 'powers that be' want to keep the parents on the back foot: just when you think you have grasped a point – it changes! However, IPSEA will have up-to-date guidance. Look in Appendix 1 for IPSEA's contact details.

Be not afraid of the COP. Yes, I know parts of it seem extremely legalistic but if you learn how to use it you'll find dipping in relatively simple and if there is something you don't understand I hope that either I or the COP itself will have pointed you toward someone you could talk it through with.

Chapter 2 of the COP, 'Working Partnership with Parents' (!), is well worth reading. For example 2.15 in talking about Parent Partnership Services states that:

> A local education authority must arrange for the parent of any child in their area with special educational needs to be provided with advice and information about matters relating to those needs.

The *old system*, which included the Special Needs Register (I quote them here because I think they may help you understand the new system better and because some teachers still refer to the old system), was as follows:

- *Stage one*
  'Class or subject teachers identify or register a child's special educational needs, and consulting the school's SEN coordinator, take initial action.'

- *Stage two*
  'The school's SEN coordinator takes lead responsibility for gathering information and for coordinating the child's special education provision, working with the child's teachers.'

- *Stage three*
  'Teachers and the SEN coordinator are supported by specialists from outside the school.'

- *Stage four*
  'The LEA consider the need for a statutory assessment and, if appropriate, make a multidisciplinary assessment.'

- *Stage five*
  'The LEA consider the need for a Statement of Special Educational Needs and, if appropriate, make a Statement and arrange monitor and review provision.'

OK, so remember the above has now changed to be replaced by the following three stages:

- Stage one: 'School Action' (see COP Chapter 5 for 'Identification, Assessment and Provision in the Primary Phase' and COP Chapter 6 for 'Identification, Assessment and Provision in the Secondary Sector'). The school provides something extra or different.

- Stage two: 'School Action Plus' (also fully described in Chapters 5 and 6 of COP for Primary and Secondary school children). The school continues to provide something extra or different but calls in external advisors.

- Stage three: the school requests a Statutory Statement.

'SCHOOL ACTION'

5:43 of COP states:

> When a class teacher or SENCO identifies a child with SEN the class teacher should provide interventions that are additional or different from those provided as part of the school's usual differentiated curriculum offer and strategies (School Action).
>
> 5:44 The basis for intervention through School Action could be the teacher's or other's concern, underpinned by evidence about a child who despite receiving differentiated learning opportunities:
>
> - makes little or no progress even when teaching approaches are targeted particularly in a child's identified area of weakness
>
> - shows signs of difficulty in developing literacy or mathematics skills which result in poor attainment in some curriculum areas
>
> - presents persistent emotional or behavioural difficulties which are not ameliorated by the behavioural management techniques usually employed in the school
>
> - has sensory or physical problems and continues to make little or no progress despite the provision of specialist equipment
>
> - has communication and/or interaction difficulties, and continues to make little or no progress despite the provision of a differentiated curriculum

To get a full picture of this I would recommend reading from 5:45–5:49.

5:50 talks about the Individual Education Plan, which is what your child should now have. This should be prepared by SENCO. The IEP sets out:

- the short-term targets set for or by the child
- the teaching strategies to be used
- the provisions to be put in place
- when the plan is to be reviewed

- success and/or exit criteria
- outcomes to be recorded when the IEP is reviewed.

'SCHOOL ACTION PLUS'

5:54 states:

> A request for help from external services is likely to follow a deci-
> sion taken by the SENCO and colleagues, in consultation with
> the parents, at a meeting to review the child's IEP. Schools should
> always consult specialists why they take action on behalf of a
> child through School Action Plus. But the involvement of special-
> ists need not be limited to such children. Outside specialists can
> play an important part in the very early identification of special
> educational needs and in advising schools on effective provision
> designed to prevent the development of more significant needs.
> They can act as consultants and be a source for in-service advice
> on learning and behaviour management strategies for all teachers.

If you read on, 5:55–5:61 will tell you much more about this process. I
sincerely wish that I had seen a copy of the Code of Practice when we
started the fight to get some help for Alice. Things would have been very
different.

From School Action Plus the next stage is where the head teacher (or parent) considers asking for a statutory assessment of a child's special educational needs.

   If the LEA considers that a statutory assessment is necessary then it
will prepare a Statement of Special Educational Needs.

   The process is similar in secondary schooling but I would urge you to
read 6:50–6:75 in the COP.

Please don't be daunted by the COP. It is broken down into chunks and
if you sit down with a cup of tea and a chocolate digestive with a notepad
and pen by your side you should find that you will be able to understand
quite a lot of it. If you don't I'd advise you to talk to your SENCO as a
starting point. If you do not get any satisfaction from them I'd advise you
to get in touch with IPSEA and talk it through with one of their advisers.

   The emphasis is on getting the schools to do everything and provide
all the 'evidences' etc. The idea is that if children get help early then they
won't need a Statement.

In one respect I suppose I can see the logic of this as children these days are constantly being assessed from Day 1 in school. Therefore, theoretically, the school should pick up on children's difficulties more easily. However, and this is a purely personal observation, all the teachers I know are already swamped with work that is not related to teaching and, while they do receive some training in special needs, I don't see how they can possibly be expected to be able to be 'lay psychologists' and fulfil all the other demands on their time.

We have to appreciate though that, whatever system your school/ LEA are running, if it is decided that your child's problems warrant extra attention then the school is going to need to find the extra money to pay for this.

The school will have to justify this to the LEA and the LEA will have to justify the expenditure to their auditors. It should therefore help you if you are following the COP course of action.

(This is the 'ideal'. I imagine that there are children out there who don't necessarily follow these stages, but it will help you fight for your child if this procedure has been followed by the school.)

So you're probably thinking 'What sort of help might my child get?'

One of the problems we had when we asked for Richard to be Statemented was because he was still officially only on Stage 3 of the register.

I have only a vague recall of what the earlier stages meant in real terms. I think when we were first told that Richard and Jack were going to be placed on the Special Needs Register (when they were still at primary school – Richard's second school) we were told that it just meant that the teacher was aware that they might need a little more attention and help.

Then when they progressed up the ladder we were told that it meant that they would be seated at the front near the teacher. It was all very casual. I'm not blaming the school. I blame myself for not knowing more at that stage about what the Special Needs Register was and what more possibly could have been done.

Learning support assistant

It may be decided that your child needs more help from a learning support assistant (LSA) either on a one-to-one basis or in a group situation. This may provide enough support to help your child cope with their problems.

Some LSAs are excellent and build good relationships with the children in their care. I think Alex must have had a LSA when he was little, and still Statemented, and it was probably helpful (but LSAs were called something else then). For some children having an LSA reinforces their feeling of 'separateness' and highlights the difference between them and their peers. Richard, as an older, teenage boy, resented the LSA intrusion and expected the LSA to do the work for him. Richard's behaviour became more extreme after the LSA was in place. However, although we argued that we did not believe that appointing an LSA for Richard would solve his problems, I cannot *prove* that the LSA was a significant factor in his deterioration. It may be coincidental that he missed masses of school when he had a LSA. In any case, it certainly couldn't be considered a success.

I also know that having an LSA can be very helpful, even vital, for other children and has enabled some to access the curriculum very successfully. I think it depends very much on the needs (and possibly the age) of your child.

Special needs unit

Some schools have a special needs unit on their campus where children may go for varying lengths of time to access extra assistance in problem areas.

Again I have mixed feelings about this. Our experience with Richard wasn't very good, which was no reflection on the quality of teaching. Our son was in such a state when this was put into action that it is very difficult to make a reasoned judgement.

Government policy at present is all about 'inclusion'; that is, including people with special needs in mainstream life. This is laudable, but if your child spends most of the day segregated in the unit because he cannot cope with the rest of the mainstream environment one might argue about the degree of inclusiveness of his or her education. However, the effectiveness of this provision may depend on the individual needs of the child and, while it didn't work for our son, it may work for your child.

A little extra help may be all that is needed to get some children back on track and keep them there. Sadly, in the case of two of our children, this simply wasn't sufficient. Both Alice and Richard required educating in a special needs environment.

By the age of twelve Alice was deeply disturbed by her 'world'. Mainstream schooling and the social skills required to survive were just beyond her abilities. Her behaviour had deteriorated so much (she was having huge – often violent – tantrums, self-harming and stealing) that we ended up paying for her to be educated privately for three years in a Rudolf Steiner school.

This wasn't a special needs school – we didn't know they existed. We both did two jobs to pay for this (with some help from a philanthropic trust) because we could not get the LEA PEP to assess her – and he 'forgot' to mention that we had a right of appeal – and we did not know that independent EPs existed.

Special needs schools

If you reluctantly come to the conclusion that your child is now 'failing' in mainstream schooling then I urge you not to delay but to investigate what appropriate schools might be alternative possibilities for your child. The type of school required will obviously depend upon your child's needs. For example:

- Does he need a day placement or a residential school which can offer the waking-hours/24-hour curriculum?
- Does he have physical disabilities which would require a certain type of special needs environment?

Depending on the problem my advice would be to contact any society linked to your child's disability. In my case I contacted the NAS and asked for a list of schools that catered for high functioning autists and those with Asperger's syndrome. I looked through to find what was available in our area.

Not a lot, was the answer!

If the LEA do actually agree that your child does need a special needs school they may suggest an LEA-maintained SN school. This may be an excellent solution for your child. I can think of at least two children I know who are in an LEA-maintained SN school quite locally and seem to be getting along fine. On the other hand, it may not be the answer. Possibly it will seem to be the solution from the LEA point of view but not necessarily from your child's. It wasn't the solution for Richard.

You will hear the term 'out of county' bandied around at this point as the LEA do not wish to pay for 'out of county' placements. What they do not seem to take into account is the fact that there may be absolutely nothing that is remotely suitable 'within county'.

How do you begin?

Go the relevant chapters in the COP regarding 'Identification Assessment and Provision in the Primary Phase' and 'Secondary Phase' (in my 2002 copy this is in Chapters 5 and 6 but it may have changed). If you read through these – bearing in mind exactly what 'School Action' and 'School Action Plus' actually mean – then you should be aware of what needs to be done. In plain English however:

1.   Talk to your child's teacher and tell her of your concerns. Ask what she, as the professional, has noticed are your child's strengths and weaknesses. Ask what she thinks would help him. Tell her if you think that your child should be assessed by the LEA educational psychologist and discuss with her why you think this is necessary. Ask about her opinion regarding 'School Action' and 'School Action Plus' for your child. If nothing else, this flags up the fact that you are aware of your rights.

It is probably a good idea to either write to the teacher prior to your appointment stating your concerns or take a well-prepared list of what you want to discuss. If you do this it is a good idea to take a copy so she can actually read what you have been talking about and take it away with her to think about. My mind tends to turn to mush when I'm confronted like this and I'm probably not alone. Remember, also, that for the teacher your child is just one of many and however good she may be at her job she is, like all teachers, pushed for time. If she has a written reminder of what you said it will aid her in assisting you when they are discussing your case with colleagues, other bodies and the LEA.

2.   Talk to the special needs co-ordinator (SENCO) at the school (all
      schools should have one teacher who is appointed to this post). He
      may be at the first meeting and in that case you can raise all your
      concerns with these members of staff at the same time. The SENCO
      should be able to help you. *A note of caution.* Please bear in mind that
      the SENCO may find himself in a difficult position. While he may
      be very sympathetic to your plight and to that of your child he is
      still employed by the LEA and his hands may therefore be tied.
          It states in COP 5:46:

> To help inform the decision on the nature of the additional
> help that might be needed by the child through School
> Action the class teacher together with the SENCO should
> collect all the available information about the child and seek
> additional information from the parents. In some cases
> outside professionals from health or social services may
> already be involved with the child. In such instances it is
> good practice for these professionals to liaise with the
> school and keep them informed of their input. Where these
> professionals have not already been working with the school
> staff, the SENCO should contact them if the parents agree.

A further change to the legislation since we tried so desperately to
achieve a Statement for Richard is that, even if the school request a
statutory assessment with a view to Statementing rather than you as
the parent, *you do have the right of appeal to SENDIST* to overturn the
decision *not* to even assess. (When we first tried, the situation was
that if the *school* requested an assessment for a Statement and the
LEA refused *you* did *not* have the right to appeal this decision. This
was an important piece of information of which we knew nothing.)

3.   If, for various reasons, you decide that you are going to write to the
      LEA, following discussions with the school, you should write to the
      person in charge at the LEA – usually called the director of
      education (DoE). If you don't know where the LEA are located, it is
      usually in your 'county town' – ask at your local library. I have
      found librarians extremely kind and helpful over the years.
          It would be a good idea to then telephone the LEA and find
      out the name of the DoE.

I am aware that legislation changes and you may be reading this book some years after I have written it. I therefore *strongly* urge you to check that this information is absolutely up-to-date by going on to the excellent IPSEA website or by writing to IPSEA. They publish downloadable Parent Support Sheets which cover the various stages of the Statementing and appeal process. I don't want you to lose out by default as we did initially. May I suggest that if you do have any independent reports – psychology, speech and language, physiotherapy – that you enclose them with this letter (be sure to state that you have enclosed them).

The sample letter on the following page is the sort of letter you should write.

The copy (cc) to the school is a courtesy naturally, but also I would advise you to try to work in partnership *with* the school as far as is possible. Sometimes the relationship does break down. This makes life a lot more difficult so I would urge you to try to keep them in your camp if you can.

You should hear back from the LEA within six weeks.

Important – do remember to keep a copy of all letters in a simple ring-binder file in date order. It could be vital to be able to refer back to your correspondence at a later stage.

Richard's first draft Statement was delayed by several tortuous months simply because I missed out a crucial word in my request. This led to a lot of heartache and wasted time while we argued semantics with the LEA. They had verbally stated that they would commence the Statementing procedure but didn't, and then argued that I hadn't asked.

I give full details of this in Chapter 10, which shows you what happened with Richard from beginning to end.

School requests an assessment

The SENCO at the school had requested an assessment for the Statementing procedure in the November. This was refused by the LEA due to 'lack of evidence'.

The SENCO had warned us that this might happen as Richard is able to read and write and is numerate. As was later revealed, he may be able to read and write but he has the utmost difficulty in extracting the

[*Your address
and telephone number*]

Mr A.N. Other
Director of Education
[*Your county*] Education Authority
County Hall [*probably*]
County Town
County, post code

[*Date*]

Dear Mr Other

Re: [*Your Child*] – [*date of birth*] – Request for Formal Assessment

I am writing as the parent of the above child to request an assessment of his special educational needs under the 1996 Education Act.

...attends...School. I believe that [*child's name*]'s special educational needs are as follows:

(a)

(b)

(c)

I enclose the following reports to substantiate this belief: [*name them*]

My reasons for believing that the school cannot on their own make the provision required to meet my child's needs are:

(a)

(b)

(c)

I understand that you are required by law to reply to this request within six weeks and that if you refuse I will be able to appeal to the Special Educational Needs and Disability Tribunal.

Yours sincerely
[*Your name*]

Enclosures:
Report from Dr Soandso, Educational Psychologist

cc [*the SENCO/head teacher at your child's school*]

meaning from what he is reading and even more difficulty formulating answers to questions posed about what he is reading.

Following Alice's diagnosis as being ASD, I asked for a 'formal assessment' for Richard in early January. This prompted some action and he was, at last, assessed in mid-January. Following that assessment the LEA EP told the SENCO that Richard should be Statemented. The SENCO telephoned me in the evening to tell me the 'good news'.

At a subsequent meeting I was told by the LEA PEP that I had 'six weeks' to go and look at alternative schools and if I wanted to get an independent educational psychologist to assess Richard now was the time.

However, when I had heard nothing further (remember I knew nothing about the 'procedure' of Statementing) by the end of April I wrote to the LEA PEP to politely ask how the Statement was progressing.

I was told that 'no request for a Statement had been made so nothing further had been done'!

After a lot of argy bargy that letter was then taken as the request to 'kick-start' the statutory assessment procedure but by then we had lost another three months. However, why had the PEP told me I had 'six weeks'? It just didn't make any sense.

Maybe you will be lucky at School Action Plus stage and your child will be given the help he or she needs by the LEA. It is a bit of a lottery depending on the county you live in. Even so you should still press the LEA to prepare a Statement for your child. Think of the Statement as a 'passport': it tells all the people that your child is going to encounter during her educational life (and beyond, sometimes) what difficulties – and strengths – your child has. The Statement also makes a, well, statement about the status of your child within the system which is recognized by other bodies – Disability Living Allowance, for example. It short-cuts the need to launch into a lengthy explanation when trying to access help for your child if you can say 'my child has a Statement of Special Needs because she has…'. Those who deal with this all the time as part of their job see this as recognition of need and it will help a great deal in the long as well as short term.

If the LEA don't reply after the six-week deadline (or if you get a negative response and you truly believe that your child requires a formal assessment and a Statement) I would suggest that you waste no further time and get in touch with one of the educational advocacy departments from one of the following: IPSEA, NAS, OASSIS or ACE. They all offer free, current advice which can be invaluable. Even at this stage you can appeal to SENDIST who can *force* the LEA to act. (We didn't know this – nobody told us our rights!)

See Chapter 6 for details about the SENDIST tribunal.

Remember, this is a legal process and your child has rights under law.

If the LEA agree to issue a Statement see Chapter 3 so that you can follow through the timing that each part should take by law. As we found out, even if they agree to the Statement it can be a very protracted affair.

I can hear you thinking: 'But this all takes so much time!' Well, you're right there. But do not let that put you off. Also don't be put off because it seems complicated. I will keep repeating, because it is worth repeating – *there are people out there who can help you.*

Don't forget (sorry to nag but this could be vital), keep copies of *every scrap* of correspondence and notes of telephone calls.

I hope you will learn something from our experience. For so many years we just didn't know what we were doing.

We couldn't seem to get anyone to do anything to help. I asked people for help but either I was asking the wrong people or I was asking the questions in the wrong way.

When we finally sought advice from a special needs solicitor (when we at last found out that such a person existed – and having lost the first tribunal) he called my husband and I 'a couple of turnip heads'!

Honestly!

And he was right to do so. We had spent so long going around in circles getting nowhere with all our children. So don't follow our example. Don't be a 'turnip head'. Don't wait. Get proper educational advocacy and advice. *Now!*

Chapter 6

The tribunal, SENDIST and appealing

It is an extraordinary sensation when you find that people in authority have paid a barrister to fight you not once but twice.

In neither incidence we had done anything wrong, yet we found ourselves up against expensive and highly trained people paid for by the LEA. All we had done was ask the LEA to admit that the school that our son was attending (when he wasn't refusing to go because he was clinically depressed) wasn't 'appropriate'.

'Appropriate' is the terminology used in the COP when it comes to deciding which school should be named in Part 4 of the Statement. What is 'best' for your child doesn't come into the equation. It is a question of 'best use of LEA resources' and 'appropriateness of the education'. The onus is on you to 'prove' your case.

We were up against a barrister because we had to appeal against the Statement. To do this you must appeal to the Special Needs and Disability Tribunal (SENDIST). You have to lay before them your reasons for appealing and then they decide whether you have a sufficient case for them to grant you a tribunal hearing.

So why would you have to go to a tribunal?

If you have received a Final Statement from the LEA which, despite your best endeavours, does not meet the needs of your child then you have a legal right to appeal against the Statement to SENDIST. You may wish to appeal because:

- the needs have not been appropriately or adequately described
- the provision within the existing school is not correct

- the placement is not the one that is most appropriate for your child.

See Appendix 1 for details on how to contact SENDIST.

How long do I have to appeal?

You have to apply to the tribunal *no later than two months after the LEA tell you their decision.* It is only possible to get the time limit extended in very few cases.

How do I appeal against a Statement or refusal to assess?

What you need to do is telephone or write to SENDIST and ask for a Notice of Appeal form. You will need to fill this in quite carefully but don't be daunted – it really is fairly straightforward. I am hoping that by now you have managed to get some help from one of the organizations I have mentioned elsewhere. They will help you to fill this in if necessary.

I hate filling in forms. I have too much of a butterfly mind to do it successfully and there are always lots of crossings out; but with all my special needs children I have to complete an awful lot of forms. I have no choice!

Notice of Appeal form

The first part of the form is mainly your name and address, etc.

In the section headed 'Your Appeal' you will see that they ask you 'What are you appealing against?' They then give you a selection of boxes to tick. You can see what questions our form asked on the following page.

So in our case we ticked box 4 and then boxes 4(a), 4(b) and 4(c). Your case may require you to tick different boxes.

We then filled in the name of the school – where Richard had been offered a place two years previously.

SENDIST then ask you to send them certain documents:

- a copy of the Statement if you have one plus the attachments – 'Advices'

- a copy of the LEA's letter giving you the decision which you are appealing against.

1. I asked the LEA to assess my child but it refused.

2. My child already has a Statement or note in lieu instead of a Statement. I asked the LEA to reassess my child but it refused.

3. The LEA assessed my child but refused to make a Statement.

4. The LEA made a Statement for my child, or refused to change it after a formal reassessment, and I don't agree with:

    4(a) what Part 2 says about my child's special educational need

    4(b) what Part 3 says about the educational help my child should receive

    4(c) the school named in Part 4 (or, the LEA named no school).

5. My child's current Statement was issued at least a year ago. I asked the LEA to change the school named but it refused. (The school you asked for must be maintained (funded) by an LEA.)

6. The LEA decided to cancel (no longer maintain) my child's Statement.

The form then states that if you have ticked box 4(c) or 5 and are asking for the LEA to change the school named in the Statement, you must provide written evidence that you have told the school. We were then sent a form by SENDIST for the head teacher of the proposed school to fill in. They state: 'The Tribunal, which hears your appeal, *must* have confirmation that a place is available at the school, normally on the date of the hearing or at the start of the following term.' (I was so terrified of losing by default that I double checked everything like this and made sure that it had arrived and been logged into our case notes by SENDIST.)

They then ask 'Why are you appealing?'

> In all cases, please explain the reasons for your appeal and give us all the information which you consider important. If you do not agree with what your child's statement says, what changes do you want? Please send us any other documents which support your appeal.

We wrote: 'Please see attached reasons for appeal.'

For the previous tribunal we had submitted masses of stuff. Even if SENDIST hadn't lost it all, there was just so much of it (because it was so complex) that it was difficult to disseminate. For the second tribunal we wrote a one-page letter to SENDIST as follows:

[*Your address*]

Special Educational Needs and Disability Tribunal
Procession House
55 Ludgate Hill
London EC4M 7JW

[*Date*]

Dear Sir/Madam

Re: [*Your child's name*] [*Date of birth*]

Please find enclosed our appeal against the content of the Statement of Special Educational Needs issued by…County Council.
    We enclose the following documents in support of our appeal:

1. Decision letter from…County Council (which had accompanied the latest revised Statement).

2. Completed Notice of Appeal form.

3. Reasons for appeal. [*We were appealing against Parts 2, 3 and 4. We sent four pages, set down in logical order, which showed very concisely the reasons we were appealing under each of the headings of Part 2, Part 3 and Part 4.*]

4. Amended Statement of Special Educational Needs dated … [*the most recent Statement*] and appendices.

Appendices to our Appeal:

Appendix A – Report from…

Appendix B – Letter from…

Appendix C – Letter from…

Appendix D – Report from…

Appendix E – Letter from…etc. [*These were various pieces of vital correspondence.*]

We look forward to hearing from you in the near future.

Yours faithfully

Mrs V. Stressed-Out

SENDIST are usually fairly prompt in replying (we heard within two weeks of appealing). They have to decide whether there is a case to answer so you must, as succinctly as possible, put a strong appeal in.

We sent in our Notice of Appeal form in July. We then received a letter from the Clerk to the Tribunal to tell us that they had 'registered our appeal'. We were granted a hearing in November. Be aware that SENDIST (as with all large organizations) sometimes lose things! As I mentioned above, the first time around they lost *all* of our Case Statement and attachments which included a video cassette and audio tapes. We didn't find out until just before the tribunal when we received 'the Bundle'.

('The Bundle' is the collated set of documents from both the LEA and yourselves. It is what is sent out to the Panel two weeks prior to the hearing so that they can consider all the evidence. You will receive a copy of the Bundle and so will the LEA.)

I felt sick. It was horrendous as I had to re-photocopy everything and we had no spare copies of the video evidence to replace the missing ones. The tribunal Panel didn't have the full time to study the case and in retrospect I think this was very damaging. However, we did not dare ask for a delay as Richard was in a very bad way and we wanted to push on.

Always send correspondence by special delivery – so that at least there is a record of when it arrived. *Always* keep a copy of everything you send.

What if the tribunal cannot deal with your complaint?

To quote the DfES again (Department for Education and Skills 2001, p.38):

> You may be able to make a complaint to the Local Government Ombudsman if your complaint is about something that the Tribunal does not deal with. For example, if your complaint is about the LEA's failure to:
>
> Keep within time limits
>
> Make sure that the help your child needs is provided as set out in the Statement.

You can find out more about the Local Government Ombudsman in a special booklet. You can get the booklet from your LEA, or from the Ombudsman at:

Commission for Local Administration in England
21 Queen Anne's Gate
London SW1H 9BU

What if SENDIST decide they can deal with your complaint?

SENDIST will give you a date by which time you must send in your 'Case Statement' to the tribunal. We heard at the end of July, exactly two weeks after we had sent in our Notice of Appeal, confirming that they had registered our appeal against the LEA's decision and giving us an appeal number. We had to have all evidence in by early October. *All* evidence really should be in by that date. It is possible to ask the special permission of the President for late evidence to be considered but if he turns you down then you are stuck.

SENDIST sound scary!

SENDIST's letter finished with the sentence: 'I hope this letter is helpful. Do please ring if anything is unclear.' I believe that last sentence is a sincere one. I found the Clerks to the Tribunal and their colleagues very approachable and helpful, and when I did have to telephone them to check details they were professional yet friendly. However, they do state 'as we must be unbiased we cannot tell you exactly what evidence to give or which witnesses to bring to the hearing'.

They will send you a video which illustrates a tribunal hearing. It was interesting but our hearing was nothing like that shown.

When will your hearing be?

SENDIST will give you a two-week period, from a certain date, within which your hearing will be scheduled. You must discuss this with anyone else who is going to be accompanying you (a representative or expert witness) and perhaps give two dates when all concerned could be available.

You have to remember that the LEA will be asked the same question, which is why it is better to give two options if possible and hope that one of those will be convenient for all concerned.

SENDIST state: 'Once we have fixed the hearing date, we can only change it in exceptional circumstances.'

You will be given an attendance form to fill in. You will have to return it by a certain date. You must decide who is going to attend with you as there is a limited number to the people you may take. You can only bring up to two witnesses. SENDIST state: 'If you do not tell us the names of any representatives or witnesses that you want to bring, they may not be allowed to attend the hearing.' This could be vital to your case so try to deal with this. However, you do have a little breathing space:

- We received this letter at the end of July.

- We had until early September to confirm what dates we couldn't make (however, this may just be because the August school holidays intervened, so do not rely on such a long time lapse).

- We had until early October to send in the Case Statement along with other evidence.

- We had until early October to return the attendance form with the names of representatives and witnesses.

- The tribunal hearing took place towards the end of November.

Once you have been granted an appeal hearing you have a little time to draw breath – but not much. This is when you really have to start making sure that you have everything that you need in the way of evidence for the day of the hearing.

Try to get as much in writing as you can so that the Panel can read your case thoroughly and understand it before you even step through the door.

'The what?'

The Panel. These are the people who on the day will hear your case, and the case of the LEA. The Panel will be made up of three people: a Chair (who is a barrister or solicitor) and two lay people (who have experience of SEN). Outside the South East appeals are heard locally so, although SENDIST are based in London, they travel around the country hearing cases.

SENDIST will also send you a leaflet entitled 'To help you prepare your case – what we need to know'.

I repeat – *I strongly urge you to try to get assistance in fighting this case from one of the organizations I've mentioned or one that is particularly relevant to your child's difficulties.*

Having received the letter confirming that SENDIST had registered our appeal I then wrote them a one-page letter.

[*Your address*]

Special Educational Needs and Disability Tribunal
Procession House
55 Ludgate Hill
London EC4M 7JW

[*Date*]

Dear [*you now have the name of the Clerk so you can address by name*]

Re: [*Your child's name*] – Appeal Number [*which you will now have on their letter*]

Thank you for your letter of … July. I would confirm that we are preparing a statement of our case and this will be given to the tribunal by early October.

We would ask that the tribunal be held on either Tuesday…November or Tuesday…November. We have checked with both our representatives and our expert witness and they are available on those dates. Please may we ask that the date is clarified as soon as possible?

May we ask where the tribunal will be held please?

We will complete and return the attendance form to you by the… October.

I am asking…School to complete the confirmation of place form. I will send it off to you as soon as we receive the completed form back.

Yours sincerely

Mrs V. Cheesed-Off

Each case is of course different. In our situation we didn't have the support of the LEA-maintained mainstream school that Richard was attending (at the time of the first tribunal hearing) but we did have strong support from the headmaster of the special needs school where we wanted him to be educated (and where Richard was by the time of the second hearing).

Not once, but twice, this wonderful but very busy man gave up his time and attended the tribunal hearing. He was not touting for business. His school is over-subscribed. He doesn't *need* extra pupils. He just felt very strongly that his school was more appropriate and could more adequately help Richard than the mainstream school.

He had stood by us in the darkest times. When there looked as though there was no possibility that Richard would be able to attend his school he would keep in touch sending the occasional email to Richard to encourage and cheer him – a joke, or a football comment – something that might make him smile. God bless him. We owe him!

He was right, the school has worked wonders, as you will see in the chapters about Richard (Chapters 10 and 11).

Preparing the Case Statement

Remember all through this procedure that the onus is on *you* to *prove* your case. You want to put together a case that is the strongest you can, but you also want to keep it as clear and succinct as possible. We wrote a simple two-page letter to the Clerk to the Tribunal, plus a three-page statement which set down all the reasons for Richard to be at a residential special needs school supported by relevant professional opinion contained in thirteen appendices. (I have explained this in more detail in Chapter 7.)

You have to bear in mind at all times that your Case Statement will initially be read and interpreted in your absence. I do tend to 'go on' a bit and I had to really rein myself in (OK – I admit it – my husband Robin reined me in!). Make it clear and straightforward and keep to the salient points. We had to forget about past wrongs and concentrate on what was central to this case.

As I've mentioned to you before we thought we'd got a strong case at the first tribunal and we lost. The second tribunal was a real education and one of the reasons why I feel able to have a shot at trying to help you.

Unexpected help

We were very fortunate (and this is why I have been urging you not to leave any avenue unexplored). I have recounted this before but it is worth re-telling if it helps and encourages you to go on. In desperation we had sent out a pile of letters begging people for advice and help. One was sent to Dame Steve Shirley, as I knew she had an interest in autism.

She sent me a lovely and very personal letter stating that while she sympathized her organization could not help individuals. However, she did make a couple of suggestions for people I could turn to for advice.

One of these organizations, Resources for Autism, turned out to have been set up specifically to help parents of autistic children to fight tribunals. I telephoned the organization and sent them a letter briefly detailing what was happening to our son and what had happened at the previous tribunal.

They agreed to help us fight and Janet was assigned to our case. I cannot tell you the difference this made in our lives. Janet had fought more than one hundred tribunals (including the one for her autistic son!). She came with a very good record of success. Her input was invaluable as not only did she know all the rules and etiquette but she also had an insight into how both the LEA and the tribunal Panel were thinking.

I hope she would agree that we were a working partnership. We provided all the information – reports, letters, a time-line of incidents, etc. We filled in all the gaps around the above documents. We did masses of ground work to find information when asked.

Janet then shaped this into our case. She was very good at extracting the 'kernel' of information from a stack of reports. She worked tirelessly. Thank you Janet (and your team).

Janet knew what sort of information the Panel would be looking for so that they could find in our favour. We built a relationship on trust. Sometimes she would ask us for information and I hadn't the faintest idea why she was asking for it but I got delving and found it for her anyway.

Every scrap of this evidence was vital to our case. It was exhausting, I'm not going to lie to you, but I don't regret any of it. Janet has admitted since that some of the preparation is guesswork. For example, we asked for and eventually received the criteria for the proposed new unit for Asperger's pupils at Richard's mainstream school. Although these criteria weren't mentioned in the decision, Janet is sure that it was taken on board, and found wanting, by the Panel.

Our son deserved justice. Richard deserved to live out his remaining school years in a place where it was possible for him to receive help that would see him through the rest of his life; he did not deserve to just miserably mark time until he could leave school.

It sounds melodramatic but I was frightened about what Richard might do. He was diagnosed as being clinically depressed. He was self-harming and cutting up his clothes. He was refusing school and hiding in his room. This was not the behaviour of a normal teenager. This was the behaviour of a deeply disturbed boy who simply could not cope with the day-to-day stresses and strains of mainstream school.

What is legally relevant?

For the second tribunal Janet helped us to present a case with the strongest evidence and enabled us to sift out what was *legally relevant*. This is very important as *the tribunal Panel can only make decisions based in law*.

It's not about logic or the Panel feeling sorry for you. The Panel cannot make decisions based on what is *best* for your child. It comes down to 'best use of resources' and 'appropriate' education. To quote the DfES yet again (Department for Education and Skills 2001, p.37):

> The Tribunal will look at the evidence and will make a final decision. In reaching this decision, the Tribunal may consider how the LEA's actions compare to the guidance set out in the SEN Code of Practice. Just because the LEA has not followed the Code will not always mean that their decision was wrong. But the Tribunal will expect the LEA to explain why they have not followed the Code's guidance when that is relevant to the decision they have made.

So what did we do next?

We got in touch with the two people we wanted to be our 'expert' witnesses, and Janet, to co-ordinate our dates to make sure that we could all be available for a date during that period of time. We gave them two possible dates where we had all cleared our diaries to be available.

A date and time were confirmed by SENDIST in early September. The location would be disclosed 'nearer the time'. We had a pretty good idea where it was going to be as we live in a rural location with few options for this sort of meeting.

We received a letter in July from SENDIST confirming that the Secretary of State for Education had approved the special needs school (this is called 'Enabling Consent'). This meant that if Richard met the criteria the 'Tribunal panel may decide to order the LEA to name the school in Richard's Statement of Special Educational Needs'. It also said: 'You will need to demonstrate that a place is available for Richard at the school. I enclose a form for the head teacher to fill in.'

We sent the form to the special needs school and the headmaster confirmed in writing to SENDIST that there was a place available for Richard.

We started gathering our thoughts and our evidence for the Case Statement. By this stage we had a ton of paperwork and we discussed at length with Janet what was the most 'legally relevant'. I've deliberately repeated that phrase – it is important to remember.

We arranged for Richard to be seen by another independent educational psychologist (an eminent professor – thank God we have a sympathetic bank manager). Janet told us it was very important that he should be assessed within the context of his new school. He was assessed in early September so we could have a very recent report ready in time to submit with the Case Statement. You will see from Chapter 10 that he had actually started there by then.

The professor's report was very important as it confirmed:

- 'Richard's primary special educational needs are related to the fact that he experiences an autistic spectrum disorder.'

- 'Richard would benefit from a "waking hours" curriculum, where his behaviour in a range of social situations can be monitored and a consistent level of appropriate skilled support can be provided both within the classroom and in the evenings.'

- 'Richard would benefit from the sheltered environment of a school which specialises in teaching pupils experiencing difficulties associated with autistic spectrum disorders, i.e. a place where Richard can feel safe.'

- 'Richard appears well placed in his present school.'

It was also interesting as it reaffirmed the 'statistically significant' scores for verbal and non-verbal IQ. If there is more than 19 points' difference between the two scores this becomes 'statistically significant' and the scores should not be added together to give a combined score IQ, which is what would normally happen. For example, at that time Richard had a verbal IQ score of 91 but a non-verbal IQ score of 67 (this is not uncommon in people suffering from Asperger's syndrome but was partially due to our intense input). The IQ in this case is then taken at the lower figure of 67.

Things are supposed to be changing but it may still be the case in your area that those with a difficulty but an IQ over 70 do not meet Adult Services criteria. Those with an IQ of less than 70 do.

The professor also stated:

> It is my opinion that Richard would be the target of bullies in a mainstream school. His speech is often laboured and pedantic, and lacks the rhythm and cadence typical of mainstream teenagers. Information in the case notes confirms that he has been the victim of bullying in his previous school.

We arranged for Richard to see the SALT who is attached to his new school to complete a language assessment.

We had all the children home for the summer so we tried to keep them happy and occupied!

We took a few days off in order to prepare for the 'big push'.

Our Case Statement

We had until early October to send in our Case Statement. The system had changed even since the first tribunal, as parents have now lost the right to respond to the LEA's reply to a Case Statement. Both parties now submit a Statement of Case at the same time. This has made the process more adversarial and it's difficult for parents to know the LEA's arguments and therefore prepare their case for the hearing.

Following Janet's advice we sent in a two-page letter and a three-page Case Statement with thirteen attachments.

Your letter should read something like the following:

[*Your address*]

Special Educational Needs and Disability Tribunal
The Secretariat
Windsor House
50 Victoria Street
London SW1H 0NW

[*Date*]

Dear...

Re: [*Your child's name*] – Case No....

Please find enclosed our Case Statement regarding our appeal against...
LEA's Statement of Special Educational Needs for our son... Date of
birth: ...
    We are also enclosing the following documents in support of our
appeal:

> Appendix 1 Report from... dated...
>
> Appendix 2 Letter from... dated...
>
> Appendix 3 Letter to... dated...
>
> Appendix 4 Photograph of... dated...
>
> Appendix 5 Video evidence dated...
>
> Appendix 6 Etc., etc., etc...

Yours sincerely

Mrs X. Orsted

This is your chance to show exactly *why* you feel the Statement is inadequate or incorrect. It is hard work but you *must* put together the very best
Case Statement you can. It has to be very strong, very concise, and very
accurate. Not easy – but it could make the difference between success
and failure. This is why I've continually encouraged you to *get help*.
    We enclosed a three-page, single-spaced Case Statement with this
letter and the appendices.

May I suggest that you begin your Case Statement with something like the following, which is ours. Naturally you will have to change the facts. I hope this will give you the gist of what you need to do. Richard was already at his new school by the time we submitted the Case Statement:

Our appeal is against the content of the Statement of Special Educational Needs issued by…County Council. We wish the information in this Case Statement to be read in conjunction with our previously submitted Reasons for Appeal [*this is the document you sent in to ask for SENDIST to consider an Appeal*].

Our child…is now…years old and has been a pupil at…School since… …LEA has refused to name this school at Part 4 of Richard's Statement.

[*We then go on to talk about the progress Richard has made since being at the new school, including reports from the headmaster and Ofsted reports of the school as appendices.*]

At his previous school, … School, Richard was very much on the outside, unable to participate in a meaningful way in the life of the school, spending time in the SENCO's room at break times and unable to join in extracurricular activities. He was subjected to repeated incidents of bullying and was self-harming, refusing to go to school and also diagnosed with depression by his GP in a doctor's note (previously submitted). In April, after the school had been made aware of Richard's diagnosis of an autistic spectrum disorder, he suffered an extremely serious and traumatic incident of assault on the school bus by fellow pupils, resulting in a period of reactive depression, withdrawal from all social contact and self-harming (see previously submitted documentation with Reasons for Appeal and also currently submitted video evidence of school bus assault incident).

Richard is a young man with an autistic spectrum disorder diagnosis who has clearly failed to thrive, or even survive, in mainstream schools. It is evident that he needs a secure, consistent environment for all of the day and evening and it is essential that he is educated in a safe environment. His social vulnerability, as a result of his ASD diagnosis, is compounded by deprivation in his very early years and he has had subsequent additional diagnoses of motor co-ordination difficulties, Attention Deficit Disorder and attachment disorder, which together produce a complex profile.

We have very recently received a report following a visit and assessment in September by independent educational psychologist Professor …of…Hospital… He has submitted his findings in a report which is submitted as Appendix 5. In summary, Professor…states:

> In his past school placements Richard has both 'self-harmed' and 'run away'. Richard's difficulties relating to autistic spectrum disorders have resulted in serious incidents of bullying.

> Teachers in his current school also report that Richard does not know how to behave appropriately within his peer group.

> Richard should be placed in a school which can offer an appropriate level of education and also has staff experienced in teaching pupils with autistic spectrum disorders. The school should offer:

> - A 'safe environment' in which Richard will not experience further bullying and will feel sufficiently secure as to prevent the recurrence of any self-injurious behaviour or desire to run away.

> - A waking-hour's curriculum where Richard's behaviour in a range of social situations can be monitored and skilled support provided both during the school day and in the evenings.

> - Since commencing at…School Richard has not suffered any incidents of self-harming nor has he been subject to any incidents of bullying or acting on a desire to run out of school.

We continued in this vein (I know I've repeated a couple of the points mentioned earlier in this chapter but I wanted to reiterate the most important facts) throughout the letter quoting a few of the most salient points from our appendices.

We also stated that we were aware that Richard had recently been visited by the LEA educational psychologist but that we had not seen a copy of his report. We said that once all the relevant information had been received we would submit our proposed amendments to Parts 2 and 3 of Richard's Statement.

We then attached the appendices, making sure that they were very clean, clear copies and marked with 'Appendix 1', 'Appendix 2', etc.

Don't forget to send in your attendance form otherwise you could find yourself totally on your own!

I gave the package a 'kiss for luck' (yes, I know – but we were desperate!) and sent it by special delivery. I telephoned the following day to make sure that:

(a)   it had arrived and

(b)   it would all be included in the Bundle.

I didn't think my nerves could stand a repeat of the previous tribunal Bundle arriving with just one sheet of paper as our evidence!

How did we find the time?

You may be thinking at this stage: 'She must be very rich or doesn't work and has access to fabulous technology to help her.' Well, I'm not very rich. My husband and I have worked very hard for over twenty years to build up our business to a stage where it doesn't make a loss. Taking on the children thirteen years ago certainly diluted my efforts towards the business and it has taken a while to recover.

I do work – often very long hours – and for some of the time both my husband and I have had to have two jobs to pay for schooling, etc.

I do have a computer which I admit has been a God-send. I would urge you to try to afford a simple one or, if not, to write up what you want to say at home in long hand and then go to one of those Internet cafés where you can type it up and print it out for just a few pounds. If you don't type, and really don't feel able to learn, then there are services advertised for people to type up notes for you. This is not a prohibitively expensive service.

Try, if you can, to get an email address somewhere that you can access often – again an Internet café can help you set up an account if you don't have your own. I had to be dragged kicking and screaming into the Internet age as I don't like 'playing games' on the computer, but this has been another invaluable tool.

So you've prepared your Case Statement. You've submitted as much evidence as you possibly can to support it. In Chapter 7 I'll be telling you what happens in the lead up to, and on, the Big Day itself.

Chapter 7

Preparing for the second tribunal

I've had to psyche myself up to write this chapter. It was a pretty grim time for us. I hope that by sharing it with you perhaps your experience might be easier. It might be useful and/or interesting for you to skip in and out of Chapter 10 while reading this as I cover a lot of the background in there.

Spookily, having put off writing this chapter for some while (as I knew it would be fairly gruelling to re-live the experience) I have just received documents from the NAS entitled 'Autism and education: The ongoing battle. Experiences and outcomes of the Special Educational Needs and Disability Tribunal'. This document has been compiled following a survey sent out to parents who had used the NAS Advocacy for Education service.

I have now received two further reports documenting the stress, etc., of parents going through the Statementing and tribunal system. I would commend them both to you. While these three reports deal with ASD tribunals I think you may learn something from them whatever your child's problems.

One was published by PACE – Parents Autism Campaign for Education (www.pace-uk.org). This is an organization that works with parents and public authorities to address the system failures that prevent children with autism accessing the education they need. The other was published by PEACH – Parents for Early Intervention of Autism (www.peach.org.uk) – a parent-led charity established to promote early behavioural intervention for younger children with autism. I wish we'd found them both years ago. They do make astonishing reading and I am drawing your attention to them not to put you off but to make you realize that *you are not alone.*

As I've mentioned before the dreadful feeling of isolation is a huge problem when you are going through this process. Our social life shrunk to nothing. I knew nobody else who was experiencing what we were and that was really hard. The more people I've met, and been able to talk to, the better I've felt about our situation.

Remember, the situation you find yourself in isn't your fault. You are not a failure either as a parent or a person. What you are doing is based in love. The love for your child.

The Peach report by Mandy Williams (undated) states:

> Most respondents had contacted and sought advice from a variety of other sources:
>
> 68% of respondents contacted another parent
>
> 61% contacted Peach
>
> 48% contacted IPSEA
>
> 24% contacted NAS (help-line*)
> *only existed for part of the period reviewed.

You will find the passion, commitment, support and knowledge of other parents to be invaluable. Please try to get in touch, even if only by telephone, with *anyone* you can find who has been through or is going through the same experience within the special needs educational system. Sympathy is one thing; empathy, something else.

Look after yourself!

As well as the COP arm yourself with some multivitamins, Rescue Remedy and St John's Wort if you can. Rescue Remedy is very good for shock and stress (both of which you may be experiencing at this point). It is a liquid which you can either take as drops straight into your mouth or you can dilute it in a little water. I was advised to put a couple of drops into a small bottle of mineral water to take into the tribunal hearing. It got me through.

I don't drink (alcohol makes all my joints hurt like heck so haven't touched the stuff for over twenty years) and Rescue Remedy has brandy in it. It is astonishing that just one drop in a whole bottle can be so potent!

I started taking St John's Wort when I took myself off Prozac a few years ago. I find it just keeps my spirits up without any nasty side-effects.

If in doubt, of course you should discuss this with your GP. In fact, it isn't a bad idea to tell your GP just how you are feeling if only so that he or she can chronicle the difficulties you are experiencing.

The Bundle arrives – eek!

When the Bundle arrives you will have to move very swiftly as you will then only have a very short space of time to refute anything that the LEA say in their Case Statement. Our Bundle was about four inches thick so, as you can imagine, there was a lot to digest!

The LEA Case Statement

Remember, you won't actually get to see the LEA Case Statement until two weeks before the tribunal hearing when it arrives in the Bundle! But just to give you some idea...

The LEA Senior Manager, Special Needs, sent a one-page letter stating that he included 'for your assistance, this Authority's statement of case and written evidence in respect of this matter'.

The evidence included:

Witness statement submitted by Mr..., Area Educational Psychologist, together with appendices.

Witness Statement submitted by..., Head of Function, Children and Families, ...County Council.

Information on relative costings of the Authority's educational provision and that requested by the appellants.

Completed SENT [*special educational needs tribunal*] attendance form.

Then what?

Immediately we received the Bundle I dashed to the nearest town and took several photocopies of it. I sent one to Janet, and one to each of our 'expert witnesses' (all sent by special delivery – the postage cost us a fortune but you *have* to do this). Everyone *must* know what they are fighting so you can all be 'singing from the same song sheet'.

What did the LEA say?

Once copies of the Bundle were in the post we took a proper look at the LEA Case Statement. I am determined not to be sued for libel so all I will say was that perhaps our LEA made some mistakes in their calculations.

For example, one of the attachments documented Richard's attendance at school for the academic year. On first reading it I didn't see anything wrong with the figures. I then sat down and read through my records for Richard's days when he couldn't go to school. They were rather different. I'm the first to admit that maths is not my strong suit (and my husband would most definitely agree – this is the woman who consistently transposes the numbers in the cheque book much to his incredulity!) but there was definitely something very wrong.

The sentence 'such a regular pattern of attendance continued up until...' stuck in my head – then stuck in my throat. When I checked my figures they had included the three weeks of Easter holiday in his 'regular pattern of attendance'! As I've said before, anyone can make a mistake – so always check *everything!*

This was obviously a very important point to refute. Richard had missed *huge* amounts of school. When we did the sums the percentage for the attendance figure was very different to the LEA's!

Another of the appendices to the LEA Case Statement was a psychologist's report from the new LEA EP who'd taken over when the original EP no longer wanted to be involved with our son. He seems to be a nice man doing a difficult job and I think he genuinely cares about his patients. It was unfortunate that his visit to Richard came at a time when the pressure of GCSE maths coursework was really getting to him in spite of the wonderful support from his new school. He reported Richard 'was in a mood' because he had torn up all his coursework and had been reprimanded and made to do it again. (Richard was quite calm from the beginning of the next term, completed all the work, and did eventually pass this GCSE as well as four other subjects.) It was a shame that this was the point when the LEA EP saw him as Richard was not being very positive about his new school (actually this has been the only time he has not been positive about the school – sod's law or what!?).

This was not the same sort of assessment as had been carried out by the professor we had approached.

The Social Services report is covered in Chapter 10. I found this report very hard to cope with. It was extremely negative in terms of our parenting skills – particularly mine. Be prepared, you may receive one like this. You may be lucky, but if you are not, remember hold your head high.

The budget figures were very interesting as it showed the investment in our son, in monetary terms, that the LEA were making, and were prepared to make, when our son returned to mainstream schooling (over my dead body!).

Janet set us some tasks (adding on other real costs for Richard's provision which had been 'forgotten') and we had to do sums of our own. I cannot find the figures at this moment but I can clearly remember that by the time we had added in the real costs of transport (which were agreed to on the day of the hearing) the sum for provision in mainstream school, which would have fallen far short of what Richard needs, was almost the same as the residential school placement which has met *all* his needs.

As a taxpayer, let alone a parent, we were outraged. The mainstream school was not meeting Richard's needs in spite of all the extra things they were doing like 'gluing on a LSA' (not our words), rearranging his timetable, removing him from lessons until he was only studying a small number of subjects, and providing a 'safe haven' for him before school and during break and lunchtime. Quite simply, the school *could not* meet Richard's needs: it did not have the right set-up or staff. This was not the best place for someone with Richard's problems.

You will need to read the LEA Case Statement very carefully so that you can ask pertinent questions before and during the hearing. However, be warned. It is much better to ask them before and to have the answers provided. It has been known for LEAs to talk to people on mobile phones during the tribunal hearing and perhaps, shall we say, the mobile distorts what is being said!

Do not be down-hearted by what I've just written. I am just trying to say that forewarned is forearmed. Fight with all your might to get your important questions answered *before* the day.

If, however, you do not get the answers, write to SENDIST and tell them. They should then ask the questions on the day of the hearing or at least ask the LEA why the questions haven't been answered.

Meeting at the old mainstream school

It is possible that you won't have to go to a meeting like this but there were many unanswered questions to which we were desperately seeking answers, so we had no choice. I found it a difficult and sad experience. Unfortunately, by the time we got to this meeting both sides had taken a position and knew a tribunal was just around the corner. Everyone was 'cagey' and for this reason there was very little constructive progress. We asked our questions, received answers to some and then left. Some of the answers were a little strange.

From what we could ascertain the LEA's was that Richard should be taken out of his residential SN school, where he was doing very well in a relaxed and happy environment, and put back into the large, noisy, mainstream high school where he had been repeatedly bullied and where his life had shrunk as he could not cope with the education regime or the other pupils. The school was about to open an Asperger's unit. It was proposed that Richard would be accepted into this unit. We had repeatedly asked about the unit and had received very odd replies which left us none the wiser.

When we arrived at the school we were met at the door and escorted to a small, narrow room with one window high in the wall. It transpired that this was going to be the much heralded unit. I have no idea whether this is a rip-roaring success. I hope for the children's sakes that it is, but I do know that for Richard it would have been ghastly.

We assumed that Richard would be in this unit all day. Not so. It transpired that Richard would have been in a normal class, with a LSA glued back on. We asked what the prompt would be for Richard to be taken to the unit. We were told that he would be taken there when he looked as though he was 'about to blow'!

We asked what new measures were to be adopted to help the other pupils understand the difficulties of the Asperger's pupils. They would be told after the child had left the classroom that 'the kid can't hack it'. Well, that would be all right then!

I do not wish to be negative. Maybe there is a unit in a mainstream school near you which does work well, in which case I'm genuinely happy for you. The fact that our LEA were at last acknowledging that their Asperger's pupils needed to access somewhere different was a step forward. However, this regime would not have worked at all for Richard and would have made him even worse. Shutting our distressed son away in a claustrophobic room crowded with other disturbed children and expecting this to help was not an idea we would have countenanced for even a moment. I felt very depressed when we emerged from this meeting.

Conciliation

Under the new rules you *have* to be offered a conciliation meeting with the LEA. Ours was not arranged until the week prior to the actual tribunal hearing. I found it very difficult, but maybe you will be luckier.

A word of warning! In our area the results of the conciliation meeting are not binding, but they may be in your area. I urge you to check before you go to any such meeting.

Our conciliation meeting was directed by SNAP Cymru Disagreement Resolution Service. There will be something similar in your area. The LEA are supposed to give you details, but if not the Citizens Advice Bureau should be able to help you. The chap conducting the meeting was very kind and kept the proceedings calm. I knew that the most important thing was for none of us to lose our rag. I'd had a hefty slug of Rescue Remedy prior to the meeting but my heart was still hammering.

It was very difficult for us as for weeks we had been asking questions of the very people present at this meeting and getting nowhere fast. My whole being was longing to shout 'For God's sake answer the blasted questions!', but I don't think that would have gone down too well!

We had spoken at length to Janet, had exchanged emails and had prepared a list of questions to ask at the meeting. We had been warned to try to 'keep our powder dry' for the actual tribunal which, as I mentioned, was only a week away.

Naturally I imagine the LEA had been similarly instructed by their barrister so it was rather a stilted atmosphere. I used to be the sort of person who couldn't bear 'gaps' in a conversation and probably like most of us I would fill them.

I don't do that now. If there is a silence I let it hang there like a line full of wet washing. Wait for the answer no matter how long it takes to arrive.

Present at the conciliation meeting were:

- The SNAP Cymru representative
- the Statementing Officer from the LEA

- the LEA educational psychologist
- the Head of Social Services (who is also 'joined at the hip' to the LEA now), who was appearing for the LEA at the tribunal
- the parents (us!).

I would imagine that your gathering would be held with a similar set of attendees.

The meeting was held in a large room at one of the LEA's 'satellite' offices. I had been to meetings in this room before and it was always tropical and I always melted. I therefore dressed accordingly. Unfortunately, the heating was turned off and had been off for three weeks! This was November. It was hard to tell whether I was shaking from cold or from fear.

Again we had a list of questions. Again we received a few answers. It was a physically uncomfortable meeting in more ways than one and we were glad when it was over. We were absolutely drained at the end, but had to go home and type up and send an email to Janet with the questions and answers so that she could help us to extract the information we needed. Even after both these meetings we still had many unanswered points.

I spent the next few days exclusively preparing for the tribunal hearing; typing up questions, collating answers and preparing, in large bold font, a chronological time line of significant events for the hearing. I wasn't going to be caught out again scrabbling through paperwork. I spent hours re-reading files and familiarizing myself with all the information and preparing a passionate statement for the Panel. Unfortunately, this was the information I could not 'read' on the day – due to stress I couldn't extract meaning from the written word so I literally couldn't read it.

The day of the hearing dawns at last

My lovely husband viewed me as a woman possessed! I would not, *could* not, give up. I felt that we had no choice but to keep on fighting. I can laugh about it now but I can assure you that at the time I wasn't laughing and neither was he!

Laughter was most definitely in very short supply. By the time we arrived at the hotel where the tribunal was held we were both exhausted and I was a wreck – but a very determined wreck.

I'm a romantic at heart and, I guess, an idealist. I suppose you could view me as a tatty little tug boat, battle-scarred, flag flapping in the wind, steaming bravely into a scrap against a gleaming, fully armed battleship. My hope was that our dogged persistence might eventually find a chink in the armour that would win the day. Well that, and being right!

The tribunal package really should really be stamped with a health warning – 'this experience can seriously damage your health'! I developed heart palpitations and a permanent twitch in my eye like the donkey in *Shrek*. If it hadn't been so serious it would have been funny. Asthma set in after we adopted the children and it was dreadful for the winter in between the Tribunals. I was in bed for nearly two months and in and out of hospital, and I managed to crack a rib during a particularly violent bout of coughing!

Since winning the second tribunal and moving Richard to the appropriate placement I've only had one small bout of asthma in twelve months. The twitch has gone and the palpitations are now under control thanks to some homeopathic iodine.

What can you expect the hearing to be like?

SENDIST will lend you a video of what the tribunal hearing day might be like. It wasn't bad and the woman in it, who used to be in *EastEnders* years ago (when I still had time/inclination to watch television), played a fairly convincing 'overwrought mother'. And they have tried to show what might happen but, however hard they try, I don't think they can really adequately portray what it is like as, although impartial, they are still seeing it from the professional point of view.

We had watched the video some months prior to the first hearing. I really do think SENDIST have tried hard to de-bunk some of the myths surrounding this event but I shall never forget the overwhelming feeling of fear when we walked into that solemn and serious place. It's the sort of atmosphere that makes you want to giggle with fear. You know that feeling?

Both of our hearings were held in a hotel in our county town. I suppose this is partly because the Panel have to travel all over the country hearing cases and they can book accommodation and the meeting room and any video/audio equipment at the same time, in the same location, which I can see makes sense. I felt slightly disadvantaged because the LEA have their headquarters in the same town, so it was sort of 'home turf' for them but nearly a hundred-mile round trip for us. This is only a small point but I'm trying to tell you what we were feeling.

THE LAYOUT OF THE HEARING ROOM

The Chair will usually sit in the middle on one side of a very long table with the two accompanying lay people on either side of him. They will have the Bundle in front of them because they will refer to this throughout the hearing.

You, your representative and your expert witnesses will sit at one end of the table opposite the Panel, and the LEA with their legal representative (it is unlikely they will *not* have a legal representative) will sit at the other end, also opposite. I found this uncomfortable as you cannot see the faces of the people in the opposing court, but by wiggling your chair around so you are at a little bit of an angle you may get a better view.

The Clerk to the Tribunal sits quietly at the back throughout the proceedings to assist the Panel. If you have any questions you can also approach him or her.

The hearing

The Chair will introduce himself, the other Panel members, the LEA and representatives and you (the parents) and your representatives. He will then ask one of the parties to give their evidence. Then the other party will be invited to give evidence.

Our tribunal was to ask the Panel to overrule the LEA decision and order them to change the Statement. This took all day. However, some tribunals are held to decide whether the LEA should even commence a statutory assessment, so they can vary enormously in length.

Both of our tribunals started at about 10.30 am and finished late in the afternoon with a break for lunch. Some tribunals are just scheduled for a morning or an afternoon if that is what the President of SENDIST has judged to be the length of time needed.

You and the Panel ask questions of the LEA and vice versa.

The decision

You won't receive the decision on the day. SENDIST hope to have it with you within two weeks of the tribunal. Those two weeks will seem like a long time so try and get a really gripping book from the library to take your mind off it all.

What happens then?

If the Panel uphold your case the LEA must abide by the decision. There are time limits imposed on this decision, but these might change so please check the current limits when you read this. SENDIST will be able to tell you this.

What if the LEA do not act?

I know that you don't want to read this: it is possible that the LEA still won't abide by the decision. Do not let your guard down until the new amended Statement is in place.

If you are still experiencing difficulties talk to the representative who helped you at the tribunal and get in touch *immediately* with the Clerk to the Tribunal at SENDIST and ask for their advice. Following that advice write a letter to the LEA copying in SENDIST.

If they still won't act get in touch with a solicitor and, if necessary, the Children's Commissioner, national press, Prime Minister or the Court of Human Rights.

What happens if you lose?

If you lose you have my deepest sympathies. I can empathize with how wretched you will be feeling. I had to shut myself away while I tried to come to terms with the injustice.

However, distressing as this is – all is not quite lost. There are still options open to you. You can appeal to the President of SENDIST and ask him or her to review the decision. A review can only be held if you believe that you lost on points of law.

However, there is a time limit imposed on how long you can wait before appealing. Please check the current regulations.

What if the President refuses to review your decision?

The final possibility here if all else has failed is to engage a special needs solicitor (if you don't already have one) and appeal to the High Court. This can be a very expensive process. In 2000/01 there were, however, thirty-five High Court appeals: thirty-one from parents and four from LEAs.

It might be possible to get legal aid for this if you meet the criteria and an SN solicitor will advise you of the procedure.

A word of warning – there are time constraints on both of these procedures so you need to act quickly.

What can you do if neither of these courses of action is open to you?

If you can't do either of the above it is a question of sitting tight and waiting. You cannot ask for another Statement within six months of the date of the last one.

Once that time has elapsed I'm afraid you have to start again. I can feel myself tensing up as I write that as this was precisely what we had to do while our son Richard was losing his mind. This time was not totally wasted as we were able to commence gathering evidence for the next tribunal. (What am I saying? It *was* wasted time and Richard was in a terrible state.)

If you look in Chapter 10 you will see what we did while we waited.

Reviewing a Statement

Your child is entitled to an annual review of his or her Statement. The school should be able to tell you when they usually conduct their reviews (they are normally all done at the same time as it usually involves the same 'cast').

The LEA will convene a meeting inviting the parents, the school and all the professionals who are involved in your child's life.

However, the *Special Educational Needs Code of Practice for Wales* (National Assembly for Wales 2002, 9:44, p.128) states that:

> where a school identifies a pupil with a statement of special educational needs who is at serious risk of disaffection or exclusion, an interim or early review should be called. It will then be possible to consider the pupil's changing needs and

recommend amendments to the statement, as an alternative to the pupil being excluded.

We were informed by someone in authority that you are allowed to ask for a review if there is any change in your child's circumstance – they have an accident or their condition suddenly deteriorates/improves, for example. In our case the change was two-fold. We had just received the second, definitive diagnosis of ASD (there was no mention of ASD in the Statement after the first tribunal found against us) and Richard was refusing to go to school for large amounts of time and thus was 'at serious risk of disaffection'.

You will need to write to the DoE stating that you wish to ask for a review of your child's Statement, setting out the reasons why. We requested such a review for Richard, but at the meeting I 'lost it'; in response the SENCO wouldn't let me read the paper we had prepared as 'it wasn't the right time'.

In a strangled voice I told the meeting I had been trying to help this child for eleven years and I asked when *would* be the right time. I was very emotional – I wasn't actually crying, but my voice was shaking – as was my whole body. I finished up by declaring I would get Richard to his new school 'if it killed me'!

My husband was wonderful and I remember him stroking the back of my hand. He was probably frightened by my outburst, and so was I. It was completely out of character for me. I used to be very reserved!

It was fortunate that we did write down what we wanted to say and copy it as we were able to give it to all those present, which included Richard's psychiatrist and social worker, so they had the information, even though we weren't allowed to read it out. It wasn't totally wasted therefore.

Tribunal tips

- Don't be afraid to ask the Clerk to the Tribunal if you are worried or puzzled by something. The Clerks are aware of how nervous you are and we found them sympathetic and helpful.

- Take the chance to go to the loo just before you go into the hearing. I know this sounds obvious, and you may have been fifteen times before, but it may be a while before you get the chance again. You will not be allowed to leave the room without permission. You can ask the Panel for a 'comfort break' but it will ruin your concentration.

- Take some water in with you. It should be provided on the table but have some with you – just in case. You will get very dry and you will end up with a raging headache. My mouth was very dry the whole time and it helped to be able to sip water (but do not drink too much otherwise you will have problems related to the tip mentioned above!).

- Wear comfortable clothes. Obviously you need to adhere to a reasonably business-like dress code as you want to be taken seriously, but this isn't the day to try out those new, very high heels or tight trousers. You need to wear something that you can forget all about so that all your energies will be concentrated on what is important.

- Wear layers for the same reason. Sometimes they completely overheat these meeting rooms and other times you freeze. Either situation will impinge on your mental faculties. Remember what your wise mum always told you and take a 'cardy'!

- Similarly, take some tissues to hand around. Although you don't get the decision on the day, emotions will be running high!

- Have a notebook and pen/pencil with you. You will need this for:

  (a) taking notes and

  (b) for passing messages to one another when the LEA are speaking.

„ I know that sounds soppy but you will probably be bursting with outrage and want to say something to somebody. You may have to wait a while before it is your turn to speak so you will need to write it down before you forget. You can also ask your representative to explain things if you don't understand. You might even find yourself doodling. I've just found my husband's tribunal day doodles. He has drawn two sketches of prison bars and written, and pencilled in, the words

'ESCAPE' and 'SCAPEGOAT'. (Freud would have a field day!) More bizarre perhaps is the word etched at the bottom of the page: 'TAPAS'. Perhaps he was getting hungry by then?

- Make sure you eat something for breakfast and again at lunch. It may taste like cardboard but you need to be functioning at the best level you can. It probably won't hurt your case, but it won't help it either if you pass out in the middle of the hearing.

- Take the Rescue Remedy in with you. Your best chance of success is if you can stay calm and be able to think straight. Remember – hysterics won't help!

- Hold your head up and look the Panel and the LEA squarely in the eye. Whatever else anyone else says you can be sure that *you* are telling the truth so you don't need to act shiftily.

- Remember you have done nothing wrong.

- Make sure you have sufficient child-care cover for your other children. The proceedings may be delayed or over-run. You do not want to have the added anxiety of wondering if little Johnny is burning your house down because you are still in the tribunal.

- Sit straight in your chair. You have nothing of which to be ashamed. Be proud of yourself. You've made it through all the bureaucracy to get to this day. You are a good parent fighting a just cause, for someone you love.

Chapter 8

Alice's story

Alice has had a very difficult time. She was on the 'at risk register' before she was born. At the age of twenty she still has identifiable reasons to be 'at risk' but very different ones.

Early problems

Alice was a cutey – a blonde bombshell – but she didn't know how to smile when she came to us at the age of six. We had to teach her that the rictus grimace she was showing us couldn't be interpreted as a smile! To be fair she hadn't had a lot to smile about. For the first five and a half years of her life she and her brothers frequently went into foster care – sometimes separately. At one point when she was just two she spent six months away from home. These periods of uncertainty and disruption would in themselves be very psychologically damaging even if you had no other problems. However, if you add on her ASD and other difficulties you can imagine what additional harm it must have done. When she was at home with her birth parents she was neglected again and so the cycle continued.

Alice now has a very good social worker (care manager) and line manager. At last, thank God, her needs have been recognized. What I find so hard to understand is why it took so long when we were literally begging the LEA and others for assistance. She had been identified when very young as being behind in her development. We only had sight of her early years' medical records two years ago, but those in authority had access to these records all along. She had displayed many telling behaviours which were documented: 'head banging', 'nightmares and screaming', 'punching own head with fist', 'facial grimaces', 'temper tantrums'.

All of these continued after she came to us and some escalated horrendously.

And yet, the professional view seemed to be that all four children had emerged from this disaster zone unscathed. How cynical and idiotic. We were left to muddle through. This was to the detriment of Alice and this family. She was, and is, and will always be a deeply disturbed person, whatever you wish to call/label her problems.

It seems extraordinary that those with access to these files seemed to think that all her difficult behaviours were going to just go away. Maybe they had their fingers crossed, but they should have swung into action when we first asked for help with her. It should not have taken ten years for her to be diagnosed and assisted. This is quite wrong and I bitterly regret the wasted years when we went round in circles not knowing the 'process' and not asking the right people in the right way.

I'm not blaming Alice. It isn't her fault that she is an autist with learning difficulties and other complicated issues. She did acknowledge to her Grandma, a couple of years ago, that life must have been very hard for us trying to cope with her. It was a very grown-up moment on her part but she was right – it wasn't just hard, it was hell.

We just couldn't get her help. We tried so hard. We loved her and cared for her and tried to make her happy. Knowing now that she is autistic I realize she must have been so confused and frightened so much of the time.

We were very aware that, as the oldest child, Alice had suffered the most trauma, but we were really out of our depth. She needed psychological and emotional support and we simply didn't have the experience to realize this. Some people look at me in total disbelief when I tell them how long it took to get the children diagnosed and to access appropriate placements and support in spite of all our efforts.

The difficulty with Alice's problems was that they were displayed as explosive behaviour and we spent such a lot of our time trying to contain this behaviour that it took our eye off the question – why? We tried all the usual sanctions when she was a child – sending her to her room, withholding pocket money, etc., when she had 'misbehaved'. It didn't work.

Alice would do such 'odd' things. You would arrange a treat and she would behave abominably. Birthdays were always particularly difficult. I used to brace myself when an 'occasion' was looming as it usually sparked truly dreadful events. She wasn't the only confused person then!

Alice was always volatile and moody, but her behaviour became more disturbed and extreme the older she became. One of the worst tantrums I witnessed erupted after a gentle time of baking for half an hour when I actually allowed myself to think, well, that was actually quite pleasant and 'normal'. She read my mind. Within seconds she was screaming abuse and it was on that occasion that I had a chair thrown at me. I had no idea why and I was pretty shaken by the experience.

We tried to give all of the children a childhood rich in good and happy experiences. A social worker reminded me that just prior to them coming home I had said that we were in the business of 'making memories'. I feel no guilt about that promise as I do believe they had many good experiences. We just didn't realize the enormous difficulty they were having in 'interpreting' the good experiences.

The LEA EP service did get involved in the fairly early days of her primary education but nobody 'did' anything. Mainstream school was a disaster.

Alice goes to primary school here

When the children first came to live with us, we were told to get them into a 'normal routine as quickly as possible'. I'm a dutiful soul so the older two children, Alice and Alex, trotted off to school for the last week of the summer term, which passed in a blur. While they were kind I don't think the school knew quite what to make of them.

The children were all pasty-faced when they arrived. That was one thing I did manage to get right. By the end of the summer holidays they looked healthy. Their hair had been cut by a talented hairdresser friend. They had run and run in the fresh air and had started to develop some muscle tone and some pink in their cheeks. We'd been for picnics to the beach (a bit of a nerve-wracking experience as Alex would throw himself into the arms of any passing strangers with a limpet-like grip much to the embarrassment of several men), and paddled in the stream and paddling pool until their toes went crinkly. They were eating three healthy meals a day with very little 'rubbish' in their diet and appeared to be sleeping well. They loved being read to. They had each grown two shoe sizes in six weeks (not uncommon, apparently, with newly placed children). We were hopeful that things were going to be OK. Yes, there had been tantrums but that was to be expected – wasn't it?

Although we were worried about Alex and Richard too, it was Alice who, after two and a half years with us, prompted our home-school experience. She threw a truly frightening tantrum whilst the children and I were out shopping, which continued throughout the half hour journey home. Well, it should have taken half an hour but I had to keep stopping to protect her small siblings as she lashed out at anything and anybody within reach. It was a nightmare – but when I eventually calmed her sufficiently so she could speak she said she was like she was because of how the other children treated her.

So we taught her at home. She still had tantrums during that time but our more peaceful, and very structured, approach did seem to help her to be calm enough to learn something.

Alice went back to mainstream primary school after nine months at home, during which we had managed to strengthen her reading, help her to learn her tables, do simple sums and improve her spelling and writing. I hoped this would be a fresh start as none of the new class would be aware of her previous tantrums. Unfortunately, they were made aware by her actions within a very short space of time.

Alice could not make friends and her behaviour was pretty extreme. She would still explode in a tantrum unexpectedly, lie on the floor, fold up on the desk and behave very strangely. The headmaster told me last year that he used to spend hours talking to Alice trying to help her.

I kept bumping into the LEA EP at Alice's second primary school, in the corridor, but all she said was 'it was a shame that Alice didn't have any friends'. No practical help or suggestions made. If I'd only known then what I know now! Statementing proceedings should definitely have been commenced without further delay.

I can quite clearly remember saying to Robin that the LEA educational psychology service was totally overstretched in our area and we weren't getting anywhere so we would have to look around elsewhere to try to find a solution ourselves. I was partly right but unfortunately we didn't know where to look. But *you* will now, won't you?

High school was ghastly. Alice couldn't cope with the work or the people. In spite of our very best endeavours she still didn't know what to do to try to make a friend and was consequently even more unhappy. The SENCO said (and I spoke to the SENCO a lot) that she was 'a loner'.

Alice started stealing money from people at school. The tantrums at home escalated. The journey back from the school was frankly frightening with lumps being kicked off the back of my driving seat by her and fists swinging wildly at her brothers. Each day was a feat of endurance. Home life was horrendous with almost non-stop tantrums (as Richard was later to display). We didn't dare mention homework. There was lots of screaming, shouting, hitting walls and herself and her brothers, breaking things, tearing or cutting clothes, soiling. I endured enormous amounts of verbal abuse. Jack, who was seven years old, had a large glass coffee jar aimed at him and thrown down the stairs. If it had hit him it might have killed him. This was a very scary scenario.

I can remember taking Alice to our GP. I asked him if her problems might have a physiological cause. I didn't really know what I meant – I suppose I was seeking a cause for this violent behaviour. He took blood tests which all came back negative. I don't actually know what he was testing for in retrospect. Again, I'm not blaming him. I've been told since by the GP that doctors in rural areas may only see one autist in their whole career so wouldn't really know what they were looking at or where to begin. I don't think the GP truly appreciated what our life was like either, so probably thought I was being a bit melodramatic.

We tried taking Alice to a homeopath, in the hope that she could calm her; she concluded, after several visits, that she couldn't help her and suggested that Alice might have a 'split personality'. She did recommend an organization which specializes in helping damaged children. The lovely lady there found her to be a very disturbed girl and really wanted to help her. However, at around that time we were referred to the local authority's clinical psychologist. He told us that we had to stop seeing this lady. Unfortunately, he completely misunderstood Alice's problems, concentrating solely on her behaviour and trying to help through a system of wholly inappropriate rewards (stars and smiley faces). I really feel that, as a psychologist, he should have had *some* inkling that Alice was autistic as we gave him enough evidence: difficulties forming relationships, lack of imagination, communication problems. We didn't know anything about autism but these signs should have rung some bells with him, surely?

We wasted an entire year while he talked to me once a fortnight. He tried to work with Alice but she would just 'wrap herself up' and not speak. Home life was dire. We were getting desperate.

We requested help from Social Services. The only suggestion that was made was that Alice should go into foster care. I have to be honest and say we were tempted as we were stretched to the limits but we couldn't bear the idea of Alice enduring another rejection. Also, the foster care being offered was in a local town where Alice would be expected to attend the local high school. We knew that she wouldn't cope as she couldn't manage in the other smaller school *with* our support and love. It would have been a disaster.

We now know that we were talking to completely the wrong people in Social Services.

I sat in a black pit of despair thinking that Alice couldn't stay at home but knew she wouldn't pass any entrance exams to go to boarding school (I knew nothing about special needs schools – and also didn't know that Alice had 'special needs'). It was then that I remembered the Steiner school in the village where I had spent some happy years of my childhood. I had attended the local school but I knew that the Steiner philosophy was a gentler one which might, just might, suit Alice.

I did tell them the truth about her tantrums but, bless them, they still agreed to take her. We managed to get a small amount of help with her fees (she had no Statement, remember) from two philanthropic trusts who assist adopted children.

Alice was relieved to be leaving the local school (another 'fresh start') and loved the setting of the new school. However, the tantrums started again. By the December we were told by the school that they couldn't keep her unless she had a psychiatric assessment. We didn't get to meet the psychiatrist who made this assessment, but Alice somehow managed to convince him that everything was fine and he did not follow up.

The school expressed more concern and told us that she had scored 7.5 out of 10 in a test for dyslexia. I tried again to get help from the LEA and was bounced around between our home county and Sussex.

Following this I wrote a begging letter to the LEA PEP. I asked if Alice could be Statemented. The LEA refused our request citing the fact that there wasn't enough 'evidence to assess'. We were not advised that we had a legal right to appeal against this decision not to assess.

The LEA's attitude seems extraordinary in the light of the copies of two letters we now have in our possession from the DoE of the county where Alice lived prior to her adoption stating that Alice was about to be Statemented at the age of six. I now know that is a very young age to commence this procedure so the previous LEA had identified her special needs. One of these letters is to the Headmistress of her first primary school and the other to the DoE in the county where we live, telling him that they were about to commence the Statementing procedure but now that the children were moving to this county they were passing on all the files to him.

How could the LEA then cite 'lack of evidence' even to assess her?

We only found these letters two years ago when Alice was seventeen. Had we had them before and understood their significance they would have changed Alice's life, and ours.

The Steiner school did their very best with her. The staff were very kind and loving, particularly her house parents. In fact it was they who first suggested that Alice might have 'autistic tendencies'. Everyone tried very hard but we knew that Alice was clinging on by her fingertips at the school.

We somehow managed to get through another difficult year, with the school starting each term with the comment that 'they didn't think that they could keep her for much longer'. They had said that Alice was 'teaching the class tolerance'!

This tolerance was soon exhausted.

By this stage Richard was also becoming very disturbed and home life was very difficult.

Camphill?

It was around this time that I found out about Camphill, quite by chance, and I finally managed to get Alice to the assessment described at the beginning of Chapter 1. I'm not a vindictive woman but I still feel (four years on) that what was said to me that day was cruel and unprofessional in the extreme.

The psychologist said that she felt that Alice should not go to the Camphill college I was suggesting. She felt that Alice 'would be stigmatized' and treated my opinions with contempt. I argued that I felt she was wrong (as has now been proven). She would not listen. I was shocked that she had spoken to me as she did.

This local authority psychologist gave Alice an IQ score of 78 (although we have never seen this report). This score was to prove very unhelpful as an IQ of 70 was considered to be the 'cut off' for accessing Adult Services. An independent psychologist later argued strenuously that this score was faulty due to an aberrant score recorded for one of the subtests.

Quite by chance I managed to get the Local (National) Health Trust's Clinical Medical Officer to listen to our story. She told me to write to her and, to her credit, was on the telephone within ten minutes of receiving the fax I sent her. She said she was appalled at the treatment we had received. She arranged for Alice to be referred to a professor in psychology. In her referral letter she stated 'as you can see many people have thrown diagnostic suggestions at this family but none seemed to have actually offered any practical support'. How true. Sadly this doctor moved away shortly afterwards, which was a shame as we desperately needed help.

Alice was nearly sixteen by now and in a very sorry state. I finally managed to persuade one of the LEA EPs to assess her. It was still a huge struggle and I remember in the preliminary discussions ending up shouting at the EP who had suggested that Alice should come back to the local school (just as they were about to take their GCSE exams!). I'm not proud of this behaviour and it is quite out of character for me but it was possibly justified as this woman did then listen to me. When she eventually did assess Alice she had the grace to look sheepish when it transpired that Alice had a reading comprehension age of an eight-year-old!

That same day I managed to at last see someone senior in Social Services. I really don't remember how. She said that she realized that Alice had a 'social veneer' and a trainee social worker was assigned to Alice's case. This lady was very kind and sympathetic but didn't have much power.

The Steiner school wrote a 'no holds barred' report (which I promised that Alice would never see) regarding her behaviour and their findings. The reports were a revelation. One said that 'as teachers we rarely push Alice into the inevitable tantrum for the sake of the class' – meaning if Alice didn't want to do something they didn't make her. I can understand why. It must have been very difficult for them every time Alice angrily disrupted a class, and they had a responsibility to these other young people who were studying for their GCSEs. This was precisely what was to happen again, this time with Richard. Long term it didn't help Alice. It didn't help Richard.

I visited the Camphill college. It felt so right to me; I just had a gut feeling that this peaceful situation with the very special ethos for helping people would be a place where Alice could feel safe and be happy.

Diagnosis at last

In January, just days away from her sixteenth birthday, Alice was diagnosed as being 'quasi autistic' with possibilities of a long-term risk of depressive illness. This has subsequently been confirmed as a diagnosis of ASD.

The quest for funding

A place was offered for the following August and we hoped Alice would 'hang on' until then, but in the February things came to a head when Alice telephoned from the Steiner school in a dreadful state to say that she 'couldn't go on'. This was a huge breakthrough with Alice as she was expressing genuine and even appropriate emotions for probably the first time in her life. We therefore took this telephone call very seriously.

I wrote to the LEA stating that Alice had to leave before she reached the legal school-leaving age and seeking financial help for the Camphill college, who managed to bring forward her entry date to the May. Extraordinarily, after all the years of turning their back on her, the LEA suddenly agreed to fund Alice's place at the Camphill college from the May to the July – as long as we paid for the transport!

A life-changing placement

Alice went straight from her Rudolf Steiner school into the Camphill college. The Rudolf Steiner school was a wonderful school, a very special school, but it was not a *special needs* school. Alice was in a terrible state, mentally and emotionally, by the time she left.

I don't blame the Steiner school. They really tried very hard to help but Alice was undiagnosed and a very confused and misunderstood young lady. You can imagine the reaction of her urbane peers when she had noisy tantrums, at the age of fifteen, to try to avoid school work which made no sense to her at all.

She could not cope with the work. She could not cope with the people. They were all becoming sophisticated young adults. Alice was an eight-year-old in a fifteen-year-old's body. It was heartbreaking to be told that she laboriously copied out the questions in exams (to be seen to be writing like the others). She didn't have a hope of answering the questions.

I swung from worrying about whether the new college would keep her as she was 'too able' to worrying about whether she would be asked to leave as she was 'too difficult'. Any sort of change is very difficult for autistic people and this was no exception. When we had taken her to visit the college I deliberately hung back to see what she thought. When I asked her what she felt (deliberately not a rhetorical question) her reply was interesting.

'I feel at home here,' she said.

And she has been 'at home' there. Being there has changed her life.

I've said this before, I know, but I feel it is worth repeating. When she was in 'mainstream' she was totally isolated as she just couldn't relate and was confused and very unhappy. Now she is in this protected, but gently challenging, environment, she has been able to integrate with the wider community because she has a good strong foundation to step out from.

The Camphill philosophy believes in teaching the spirit as, no matter how 'damaged' the body or mind, a person's spirit is intact. Alice has just finished her third year. They have helped give her life meaning. She has dignity and her self-confidence has grown enormously.

Whereas before she *constantly* had tantrums (even up to the age of sixteen) now she rarely does as she has found some inner peace. It sounds a bit 'airy fairy' but it isn't. She is still autistic, and always will be, but working from a basis of calm she has been able to discover just what she is capable of. She has at last experienced success rather than failure.

This has been achieved through the consistency and commitment of the people at this wonderful college, and Alice's hard work. Practical work (they do very little theory) is the basis of what they do each day. Everyone helps by doing what they can. House parents live with their own children, co-workers (who are volunteers from all over the world) and a small number of students in one of the houses that are dotted around the 400-acre farm. Students go out into the wider community as much as they are able.

Alice isn't 'in a home', she *is* 'home'. The atmosphere of the houses is very much one of 'family' and not in the slightest bit 'institutionalized'. Alice discovered her worth as a human being and this changed her life. We were right. A gentler, sweet girl began slowly to emerge from the confused chrysalis. A girl who would willingly help the less able students and was appreciated for it.

The college is run along Christian principles but in the best sense. I think Jesus himself would feel very at home there. Life is simple, structured, orderly and hardworking. People are taught to respect and be kind to one another. We don't think that is a bad thing and Alice has thrived within this structured and happy environment.

Each morning the students have breakfast in their house, help to wash up and then go off to work.

Alice worked on the farm for her first year (and in spite of her reservations she was rather good at looking after the cows, sheep and pigs!) as well as learning crafts and other skills. The green woodwork is amazing (based in a little round wooden house in the woods where the students use pole lathes to produce wheel-back chairs, etc.) and the candles that these young people make are glorious.

Alice (the girl who could do virtually nothing previously as she could not take instruction without erupting) can now weave colourful creations, create felt handbags (which would sit unashamedly in any craft fair), make breathtaking baskets and cook fabulous bread. She also attended mainstream college one day a week and completed a care course and first aid course which gave her a chance to dip her toes into the wider community. She found this day exhausting but Camphill understand her need to be quiet on her return to recover her equilibrium. In her second year Alice worked in the local Steiner kindergarten helping with the children four mornings a week. She was good at this but found it very tiring. In her third year Alice asked to work in the local old people's home, first for one day a week then two. She enjoyed this but again found it 'tiring'.

All the students return to their houses for a proper cooked lunch – which will have been prepared by the house-parents, co-workers and students, who take it in turns to help with cooking. Life skills are a very important aspect of the curriculum. The college has very productive organic gardens and also produces their own organic meat on the farm, so being invited to lunch is a treat!

Alice used to be rather unhealthy-looking (she comfort-ate when she was unhappy). Now she has a much improved complexion and looks good from the exercise she gets from all her outdoor activities.

Learning how to socialize is an important aspect of life. It cannot be learned through theory. Alice didn't have any friends until she went to this college. She was very aware that she was somehow 'set apart' from her peers. This made her feel more lonely and inadequate. Now she will visit other houses for lunch with a friend, join in an evening of dancing and fun, perhaps enjoy a sporting activity, rehearse a play or go off to the pub for a shandy and a game of pool. Wonderfully, she has a 'life'. This has helped diminish her feelings of inadequacy and as her confidence has grown we have seen amazing things from her. She came home at Easter and presented us with a beautiful new house sign which she had carved out of a large piece of oak. She also showed us the handbag she had woven, having dyed an old sheet first to rip up and weave!

I am always very moved when I visit. One of the other students is an autistic young man. He has no speech and was very much in his own world when he arrived. His mother has taught him to use a simple laminated piece of card (representing the 'querty' keyboard), held in his hand, to communicate. She was asking him all sorts of questions to try to draw him into the 'conversation'.

'Do you like Alice?' she said.

The young man thought for a moment. Having just watched him being fed by one of the co-workers I didn't hold out much hope of this eliciting any sort of response. I was wrong. He seemed to re-focus and pointed at the printed card.

'Yes. N i c e b e c a u s e k i n d,' was laboriously, and phonetically, spelled out.

It makes my hair stand on end just recounting this. As I told Alice later, we may never know what it was that she had done for this young man but he had recognized it as 'kind'. I was *so* proud of her. Never mind GCSEs and A levels, she had come so far as a human being.

We are very proud of all she has achieved. I dearly wish we had found out about Camphill so that she could have gone to a Camphill school and not suffered for all those years, but we are very thankful that we found this place eventually and quite by chance.

Not all plain sailing

At the time of her eighteenth birthday (when there should have been a 'seamless transition' to Adult Services) arguments raged as to who was going to fund her placement in the long term as the LEA had only agreed to do so for three months. Had we not been able to resolve this Alice would have been forced to leave. There was a 'multi-agency' meeting which we were not allowed to attend. It was apparently a very nasty-tempered affair. Education and Health were also represented but the representatives of both these services walked away from the situation saying that 'there was nothing wrong' with Alice, so why should they support her?

Part of the problem was the erroneous IQ of 78 that Alice had been given in the infamous assessment. This was to involve a very large fight that required me to trek to meetings, write many letters and speak to numerous people on the telephone. Eventually we managed to persuade the authorities that Alice should be reassessed and, following this, it was found that Alice has an IQ of 68 and at eighteen the mental age of ten years, six months. It was agreed that the funding council and Social Services would continue to support her. Social Services alone have now taken over that role as the funding council have fulfilled their brief and Alice's 'Needs' appear to have been recognized at last.

We don't know how long Alice will be in this particular placement (she is still very fragile emotionally but receives the support she requires to have a good life). We are looking to the future when, at some point, we hope that she will be ready to move to a Camphill community to continue the good work that has begun in the last few years. She will still be under the 'umbrella' of Camphill but access the wider community as and when she is able. We think she could continue to live the happy, worthwhile and fulfilled life that she so richly deserves after all the distress and mess of her childhood.

Chapter 9
Alex's story

'I'm surprised that the local primary school is prepared to take Alex,' said his foster mother.

In hindsight, that horrible word again, she summed the situation up rather well. We just didn't know it at the time.

Alex was just five years old and we didn't have a clue really. I remember tucking him into his bunk bed one night on one of the first few days after the children arrived 'home'. I was kneeling next to the bed. I kissed him goodnight and gave him a cuddle. His hair was much too long and very straggly (all the children had raggedy hair as nobody could get them to sit still). I stroked his head and then lifted his hair with my hands to properly reveal his face.

He was gazing at me quizzically. He couldn't say much then as his speech really entailed grunting and screaming but I looked into his eyes and thought, there is 'somebody' in there – and we're going to set him free.

How was his autistic diagnosis not picked up?

Alex can be a lovely boy, kind, sweet, innocent, with old-fashioned manners and loving (in his own funny way). However, as he's grown older and is more in the adult world his lack of understanding of situations has caused difficulties as he is easily led and tends to fly off the handle following often imagined 'slights'. He's also tall and quite good looking, which can be a problem as people expect more of him than he is capable of. He was always quite a cheerful child, in his own world really, and I think that helped him chart his way through mainstream school. We gave him a nice strong framework and he just about managed within that.

Alex was the child with the more 'obvious' problems. Sorting these out somehow masked what turned out to be life-long problems. He had been very deaf in early childhood; had suffered from glue ear and had grommets inserted (the specialist said he would have been hearing as though under water at the swimming pool); he also had ghastly adenoids and tonsils (which were whipped out) and a short soft palette which we thought were causing his communication problems. We were at least partly right.

Alex did receive a Statement (of sorts) in May 1991. It was based mainly on his 'speech' and hearing. I have only a hazy recollection of the procedure. Our input to the Statement seems to have been minimal. However, this Statement was being prepared during the first few months that the children were with us and we were a little overwhelmed by suddenly having four children to care for, so it is hardly surprising.

Re-reading the Statement now, it seems extraordinary that he was unStatemented so soon afterwards – in May 1993. The medical Advice does talk about:

- 'poor concentration span'
- 'problems with fine and gross muscular coordination'
- the fact that he was 'incoordinate and has difficulty with balancing skills'
- 'mixed laterality (right-handed, right-eared, left-eyed, left-footed)'.

Now I've seen what a proper Statement should look like I realize he was very badly let down. We weren't aware of the power that this should have given us regarding Alex and his education. We really were green-horns!

He was unStatemented at the age of eight based on a 'Verbal scale general abilities test', during home-school time. We were so stupid and naïve we congratulated him!!! Well, he had worked hard and so had we – we never stopped stimulating him, we sang with him, read with him, talked with him, did his exercises, did anything to make him interact with us and practise speaking. He had improved enormously from the funny little unco-ordinated 'bag of sticks' who'd been handed to us on his fifth birthday.

We now know that he was illegally unStatemented. We just received a letter saying that he had reached the speech quotient required and he would therefore no longer be in receipt of a Statement.

However, if his Statement had been adequate and continued:

1.   He would have received more help throughout his educational career. What he learned in mainstream would seem to be largely irrelevant to the life he will probably live.

2.   He would have been reviewed annually by the LEA EP at least, who surely would have eventually picked up on his semantic pragmatic problems and thus may have secured the accurate diagnosis earlier.

3.   We wouldn't have had to fight every inch of the way to secure funding for his post-16 placement.

4.   He might have been spared some very unpleasant experiences.

We should have resisted with all our might this travesty of justice but we simply didn't understand the implications. Alex turned out to have an IQ of 67. Surely it shouldn't have taken until he was seventeen years old for him to receive an accurate diagnosis of ASD?

All through his childhood I was kept busy ferrying Alex to speech therapy, physiotherapy, hearing clinic, doctor's appointments, special-ist's appointments (he also has a heart murmur) – a never ending stream of hospital corridors.

I was at the primary school so often (either taking him or delivering him from somewhere) that I once heard a small girl in a queue say to her friend in a stage whisper, 'Who is that lady?'

So I was 'the Mummy of Mystery'!

GCSEs?

Alex managed to achieve some GCSE passes mainly by laboriously copying out scads of work for his coursework and with loads of support from us and the teachers. His diligence got him through. His SENCO said that he was the best register monitor he'd seen and took his monitor duties very seriously 'as though he were carrying a cheque for £1000'.

We were very proud of Alex but frankly bemused. We could see that he hadn't understood what he was copying out. But he was muddling through and we still had two far more pressing (and noisy and violent) problems in Alice and Richard to sort out. That's my defence and I'm sticking to it – OK?

So Alex's school days came to an end with people probably thinking 'odd chap – but quite cheery'.

Beyond school – life gets difficult

Alex commenced on a care course at the local FE college. Well, he is quite a kind and caring boy so it seemed like a reasonable idea and he'd just scraped enough GCSEs.

Sadly, just a couple of weeks into the course, he was behaving very strangely. As I've mentioned before we now know that when the children can't cope with a situation they start doing very odd things – sending sort of non-verbal messages. I raised concerns near the beginning of his course regarding his strange behaviour which our antennae saw as his non-verbal message that he was not coping and was not happy. I was not heard – again!

I'm trying not to be antagonistic here so I'll just say that there was a difference of opinion between the FE college and us. We later found out that our concerns were very well founded, had drawn him into a situation which was potentially very dangerous and the police had to become involved. There is no joy in being right when you see your child suffering – especially if that suffering could have been completely avoided had your voice been heard.

A word of advice here – never give up, never shut up.

The disastrous FE year ends

Towards the end of this time, by a strange quirk of fate regarding Richard, information came into our hands from the local day centre for people with 'moderate' learning difficulties.

It transpired that the manager of this centre had given a report to the FE college the previous autumn (at the time when my concerns were being side-lined) which stated that Alex was not college work-placement material. The staff at the centre had realized that he needed such a lot of support that he was actually 'a service user'! This confirmed our fears that Alex, once removed from the firm framework of school and home, basically couldn't function. He left college with another set of more or less worthless qualifications gained with huge amounts of support which he was again, seemingly, unable to put into practice.

It was at this point that I applied to Derwen College. God bless them: this was the third time I had approached them to take one of my children. Ironically, on my first visit (when I was looking on behalf of Alice) I had said that I thought it was too 'busy' for Alice, who definitely needed peace and quiet. However, I had said that I thought that Alex would love the atmosphere. We even wrote to ask if he could do work experience from school there!!! Our stupidity confounds me sometimes.

The wonderful woman who handles admissions at Derwen listened patiently to my latest tale of woe (Richard had already been assessed and had a place at Derwen the following January, so she knew me of old!). She regretted that all 'assessment' slots were full for the foreseeable future. I sent her a copy of the report from the manager of the day centre. And then – our prayers were answered – someone cancelled and Derwen fitted us in within weeks of my call. They accepted Alex without any hesitation once they assessed him.

The other student being assessed at the same time as Alex was looking at a place two years hence. This is the norm. But we needed something for Alex in the next few months. I did something which is *totally* out of character for me. I told Derwen that, now Richard was at Cruckton Hall School, we wouldn't be needing the place they had offered him. Could they possibly offer it Alex? I shrivelled inside at my cheek – but we were desperate!

They said no. Quite reasonably. It would mean jumping ahead of a queue. I accepted their decision: it was quite fair. But what the heck were we going to do with Alex now? Again our prayers were answered and Derwen, God bless their cotton sports socks, offered Alex the place for January. Now all we had to do was secure the funding!

A community care assessment

Up until this point Alex didn't have a social worker. When the report came in from the manager of the day centre (herself an employee of Social Services, so I thought it most courageous as she was speaking out and disagreeing with the Authority who employ her) we knew that he would need one – and urgently. I didn't waste any time; I went straight to the Children with Disabilities Team (CDT) in our local town who had Richard as a client, so knew our family circumstances.

The CDT had seen what we had been through and in what state Richard had been until his move to the SN school. We were lucky the social worker I saw recognized the fact that our family had a genetic pre-disposition towards autism and didn't now question our concerns.

After some discussions with Social Services it was agreed that Alex would be taken on as a 'client'. Because he was now just seventeen years old (theoretically he would have been in transition had he been diagnosed earlier) it was decided that the Adults with Disabilities Team (ADT) would lead and the Children with Disabilities Team support.

During the summer both Alice and Alex were called in to the office of the new care manager from the ADT. She is a very nice woman and has a sympathetic way about her when dealing with them.

She interviewed Alex who was very bouncy, but like a five-year-old! This was in direct contrast to Alice who sat and cried during her interview. The care manager took into account those assessments we had to hand, our opinion and hers based on the information gleaned.

She concluded that Alex was 'at risk to and from the community' and was very 'gullible'.

Supported employment

In the September we managed to secure some supported employment for Alex as a stop-gap while we waited to hear about funding. He worked at a place that also employed, on a government scheme, young people with learning difficulties and other problems. We knew the kind lady who ran the scheme and felt that she would keep an eye on Alex for us.

He worked there for three months and was kept very busy. It was an interesting experience for Alex and gave him the dignity of 'going off to work' every day. He also received an allowance of approximately £40 for the week's work – travel expenses were paid. This money was saved for his 'college fund'.

Alex would come home every single day and asked if we had heard from the funding council regarding the funding for his place at Derwen. He was very anxious and his anxiety grew as the months passed with no news. When we heard that he had been turned down, in December, he wept openly on my shoulder. I promised him I would fight on.

Alex was going backwards and getting more and more frustrated and angry as time wore on because of his inability to be a young man and have a life like other young men. We'd had to gently talk to him about the fact that we thought that driving lessons ('but all my friends are having driving lessons') really weren't a good idea bearing in mind his lack of co-ordination, anticipation, empathy, etc. He has now quite rightly realized he would find it very frightening to be in charge of a heavy metal object moving at speed. While we encourage as much independence as possible in all our children we really thought this was a 'bridge too far'.

Another fight for diagnosis

While we were trying to get a diagnosis for Alex and funding for his place at Derwen (more appointments with specialists, etc.) I had to write a letter to the local child and adolescent psychiatrist to tell her more about him and his early years to help with the diagnostic process. It was a difficult letter to write as we both knew that I had by then read up on autism and it would have been easier, but not very honourable, if I had just written about a 'text-book' boy. I couldn't do that. I wanted to be honest just as I would want people to be honest with us.

As a template for writing a letter to your psychiatrist you need to refer to the information on writing the Parental Advice for the Statutory Assessment in Chapter 3. I hope that you will not have to wait until your child is seventeen before you are writing a letter to the psychiatrist. In all likelihood you will be sent a form by the Community and Mental Health Service (CAMHS) team and you can then put all your information in there. Nearly two years on from writing this letter regarding Alex I have just had to fill in a large form on Jack's behalf. Actually, thinking about it, I have also just sent a seventeen-page letter to fill the psychologist in on details that weren't touched upon in the form. So you see it may seem long winded, but how do you précis the life of a sixteen/seventeen-year-old and squash it all onto a form? If the psychologist/psychiatrist is to form a reasoned judgement they do need to know how the young person handled situations through their lives. They cannot base their diagnosis purely on how the person behaves in their office or even on how the person scores in an assessment in their office. Yes this is important as well, but it is how the person reacts to real-life situations that is very relevant to diagnosis.

Appendix 2 is an extract of the letter that I wrote to the psychiatrist last year about our eldest son. I have included a large part of this long letter because you may recognize some of the incidents I mention and it may help you find the missing part of your child's jigsaw puzzle.

Desperate days

SALT

An extract from the SALT 'language' report follows. There is a big difference between a 'speech' report and a 'language' report. Language tells us just what he does and doesn't understand – which is critical, especially for a diagnosis of autism.

The SALT had some problems as formal tests for Alex's age group are few, therefore some assessment was carried out informally and by using tests standardized on a younger age group.

The SALT asked Alex to explain two idioms for her:

> First, 'pull your socks up' and, second, 'it is raining cats and dogs'. He described the literal meaning of the first and then had a good go at describing the second meaning... The second one he found more difficult, giving a reply of 'Beware of cats and dogs'!!

I am aware that I think more carefully about what I say to all my autists following this revelation! Everything is taken literally.

In the summary the SALT comments:

> Alex presents with a severe delay in his language skills, in particular he finds the semantic aspects of language difficult and from report also has difficulty with the pragmatics of language.

> On the surface Alex's language skills are functional for everyday needs but on spending more time with Alex his difficulties become more apparent.

This was a very important assessment and highlighted enormous gaps in Alex's understanding.

I had spent months putting together a case for the funding body to secure funding for his place at special needs college. We had been compiling evidence throughout that time.

Physiotherapy – again!

Alex was first referred to physiotherapy by his headmaster in May 1994 when he was eight years old. The first physiotherapist's report stated: 'It had been noticed at school, at which he had just started, that he was ungainly in his movement and was having difficulty in sport.'

He was assessed by the physiotherapist who found that 'he had hyper mobile joints, a head lag and poor head righting to the right'. She queried a very slight increase in tone on his left side. She said he had very little counter balance. He had difficulty in hopping especially on the left. He had 'poor hip and shoulder stability'.

The physiotherapist gave Alex loads of exercises to do with baked bean tins. He started off with five baked bean tin 'lifts' a day and we encouraged him to extend himself daily. By the time he finished, after about eighteen months, he was up to one hundred and fifty lifts per day!! Diligent, as I've said.

He had to do all sorts of other exercises and slowly his muscle tone improved. In the autumn of 2002 I managed to arrange a physiotherapy assessment for Alex, which we hoped would help to gain a definite diagnosis. In spite of all our efforts over the years to get him stronger, the physiotherapist concluded in this assessment that Alex's physical difficulties would come 'under the umbrella term of Developmental Co-ordination Disorder'.

The correct diagnosis – at last!

From the SALT assessment, the physiotherapy assessment, our comments, and the psychiatrist's own assessments it was concluded by the latter that:

> It is my opinion, therefore, that in conjunction with his difficulties in social, motor and cognitive development, that Alex's symptomatology would attract a diagnosis of high function autism on both DSM-IV and ICD-10 criteria for this disorder.

At last we had the diagnosis which might help him to access assistance. He was over 17 ½ years old. We weren't home and dry yet though!

Dark days of winter

I sent off the report to the funding council and hoped that now we had a definitive diagnosis his funding would come through in time for the commencement of the new term which was only just over a month away.

Sadly, we received a letter from the funding council which crushed our hopes. They said there 'wasn't enough evidence'.

When I spoke to them on the telephone to plead his case, pointing out all the other evidence, they agreed to review their decision if I could get confirmation from Social Services and the psychiatrist that Alex needed to be at Derwen.

The psychiatrist had finished work for Christmas.

We then entered another twilight zone with Social Services ADT saying they wouldn't support this application and the CDT saying *they* couldn't because ADT said they were no longer part of the picture.

I had nails bitten up to my elbow. I knew that if Alex missed the January slot there might not be another place for two years and Alex was extremely upset all the time – both at home and at work. He was very short-tempered and miserable. He had pinned his hopes on going off to SN college.

He may have learning difficulties but he isn't stupid. He had realized that this was an opportunity to be in the correct environment – an environment where he could be 'at home' and thrive. We were having to live with his upset and it was very difficult.

Ghastly news!

I asked Alex's supported employment manager if she could write an accurate account of what Alex was like in the workplace. Bless her, she worked late and at eight o'clock at night she rang to say that she was faxing it through.

'You're not going to like it,' she said.

Her report had unexpected repercussions. It was very honest, but aside from stating that while a 'lovely boy' (this is a term often used regarding Alex) she did point out the problems they had experienced in working with him. He was obviously very willing but even this fairly undemanding job was too much for him and his behaviour had deteriorated towards the end of his term there.

I don't want to go into all the details, but as a result of the psychiatrist's letter we discovered, again quite by chance, that Alex had been targeted by a local paedophile. He'd been introduced to this man by one of the other students with learning difficulties that he met at the local further education college (if you recall I had said I was worried to the college at the meeting where I was 'mashed into the carpet'). It made us fully appreciate just how vulnerable and gullible he was even at seventeen years of age. Alex was so desperate for a friend, and this man said he was his friend, that he let him do some extremely inappropriate and potentially dangerous things to him. It meant that my husband spent most of Christmas Eve at the police station helping Alex to make a statement. This man was known to the police but because of Alex's age they thought that it was unlikely that they could get a conviction in court. Alex has a mental and emotional age much younger than his chronological age. Following their advice we dropped the case as it would have meant Alex having to appear in court and being cross examined. Even though this man is now on the Sex Offender's Register (based I believe on previous incidents as well as this one with Alex) he is able to walk freely in the local town. We cannot allow Alex the same freedom and I wonder how many of the other vulnerable students with learning difficulties at the local further education college he will prey upon before he is stopped.

Thank God, Social Services changed their mind and said that not only would they write to state that Alex should be at SN college but they would support 50 per cent of Alex's funding for Derwen.

The psychiatrist intervenes

In early January we received a copy of the letter from the psychiatrist to the funding council which stated:

> I should like to recommend that Alex has a residential educational placement in order that he is able to gain appropriate social and independence skills. His learning difficulties are such that he needs intensive 24-hour support and education in order to gain these skills. He is currently extremely vulnerable to exploitation as he does not have the ability to protect himself. This has already resulted in him being in a sexually vulnerable position… I would support the application for a place at Derwen College.

Alex packs his bags – in a hurry!

Alex was due to start on a Monday early in January. We finally heard from the funding council at twenty to five on the preceding Friday. Alex could go to college! I spent the weekend manically sewing in name tags and helping a very excited Alex to pack.

He is now successful, hard working and very happy. He is learning new skills through practical application which he really enjoys. He has the dignity of work and an appropriate social life. He has a chance for the future.

He is thriving and happy now he is in Derwen College mixing with a wide group of people with a range of disabilities and abilities. He plays wheelchair basketball (he doesn't need to use a wheelchair, this is just for fun), football, water polo and table tennis, and his social life has improved beyond his wildest dreams. Alex didn't have a proper friend either until he started at Derwen. Now he has lots – and a girlfriend!

This is the right placement for Alex. The fight was worth it.

Chapter 10

Richard's story

I want to start this chapter with a couple of really positive sentences. This weekend Richard came home from his SN school on the train (by himself – for the first time!) and we had a happy, peaceful time. He was pleasant, relaxed, polite, helpful and humorous – it was wonderful!

We've come a long way down a very rocky road. Perhaps we appreciate the good days even more because of all the ghastly times.

Richard, like his siblings, did suffer early years' neglect and deprivation. We know this and do not dispute it. What we've had to dispute for a long time is that this early years' deprivation was the *sole cause* of Richard's confusion and angst. By not naming the beast the LEA were able to do very little to help our child as he descended into a dreadful state. Looking at his early years' medical records now there were obviously signs then that there were going to be long-term problems but these were glossed over and we didn't know any better. We didn't get to see the early years' medical records until autumn 2001.

I'll attempt a sort of time line. Maybe you'll recognize something here and it might help.

Once upon a time...

Richard came home to us when he was three years old. My aunt commented that he always had 'worried eyes', an extremely prescient observation.

He attended playgroup two mornings a week followed by our village school from the age of four. He was a fairly cheerful little boy but one who simply could not be persuaded to do things if he didn't want to and things had to be 'just so'. He was very 'stubborn'. Richard's speech was very poor, and still is to an extent. He is just not comfortable with language. He found it very difficult to string a sentence together. Tense was a mystery to him and remembering the most simple verbal message was impossible.

We assumed, initially, that this was partly due to lack of stimulation but also the fact that he had probably learned from Alice, whose speech was snuffly and indistinct, and Alex, who couldn't do anything other than grunt and scream even at the age of five!

We've just bought walkie talkies as we live out in the country and when the telephone rings one of us might be in the workshop and unable to hear. Richard loves these. He will communicate far more with us on the handset than face to face. Wish we'd had them years ago!

The children's co-ordination was awful and we spent a long time practising catching, throwing and kicking a ball. Richard, having mastered this, couldn't be separated from his ball. As with his older two siblings, he was unable to play ordinary imaginary childhood games in spite of being repeatedly shown and encouraged.

Milestones? What milestones?

The older three children were very behind in their 'milestones'. They had very poor muscle tone and looked as if someone had tied their knees together as they were very pigeon-toed. We enrolled them at ballet. It worked very well. A year of ballet lessons and their legs straightened up beautifully.

Richard still ran on the outside edge of his feet and it wasn't really until he got into playing football in a big way that we managed to correct this. He could run quite fast but didn't seem to get anywhere on the football field until we realized that all the other players were going past him. We showed Richard the studs on the bottom of the boot and pointed out that he would play better if he could really try to run in a different way so that the studs would stick in the mud. We did all sorts of exercises to help him.

It took us a year of blood, sweat and tears (his and ours) trying to teach Richard to ride a bike. Even with stabilizers he found it incredibly difficult to co-ordinate and would disappear into the hedge when we let go of the handlebars. It could not be described as a particularly happy experience and once learned the bike was soon left. In contrast, Jack, our youngest son, just got on the bike and pedalled off at a much earlier age.

Problems begin at primary school

There were lots of problems at the village school with Richard and his two older siblings. Almost every day the school reported some misdemeanour to me. It was very difficult (the children would arrive home in the school minibus like wild animals) and I would spend ages trying to calm them all down.

This was odd because at home, while they were a handful, they weren't too bad. This sounds strange but we had worked out very quickly that the children really needed a very structured routine so this is what we gave them. Everyone sat down to lunch and supper at the same time. We organized a very regular bath- and bedtime and always had a long 'quiet time' when I read to them and sang to them before sleep. This relaxed them and at that time they slept well.

We thought that this was needed because of the disruptive years they had endured pre-adoption and we were partly right. We were lucky that what we gave them was exactly what they needed – by some gut instinct. The autistic children could cope with their lives when they were so structured and had such a strong framework around them. It was as they became older and the entire framework shifted both at home and at school that they simply couldn't cope.

On one occasion I was disturbed and appalled when the teacher told me it had 'taken three teachers to hold Richard down'. For some minor transgression Richard had been told to stand in a hoop (the class punishment). He couldn't do it and when the teacher caught hold of him he struggled and panicked. By the time the three teachers were holding him down he was screaming his head off and still struggling.

In retrospect we didn't protest enough at this treatment. I had told the teacher when he joined school that Richard couldn't stand to be restrained physically. This was something I'd noticed before we even brought him home and had witnessed a screaming, distressed child when his foster mother had tried to restrain him. I'm claustrophobic and thought that this was perhaps his problem too. I now know that for autistic people even the lightest touch can sometimes be felt as the most excruciating pain.

And now for something completely different!

In early 1993, when Richard was five years old, following a very violent outburst by Alice, we took the decision to 'educate the children otherwise' – at home. We believed that the constant upsets at school were very detrimental for the children and they didn't seem to be learning much. The largest amounts of progress seemed to be made in areas where we helped them anyway. The school were, in retrospect, out of their depth with these weird little children and we often felt that we were in opposing camps – very dispiriting to a new mum struggling to make a success of her 'instant family'.

I can assure you that the decision to home-school wasn't taken lightly. The responsibility felt enormous. We home-schooled Alice for nine months and the boys for approximately eighteen months.

When we first brought them home to join Jack I thought I should just let them play so they could recover. I quickly discovered this wasn't a good idea and that they had to have a structured day. So we would work on maths, science and English during the mornings, with a fifteen-minute break to run around outside. We would also be preparing lunch, making it part of the lessons. I quickly became aware that they picked things up much more quickly if the learning was of the 'doing' variety rather than theory and particularly so if it related to food. Our children had been neglected prior to adoption and filling their stomachs was an important issue. I always knew I would get their attention if food was involved.

Fractions were baffling until we baked little muffins and I put them all in a tin. 'There are fourteen cakes in this tin,' I announced. 'There are four of you. How many cakes will you each get?' Hands would excitedly shoot up and they would be rewarded with their 'fractions'. If I put the same sum on paper they would look blank.

After lunch, which was paid for with toy money and a till (they had no concept of money), we would try to do more artistic or active and social pursuits. I took them all to gymnastics, swimming lessons, drama, ballet, piano, football. Occasionally we would join together with other 'home-schoolers' but this was not particularly successful: I couldn't understand why at the time but do now. In spite of our best efforts to get them mixing with other children in a relaxed environment, none of our older children seemed concerned that they had no friends.

Richard was very happy doing spelling tests, which we did a lot. He learned his tables and absolutely loved sums. I could set him pages and pages of sums. Like most Aspergers, he didn't like being corrected when wrong, however gently we did it.

In retrospect Richard was an odd little boy but I'm sure you'll know what I mean when I tell you that we sort of adapted our lives to suit his oddities (and those of his older siblings). We came to accept the things that were absolutely rigid for him and tried to work around them. We also tried to 'accentuate the positive'. We had no idea of what we were all about to endure with him as the pressure in his educational life mounted and his life became very difficult.

Once Richard had learned to count he counted everything. If we were out he would be counting stairs where ever we went. I couldn't say 'I'll be back in a moment'. Richard would have counted the 'moments' I had been away for and I would be met by a storm of accusation!

A new beginning, a new primary school

When the time felt right we took Richard to the new primary school. He joined in the last week of Year Two and then moved up to Year Three in the September. It was a school with more structure than his previous one, which helped.

Richard was fairly quiet in class and because he had joined school able to read and spell it took a while before we all realized that he understood very little of what he was reading. Yes, I know that sounds crazy but you have to put this picture in the context of Richard as the third child with the older two children still behaving very oddly. The school had a very caring headmaster and teaching staff and they were trying very hard to get these two other children some help.

However, Richard still loved numbers, sums and jigsaw puzzles and one of his teachers said that he was able to see 'patterns' in sums, which is quite uncommon.

Richard still didn't have any friends in spite of all our endeavours to help 'create' friendships, but he played football at break time which eradicated the need to converse.

Richard takes his first step on the special needs ladder!

Richard moved up in the school and I think it was in Year Four that he was placed on the Special Needs Register (see Chapter 5). I was told that this just meant that the teachers were aware that Richard needed a little more help than some of the class.

By Year Five we were aware that Richard couldn't tell us what he'd been doing in school. Whereas Jack would come home and tell us almost verbatim what had been taught in class, Richard would be virtually blank. This created problems as he was being set homework but didn't know what he was supposed to do.

My letters to Richard's teacher become very concerned about his lack of comprehension when he was in Year Six. One stated that Richard didn't seem to know what he was doing most of the time. Richard's teacher told us it was better to wait until Richard was at the high school where they would 'sort it out'! He had been moved up another notch on the Special Needs Register to Stage Two but I was still not aware of what this really meant.

The situation with Alice was horrendous and other priorities were taking massive amounts of our time. Our focus was therefore very much on Alice and Alex. My husband was away on business a lot at this time and it was very stressful and exhausting.

High school, high stress

From the outset Richard was very unhappy and under stress at high school. This school is a good school with an excellent record of academic success; however, they pile on the homework from the first day to sort the wheat from the chaff. Richard couldn't cope with the volume of work and I remember very unhappy scenes when it came to homework time.

Richard was moved into the remedial set for English but was in the low mainstream set for the rest of the subjects. During that first autumn term I spoke to the SENCO about our concerns. He said he didn't think that the LEA would be interested in helping as Richard could spell, read and was numerate.

However, he did comment that he had noticed that Richard seemed to be 'a bit of a loner' at break and lunchtime but that he hadn't heard any complaints from any teachers regarding Richard's behaviour or lack of homework being handed in. This was because I, wrongly as I now see, would insist that Richard keep going on his homework until he had something to hand in. The school had no way of knowing, until we told them, that Richard's homework, which would have been completed by most children in twenty minutes, had taken him all weekend to complete – accompanied by many tears and tantrums.

We continued to keep in touch with the SENCO by telephone and with appointments but we still knew *nothing* about the special needs system and our children's rights. Richard became more unhappy, confused and difficult.

At last, a glimmer of understanding!

In the summer of 1999, at the end of a nightmare Year Seven, we had a small breakthrough regarding Richard's diagnosis. We had been taking him to Scouts as Alex had enjoyed this social activity. We can't say Richard was wildly enthusiastic but we were still trying to 'engage' him with other young people out of school. The Scout leader wouldn't take Richard to camp, which was disappointing. When I asked if that was because he was too young the Scout leader replied that it was because he couldn't get Richard to understand what he wanted him to do!

By this stage we were convinced that there was something definitely 'wrong' but we still didn't know what. Quite by chance, I managed to find a residential dyslexia summer camp. I had seen a banner advertising the previous year's camp when driving past and had registered in my mind that this might be helpful. It was.

First, Richard enjoyed the camp which was held at a school for dyslexics (now closed). Second, they identified that he did have some form of learning difficulty. It was the first time I heard the phrase 'semantic pragmatic disorder'. I didn't know what it meant and had to go and look it up.

Semantic pragmatic disorder is described in Lorna Wing's wonderful book *The Autistic Spectrum: A Guide for Parents and Professionals* (1996, pp.72–3):

> A condition in which speech production is fluent and grammatically correct but there is a serious deficit in the understanding of speech. There is much repetition and often immediate and delayed echolalia. The children have good memories and may read precociously but with poor understanding. The pragmatic aspect of language is its use in social conversation and its relevance to situations. This is markedly impaired in the syndrome. Some have special interests and repetitive routines. As pointed out by Sarah Lister Brook and Dermot Bowler, who compared the published studies on this subject, this is a description of the 'active but odd' group among the autistic disorders, including those who can be

diagnosed as having Asperger's syndrome. Some professional workers who are specialists in linguistics or language therapy insist that the semantic-pragmatic disorder can exist separately from the autistic spectrum. This is usually because they concentrate on language without examining the whole pattern of behaviour and the development from infancy of children given this diagnosis. Most people in the field of autistic disorders do not consider that there is any value in separating semantic-pragmatic disorder from the autistic spectrum. The disadvantage of doing so is the failure to recognize the child's whole pattern of disabilities and therefore a failure to address all their needs. It is also most misleading for the parents.

It is thought that follow-up studies into adult life would be helpful to clarify whether there are any real differences between semantic pragmatic disorder and autistic spectrum disorder. It is suspected that the prognosis may be the same for both.

The dyslexia school wrote a thorough report laying out their findings and disclosing the tests that had been carried out. One of these was an audiometric test which showed that, while there wasn't anything wrong with Richard's hearing, there were great problems with his audio processing – that is, what happens once the messages from the ear arrive in the brain. I described it to Richard as 'scrambling' which he understood and I think he was relieved and hopeful that someone might now help him. I too felt heartened when we left the summer camp. Richard was calm and happier than I'd seen him in a long time. I also felt that we had some ammunition to go back to the LEA with.

Wrong! The report has been consistently totally ignored by the LEA. This is difficult to accept as it should have helped the LEA EP to better understand Richard's problems.

We really tried to get it right. This was our wake-up call with Richard. I wrote to the SENCO immediately enclosing a copy of the report and asking that Richard be assessed.

The school request a statutory assessment

In October 1999 the school sent a 'Combined School Referral for Statutory Assessment' to the LEA. Just after this, I wrote to the SENCO pointing out that Richard was really struggling again and that his 'shoulders were going down'. It was also when I first pointed out to the

SENCO that Jack was having problems too (approximately six weeks after joining high school). We also therefore asked that Jack be assessed.

In November 1999 we received a letter from the Director of Education. He told us that Richard and Jack were 'not deemed to require statutory assessment'. He was unable to determine that they had 'significant physical, sensory, emotional, behavioural difficulties'.

We wrote again to the SENCO in December as we had just received the long awaited, and fairly shocking, EP's report regarding Alice. This reported that she had the reading comprehension of an eight-year-old. We reiterated that there had always been large similarities between Alice and Richard. We also pointed out that Richard, while being able to read, *wouldn't* read in spite of all our best endeavours; also that if he were watching even a fairly simple television programme he didn't seem to be able to understand the plot.

This letter was passed on to the LEA but nothing was heard from them regarding the contents. At this point it was suggested by the SENCO that both Richard and Jack be 'disapplied' from a non-core subject to allow them time to go to the special needs unit to work with the specially trained teacher.

The autistic diagnoses begin

It was in early January 2000 that I took Alice to see the professor in psychology who told us that she was 'quasi autistic'. Whilst this was sad and stunning news it stiffened our resolve to get help for Richard. I immediately wrote again to the PEP.

Warning – be very careful how you word requests. I know now that I made a mistake in the wording of that all-important letter. I did not mention 'statutory assessment' when asking for Richard to be assessed. This was later to cause problems with the commencement of the Statementing process. What I actually wrote was:

> May I formally request therefore, especially in the light of this report regarding their sister, that Richard and Jack both be properly assessed, either by yourself, or by the EP who had assessed Alice, who now has the family history on file so that appropriate steps can be taken to secure the very best help for their futures.

At last Richard was to be Statemented – or so we thought!

Richard was assessed in mid-January. The SENCO telephoned me in the evening and told me that the PEP had said that Richard should be Statemented – this was later denied by the PEP. He had also apparently said that I 'was quite justified in drawing his attention to Richard's problems'.

A most peculiar report was produced, placing Richard in the: 0.3 centile for 'general conceptual ability', less than 0.1 centile for 'verbal ability' and second centile for 'non-verbal reasoning'! (Centile refers to the percentage of the population which is at or below the IQ attained by the child in question. For example, Richard's second centile means that 98 per cent of the population would score better than him.)

It was peculiar because, as the PEP pointed out, 'it is significant to compare his general conceptual abilities with his achievement with number skills, spelling and word reading. His achievements were higher than might have been predicted from his general conceptual ability.'

This report came two months after the LEA had considered that Richard did not warrant further investigation!

The PEP also stated that 'this psychological investigation gives further evidence that Richard's special educational needs are significant because his level of ability falls within the bottom 2 per cent of children his age'.

Beware – man speaks with forked tongue!

Following this report we requested a meeting with the PEP to discuss his findings. It was at this meeting (which I attended with the school SENCO) that I was told by the LEA PEP that Richard should be Statemented, which I agreed with.

The PEP asked if I considered that Richard's current school was the right place for him. I said no, I didn't think it was the right place for him.

I was then told by the PEP that I had six weeks to prepare our side of the Statement and find an alternative school. I was also told that if I wanted to get an independent educational psychologist's assessment this was the time to do it!

I had just arranged for exactly such an assessment following advice from the dyslexia school but we thought it a very strange comment.

The independent educational psychologist – and Asperger's syndrome

I took Richard to see an independent psychologist in March 2000. We spent five hours with him and his associate. They both tested Richard very thoroughly, then came to talk to me.

'Have you ever heard of Asperger's syndrome?'

The first time I'd heard of this was at the meeting at Alice's prospective SN college, just a few months previously, where they mentioned their belief that this was what Alice was suffering from – otherwise I wouldn't have had a clue. It appeared that Richard fitted the profile for Asperger's syndrome too. I said that I imagined a sort of rollercoaster track if you charted his abilities on a graph.

The independent EP pulled out a piece of graph paper from his assessment forms with little dots marked for Richard's scores. He joined 'the dots'. My jaw dropped. It *was* a rollercoaster!! In some areas Richard was perhaps only just below average ability. In other areas there appeared to be nothing going on at all.

This visit cost us £250 and was worth every penny. We couldn't really afford it but we put it on the overdraft. Do not be put off if your immediate thought is 'Where would I get the money?' because you may be eligible for a carer's grant.

Carer's grant could possibly help you pay

If you look in Appendix 1 you will see that I mention the local carers' association. I know that our local branch has funded just such an independent assessment for a desperate mother using a carer's grant. Of course we didn't even know that we were 'carers' at the time of Richard's assessment.

Do you know that you are a 'carer' with rights in law and possibly benefits? If not, have a look at the information in Chapter 14.

Looking for schools

LEA-maintained schools

I am very dutiful so, following the PEP's instructions, set out to find alternative schools. I visited the local LEA-maintained SN school. I took with me the PEP's report. The headmaster took one look at it and said that Richard was much too bright for his school! He also said that because he was too intelligent for the school that he would resent the placement and his behaviour would become worse. As this was a man with many years' experience we respected his opinion.

This headmaster was later reprimanded by the LEA for telling me this!

Independently maintained schools

There were no other LEA-maintained schools that were even vaguely suitable for miles and miles. I then started investigating independent schools through the National Autistic Society.

At this point I hit upon some good fortune. The next school I telephoned was only 1¼ hour's drive from home and I was immediately able to speak to the headmaster.

'Do you take boys with Asperger's syndrome?' I asked him. There was obviously no point in even continuing with this discussion if he didn't. I half expected him not to know what Asperger's syndrome was, so it was a great relief when he replied that a very high percentage of his boys were 'Aspies'.

I made an appointment to see him, taking the PEP's report with me again, and also the report from the independent EP. The headmaster looked at the reports and talked to me about Richard and his difficulties, and strengths. He said that the peculiar educational profile was very usual in people with Asperger's syndrome. He then asked a couple of the boys to show me around.

Being totally honest I have to say that I wasn't frightfully enthusiastic at the prospect. The way things were at home at that point I'd had my fill of 'boys'.

How wrong can one be?

Two boys were 'volunteered' to show me around. They were polite, funny, informative and clearly very proud of their school. They showed me all the bedrooms (very neat, very minimalist, *very* suitable for autists) and bathrooms, dining room (very homely) and the games room. Other boys we met *en route* seemed industrious, happy and calm (Richard was none of these things at that time – far from it). In fact the whole school seemed happy, industrious and calm.

The boys also identified everyone's clean washing which was in tidy piles by the bedroom doors (which made me smile!). They were great and I was convinced. I must have returned to the headmaster glowing, hopeful, praying that he'd offer a place at this school.

We arranged that he should meet Richard at the school fete a few weeks hence. Cunning plan eh? Richard didn't even know that he was being scrutinized. We didn't want to unsettle Richard even more by telling him about this wonderful school that we had found for him. We didn't want to raise his hopes when we didn't know what was going to happen about funding. How right we were to take that attitude.

Having met Richard, the headmaster didn't have any hesitation in offering him a place. He felt that Richard would fit in. All we had to do was arrange funding – ha, ha.

Forgive the hollow laughter. Richard was thirteen when he was offered that place and he was 15 ½ when he finally was able to take it up!

The twilight zone

It was during this time that we entered a sort of 'twilight zone' and I became increasingly frustrated and bewildered by events.

We were under the impression that the Statementing process had begun. My reasons for thinking this, if you remember, were:

1. The SENCO had told us that the PEP had told him that Richard should be Statemented.

2. The PEP had told us that we had six weeks in which to find a new school and arrange an independent assessment. The 'six weeks' is significant. If you refer to Chapter 3 on the timing of the Statementing process you'll see why.

3. The PEP also said meaningfully we'd be hearing from him 'shortly'.

We thought therefore, as you might be entitled to, that wheels had been set in motion and that things were progressing. Wrong again!

What was happening meanwhile with that Statement?

As we hadn't heard anything I wrote again to the PEP in mid-April to ask what stage the Statement of Special Needs had now reached.

We were astonished by the PEP's response. I spoke to him on the telephone (three months had elapsed since the assessment in January when he had told the SENCO that Richard should be Statemented) and he said that he had not heard from the school formally requesting a Statement and therefore nothing had been done!

Unbelievable!

He then told me that my letter in April would be taken as 'Parental Request for Statementing' to start the process.

The SENCO telephoned to say he was 'baffled' by the PEP's comment as it had been his understanding that a Statement was being prepared for Richard and he could not understand why nothing had been done since.

The LEA 'out of county' policy

I mentioned to the PEP that I had been impressed by the special needs school in Shropshire. The PEP said that 'generally it is LEA policy to accommodate children with needs similar to Richard's within main-stream or at least within county'.

When I asked him what was available 'within county' he named two schools which were for severely disabled children and clearly would not be appropriate. He admitted this. He also said that I 'had to bear in mind that the budget had to stretch to meet the needs of all the children within county'.

I politely pointed out that our experiences with Alice meant that we were well aware of this and were also adamant that Richard should not suffer in the same way that she had simply because of LEA policy.

Do not take anything for granted or assume it is being done. Keep in touch regularly with the LEA by phone, letter and fax.

Appropriate wording in the Code of Practice

Check out the Code of Practice for your part of the UK. On page 77 of the Special Educational Needs Code of Practice for Wales (National Assembly for Wales 2002) it states in 7:21 the following:

> Parents may ask the LEA to conduct a statutory assessment under section 328 or 329 of the Education Act 1996. The LEA must comply with such a request, unless they have made a statutory assessment with six months of the date of the request or unless

they conclude, upon examining all the evidence provided to them, that a statutory assessment is not necessary.

Check the wording in your current COP and quote it exactly. When I wrote to ask for a 'formal assessment' I should have phrased my letter thus:

> We wish to request a statutory assessment under section 328 or 329 of the Education Act 1996.

If I had done that the LEA would have had to get on with it then, instead of which we wasted months arguing semantics with the authority.

The Statementing process begins – at last!

By this stage Richard was becoming increasingly frustrated and aggressive and we were seeing more and more tantrums. I notice that I describe his behaviour at that time as being 'more extreme'. He was becoming increasingly 'manic'.

In May we finally received a formal letter from the Director of Education at the LEA stating that they had received a referral (from the school – which was incorrect) that a 'statutory assessment is proposed for your child'. It set out the rules (under Section 167 of the Education Act 1996) and gives a brief outline of the timing, Advices, etc.

> We hope that the Statutory Assessment will be a positive and uplifting experience for you and your child. We want it to be a positive experience. We want to treat every child as an individual. Please consult with us whenever necessary to ensure that this happens.

No comment!

Advices, Advices!

The LEA psychological Advice was prepared in June. It was an odd report with which we took issue later. It did not mention that our independent EP thought that Richard had Asperger's syndrome but at least it did state 'he does not relate well to other children'.

We were asked to prepare our parental Advice.

The LEA 'Named Officer'

The LEA 'Named Officer' is supposed to liaise with parents and the LEA over 'all the arrangements relating to the statutory assessment and the making of a Statement'. I made an appointment with our Named Officer.

This appointment was held on the same day as my husband's first visit to the proposed new SN school. Unfortunately, my husband had a business appointment in the morning, so once again (when will I ever learn?) I went to a meeting on my own.

The Named Officer seemed to be a nice man who had many years' experience as the head of an SN school. When I arrived in his office I started to rummage in my overflowing bags for Richard's files (remember, we're called 'Carrier Bag Mums'!).

'It's OK,' said the Named Officer (NO). 'I've read your son's file and I recognize him.'

Well that fair took the wind out of my sails! I was so used to having to explain in detail all of Richard's peculiarities in the hope that someone would give us some answers that this was a first.

The NO was very helpful and actually answered some of my questions. I asked him why Richard had just about managed to get through primary school yet things had accelerated into the abyss when he hit high school. He explained that it was just about possible sometimes for ASD children to make it through primary school because there you have:

- your own teacher all day
- your own classroom virtually all day
- your own seat and table/desk in the classroom
- your own box with your work in that classroom
- your own peg to hang your coat on
- your own structured space, basically.

When the child arrives at high school all of the above disappear and the child starts to flounder immediately, thrown into a maelstrom which is just too chaotic for these sensitive children to cope with. They have sensory overload *big* time. They are constantly expected to be in different classrooms with different people. Most high schools are on large, sprawling sites with high numbers of pupils and very noisy corridors and playgrounds. Autistic children are bombarded with information all day long and, having struggled to make sense of the work, geography and social demands, they then find that they have a pile of homework to complete on arrival at their only refuge – home. This can then lead to difficulties in home relationships as parents struggle to try to keep their child on track with the work.

So the NO and I had a full and frank discussion. I can quite distinctly remember saying to my husband when I met him at the car that it had been the best meeting I'd ever been to as I had learned so much. Progress at last, I thought, and someone who didn't seem to regard me as either:

- a hysterical mother who knew nothing
- the enemy.

I looked forward to being able to 'liaise' with this man with whom I felt I had established a working relationship.

Oh dear!

Throughout the rest of the Statementing process we never managed to speak to the NO again. He didn't respond to any of our calls, and all the letters we wrote to him were answered by the Statementing Officer.

Difficult to liaise with someone if you can't communicate with him!

I think part of the problem was that I had discussed the knotty bone of contention regarding when the Statementing process should have commenced. He agreed with me that things should have been started in January and promised to bring up the subject the next time the Statementing Panel met.

Obviously we do not know what happened but you couldn't blame us if we felt that possibly he had been 'knobbled' for daring to ask this question? Whatever the reason, it was a great shame and made the whole process even more difficult.

Special needs school camp

One of the reasons why initially I tried to talk to the NO was that the proposed new school had offered to take Richard away on their annual camp. I just wanted to tell the LEA what had been proposed, as a courtesy, and that it wasn't going to cost them anything and didn't commit them to anything. I telephoned many times, leaving messages, and received no response.

Richard was having such a miserable time at school that eventually we made an executive decision as a week away could only be a good thing. Which, as it turned out, it was. Richard had a great time. He was very relaxed with the staff and other boys. He also showed courage as it turned out that he had gone away with an undiagnosed fractured arm.

Yes, I know it sounds strange but autists feel pain in different ways. Some feel pain if you brush against them, others feel pain but elsewhere away from the site of the problem and some don't seem to feel it much at all. Richard carried on playing football, canoeing, etc., for *four days* before he mentioned, in passing, that throwing the ball was a 'bit painful'.

Before you rush to telephone the NSPCC I have to defend myself. Richard had been watching a game of football at the church fete when it happened. He was hit on the arm by a heavy leather football. I had popped off to pick up some baking and on my return a friend told me that Richard had said that he had broken his arm but, in the same breath, had announced that he was 'just off to the bouncy castle'! She didn't know whether to take him seriously or not.

He continued to enjoy the rest of the afternoon playing on the bouncy castle and watching football. I examined his arm. I compared the good arm with the bad arm, there was no swelling, he wiggled his fingers and wrist and apart from a small amount of bruising seemed fine. So I just gave him some arnica pillules for the bruising and we carried on with life.

I was very relieved to hear when I was told of the visit to casualty that the doctor had initially refused to x-ray his arm, having carried out exactly the same procedure as I describe above. Even with his arm in a right angle with plaster from upper arm to wrist he enjoyed the rest of this camping holiday, including climbing Mount Snowdon. This trip totally reinforced the headmaster's belief that Richard should be at his school. He wrote in his report:

> Richard is a highly sensitive young man with a poor understanding of the protocol and taboos of the outside world. As he enters adolescence this will become more exaggerated among his peer group and raise his personal anxiety levels about himself, his family, his school and his peers. The knock-on effect being the degradation of his self-esteem and self-image.

This week away turned out to be the last peaceful and happy time that Richard enjoyed for a very long while.

The Scout camp disaster!

Not long after this Richard went away with the Scouts (the leader relented that year). The Scoutmaster, unfortunately, turned out to have been absolutely correct the previous year in his decision not to take him away to camp. It was an unmitigated disaster.

We had picked Richard up from the trip away (living in a tent, doing outdoor activities) with the proposed SN school, happy, relaxed and smiling – in a wonderful mood.

We collected him from Scout camp (living in a tent, doing outdoor activities) in the most dreadful state. He was sobbing and hysterical for the entire journey home in the car. It took a long while to calm and settle him. Apparently, the Scoutmaster said, Richard would not take instructions and had tantrums, damaging a tent in the process.

Given that this was an almost identical holiday situation it would seem very weird. However, the headmaster of the SN school had also written in his report:

> Richard always needed careful direction from staff with clear explanations. There seemed to be a difficulty in completing more than one instruction without a repeat, his usual pattern was to rush off to complete the first request and then return for the second. This was very interesting when the boys set off for an orienteering exercise where they had to follow a sequence of instructions.

The headmaster said his pattern of movements would have looked like a 'spider's web' as he dashed back and forth for the next set of directions.

The special needs school group totally understood what Richard's needs were and met them so he could be relaxed and confident in his surroundings. It really showed us how two apparently parallel situations could have such different outcomes.

Quite understandably this was the end of Richard's Scouting days and his world grew smaller still!

OK – so anyone can make a mistake!

Richard was referred to the professor who had told us that Alice was 'quasi autistic'. He was a leading light in ASD diagnosis. When we went for the appointment with him it was all very odd. I had expected quite a lengthy appointment but Richard was only in with him for approximately five minutes.

The professor then spent some time talking about 'neonatal alcoholism' and we ended up having quite a heated discussion when nobody seemed to be listening to our point of view at all. Richard told the professor, when questioned, that he had lots of friends! This was such a blatant untruth that I 'harrumphed' and cleared my throat very pointedly.

'Nasty throat you've got there Mum,' Richard said.

That clinched it for the professor and his assistant. We had told them that the independent EP had thought that Richard had Asperger's but they thought that Richard couldn't possibly be autistic as he had displayed humour.

What the professor didn't understand was that this was a family joke, very well practised over many years. I had honed my throat-clearing method of communication over years of being in church or other places where I would need to convey something to all four children when in a crowd, without shouting.

'Nasty throat!' became the traditional response as they got older when admonished in this way. This sounds a bit weird as I write this. Perhaps you had to be there, but it had been a jolly effective way of letting a child know that I could see that they were misbehaving in some way. They would turn to look at me across a room and I could diffuse a situation by the raising of an eyebrow, a shake of my head or a finger to my lips. Similarly I would use it to encourage if I could see a child floundering in a crowd and a smile was all that was needed to help them on.

This was the assessment during which no diagnostic tests were done except a scribble on the back of an envelope.

It caused us *endless* pain and led to us losing the first tribunal on the strength of this professor's feeling that Richard wasn't Asperger's in spite of the fact that he hadn't run any proper tests and the independent psychologist had! The professor said that a lot of Richard's problems could be down to his low IQ (as I've mentioned before, because people with Asperger's have 'patchy' knowledge IQ assessments can yield strange results). The professor said he couldn't conclude that Richard had Asperger's as he 'wasn't bright enough'.

A dichotomy! On the one hand we were being told that Richard was too dim for an Asperger's diagnosis, and therefore not worthy of extra help, and on the other he was too bright for the LEA-maintained special needs school! When I asked how it was possible for Richard to be able to achieve more than his capabilities the professor talked about 'over-educated simpletons!'.

We were very depressed. The independent psychologist was astounded by the findings of a man he respected and he argued our case – to no avail. The LEA of course fell upon the professor's report with glee as it meant they were able to refute the fact that Richard was autistic.

Try not to get involved with arguing 'semantics' with the LEA!

We found this out to our cost after we had written a lot of letters and wasted masses of time and effort. It gets you nowhere. Unless you are prepared to go to argue your case with the ombudsman you just exhaust yourself. If you are prepared to take your case to the ombudsman, and you win, I suppose you will have the moral satisfaction of witnessing the LEA receiving a slap on the wrist. However, will it help your case? Probably not.

The Clinical Medical Officer tries to help

Not long after the meeting with the LEA PEP in February the Clinical Medical Officer (CMO) saw Richard, at our request. You can get to the CMO through your school nurse or call your GP's surgery. They wield quite a lot of clout so they are worth getting on board with your case.

The CMO wrote: 'Richard obviously has a discrepancy between what he has achieved with his language and what he comprehends. This is causing him a great deal of difficulty at school.'

The year dragged on. In July I wrote to the LEA Named Officer to tell him that Richard had been offered a place at the SN school from September, subject to funding. I state in that letter, enclosing our Parental Advice for the Statement, that I had been told by the PEP that all the other Advices had been submitted apart from Health but that, as Richard had been put through a full medical with the CMO fairly recently, this shouldn't be a problem.

At this point I was writing to the educational adviser at the NAS and railing against the injustice done to these children that it had taken years to even get to that stage. Our daughter's childhood and schooldays were over before we could persuade the authorities to do anything at all.

Finding the right department within Social Services

We were still trying to get Social Services involved and desperately trying to get help and support with Richard. We got nowhere. I have mentioned elsewhere that you must make sure that you have contacted the right department of Social Services. I know it probably seems obvious but it took a long time before we discovered that we were talking to the Families Team, who are involved with child abuse, etc., instead of the Children with Disabilities Team. We were very low priority indeed for the Families Team and we got nowhere even though I had given them a copy of the independent EP's report.

You might think that you don't need a social worker. Think again. Without a social worker you will find it extremely difficult or downright impossible to access help for your child. Don't argue. Just trust me on that one. And forget stigma. I felt terrible but there really is no stigma. Just a simple fact: your child needs help. Social Services can assist you in accessing help.

Your MP

In August our MP became involved and wrote to the Named Officer:

> I write to urge you to rectify this as soon as possible. I feel that if Richard were not to be assessed in time to be admitted to ... School in September this would have a very damaging effect for him emotionally as well as the further disruption to his education. I am sure that this situation can be rectified in time to prevent this from occurring. I write in support of my constituents and in the best interests of Richard, whose welfare is central to all our concerns.

The LEA wrote back to him and suggested that 'a number of issues need to be addressed in order that you may have an accurate account of this particular case'. They went on to write that 'the LEA is well within the statutory time limits for the issuing of this Statement'. Bit rich don't you think? We found the implications of the phrase 'accurate account' quite insulting and wrote and told the MP so. The MP was very sympathetic but this got us nowhere.

It is interesting for me to see as I am looking through the file now that at this stage my husband starts to write letters to the DoE. I seem to recall spending a lot of my time saying 'but I'm not making it up. He did say that.' It was a very frustrating time.

In one such letter written in early September my husband states, regarding this on-going quarrel about when the Statementing process had begun,

> regretfully we cannot agree with your interpretation of events. It is our opinion, the opinion of the legal advice we have received and the opinion of the teacher involved in the discussions in January 2000 that we had requested a statutory assessment. Indeed, my wife's discussions in January with the PEP at that time left her – and others – in no doubt that the process had begun.

He also wrote:

> However, we see no value in pursuing the question of the timing of our request for a statutory assessment at this stage. Our concern right now is for Richard's future to be properly considered and with this in mind look forward to a very fast response from the Education Department from this point on in the hope that Richard can swiftly take up the more appropriate placement that has been offered.

It got us nowhere of course, which was very dispiriting!

At around the same time we received a letter from the CMO. She enclosed Richard's Statementing medical where she tried to emphasize his difficulties with comprehension and behaviour.

She tried to contact the PEP to talk to him about arranging a meeting with

> health, education, and social services, to see if it is possible to draw up a plan to address Richard's emotional and social needs. I hope we will be able to arrange this in the near future. I have also referred the family to the psychiatric services as I feel that Richard is going to need long-term psychiatric support and that as a family you have struggled along for a long time without advice on how to deal with these very difficult children, although I feel that you have probably done as good a job as is possible under the circumstances.

These comments meant a lot to me as my parenting skills were really under attack at that time. To have a professional praising us for what we'd done was a real boost.

The CMO also referred Richard to the physiotherapist as 'he does have some difficulty with integration of his movement patterns and it will be interesting to read her report'. She said that she felt that Richard's 'situation would be much worse if he hadn't had such intensive input from yourselves to try and improve his social and emotional skills'.

This voice in support of us was appreciated. Sadly for us, the CMO left her post shortly afterwards to go and live in India. The meeting she suggested never took place.

Was this what all the battling was for?

In mid-September we *finally* received the draft Statement. Following advice from the NAS advocacy service we immediately wrote to the DoE stating that we did not agree with the contents and expressing our preference for Richard to attend the SN school.

We also requested a meeting, which is your right by law, with officers from the LEA to discuss this. We wanted to bring along other people to give evidence to support our reasons. This was denied, although the authority had no objection to the inclusion of reports.

This, as usual, turned into a farce with my husband being forced to write a very tetchy fax to the DoE chasing him to get this meeting arranged, nearly a month after we had written asking for the darned thing. I notice in this fax my husband says that:

> My wife and I are extremely dissatisfied with what we see as inordinate and unnecessary delays in Richard's Statementing process. Far from being the 'positive and uplifting experience' referred to in your letter of May 2000 it has to date been negative and demoralizing almost entirely due to your authority's perceived lack of empathy and apparent inability to deal with issues in a timely manner.

We weren't happy and Richard was having a very bad time. By this stage he was deliberately cutting large holes in his clothes and he was manic – either very low or very high and was irrational.

Following advice from the NAS advocacy service we wrote a sixteen-page letter setting out all the reasons why we did not agree with the draft Statement. There was so much wrong with it. They had left out so much vital information. Advices that *should* have been in *weren't* (language assessment, physiotherapy assessment and psychiatric assessment as recommended by the CMO, for example) and others that *shouldn't* have been there *were*; that is, the insulting report from the social worker who had met neither Richard nor my husband but was suggesting 'alternative parenting methods' because of the 'stressful relationship between him and his parents'.

We finally received the meeting that we were entitled to by law. It was very disappointing. Having asked for various representatives to be there we ended up with the PEP and SENCO – that was it! And in case you're wondering, the Named Officer wasn't there either in spite of the fact that the LEA had plenty of time to arrange it with all parties.

Following the 'meeting' we were asked to comment on the revised draft which was prepared. One of the things we protested in a letter in November (nearly two months after the draft Statement) was that the report from the independent psychologist

> based on a thorough five-hour assessment is selectively edited whilst the professor's report based on a fragmented thirty minutes with my wife, myself and Richard and some five minutes with Richard alone, is quoted virtually in its entirety. We have stated before that there is absolutely no evidence of Foetal Alcohol abuse. We would like Richard's Statement finalised as soon as possible in accordance with the *Code of Practice*.

That last sentence is a telling one. We had at last realized that we were falling into their traps all the time and meanwhile they were able to argue and prevaricate. Forgive me if that seems antagonistic but that was what it felt like from our perspective.

This farce continued with another meeting at the LEA-maintained school in November that I had first visited in April. It was at this point that I found out that the headmaster was 'uncomfortable speaking to me' as he had been reprimanded for telling me that 'Richard was too bright' for his school. He seemed a nice chap in a very difficult position.

We were made to go along again to see him, this time with the PEP and the SENCO. The LEA-maintained school seemed very nice but we had already been told that it wasn't suitable for Richard so we had to conclude that this was a bit of a waste of time.

The SENCO from the mainstream school seemed baffled too as Richard was working on GCSE coursework at the time and it was predicted that he would pass 'a full range at grades A–G' (if he didn't do something terrible first). The LEA-maintained SN school didn't offer GCSEs for any of its pupils and had no plans to do so! Again we were mystified at the time as the LEA PEP, a frequent visitor to the school, must have been aware of this.

It was a very odd meeting as we all sat there looking at each other and not knowing quite what to say. It was obvious to all of us that this wasn't going to work for Richard and that we were just 'going through the motions'.

It was sad that this school hadn't been mentioned before when I was trying for all those years to get Alice helped, as she could possibly have been happy there. GCSE coursework was beyond her and therefore irrelevant.

We finally realized that we could be on this mad merry-go-round for months and we asked the LEA to finalize the Statement so that at least we had something to appeal against.

Even then it all seemed very odd to us. This is why having some help/advocacy is *invaluable*.

My husband wrote:

> Seventeen months of Richard's school life have now passed by since the initial Combined School Referral for Statutory Assessment and some thirteen months since the second Referral following our parental request for formal assessment. We adamantly believe this matter can only be finally resolved at a SEN Tribunal and would urge you to immediately finalise the Statement so that this matter may proceed.

At this time we also tried writing to our county councillor to ask him to try to get the LEA to finalize the Statement. We then started faxing the LEA DoE daily asking politely when we could expect Richard's Statement to be finalized.

At the end of November we received the Final Statement at last. It was, as anticipated from the draft we had seen and the subsequent discussions, not appropriate in our view and did not adequately meet or accurately describe Richard's needs and so the next phase began – the Appeal to the Special Educational Needs Tribunal or SENDIST.

Chapter 11

More of Richard's story

You may be losing the will to live here as I continue to recount the long, sad tale of Richard's saga, but if you can bear it please plod on. I am putting as much of the detail in as it is possible that one of these situations will ring a bell with you and it may be of help. Sometimes I have found a solution to a problem in a 'throwaway' remark made by another parent and I have been able to resolve a seemingly unsolvable problem and move on. Go and make yourself a cup of tea, or something stronger, stroke the cat, and hang on in there. Maybe you'll read something that strikes a chord.

Some of this chapter cross references with Chapter 7 as it describes the tribunal.

So there we were, after all the months of waiting, in receipt of a Final Statement which was of no use.

Parts 2 and 3 appeared very odd and it continued to name in Part 4 the mainstream school which we maintained was not appropriate for Richard.

Things were very hard at home. Richard was behaving more and more strangely and his behaviour was impacting on the other two boys. We were living in a war zone with me constantly having to interject, often physically, which wasn't funny. My sons are *big*. It was exhausting. It didn't seem to stop from the moment they woke. Our bedroom is located above the kitchen and my palpitations would start with a lurch as I heard the first one of them scrape their chair across the wooden kitchen floor in the morning.

In spite of all our hard work to help Richard we seemed to be 'losing' our son. We had to try to keep life on an even keel. We couldn't explain to Richard that we were fighting to get him to a new school. It would have been too unsettling. There were no alternatives for Richard so we were trying hard to keep his respect for the school he was still at.

First we had to battle to get him to go to school and then we had to battle with him when he returned from school in a terrible mood.

The NAS Educational Advocacy Service

The NAS are great people doing a really difficult task and all of them are trained volunteers – usually those who have experience of special needs either professionally or personally. They told me that we had to fill in the appeal form (as mentioned in Chapter 6). Part of this form asks for 'Reasons for Appeal'.

I spent the day after Boxing Day in bed with bronchitis and it was there that I started writing this part. We really know how to have a good time in our house!

For this first appeal we wrote far too much but it is so difficult to know what to leave out. I think in retrospect we dwelt far too much on the length of time taken to prepare the Statement, semantics, etc. The 'Notice of Appeal and Reason for Appealing' was six pages long but the whole appeal form was approximately 129 pages!

Richard had to go to see the physiotherapist and so the New Year started with yet another visit to a specialist. She felt that Richard was 'quite difficult to work with in that his face is usually expressionless and it is quite hard to get him to smile or talk'. He was nearly 14 ½ by then but scored poorly in tests that are only scored up to the age of twelve years. The physiotherapist also stated that he had 'definite motor co-ordination problems both with fine and gross motor skills'.

Options?

We knew things were very wrong in the mainstream school, and the reality of it was highlighted at a Year Nine parents' evening at the school during April. We had helped Richard choose some GCSE options. It wasn't really a choice, more a case of what he could possibly cope with within the confines of the state system. The LEA should have been looking at a different provision for Richard, rather than saying every-thing was fine. It was clear that Richard's Asperger profile really flummoxed some of his teachers. They were a decent bunch of human beings, trying to do a difficult job but most of them really didn't understand what they were dealing with. And why should they? It is a very strange and difficult disorder.

Richard had somehow managed to do quite well in his French exam (the highest mark he achieved for any of the exams at this time) but we were told with genuine kindness that Richard could not possibly take the GCSE.

We had also opted for history, as the only other option in this section was geography and Richard had been 'disapplied' from geography the previous year to give him more time in the SN unit at school (although bizarrely I notice that he had done very well in a geography exam that he was forced to take even though he no longer studied the subject!). We were told by the history teacher that he couldn't take the exam, as unless she worked with him 'one to one' he didn't seem to know what to do. She said that she had the rest of the class to deal with and this was not possible.

Another GCSE option we had chosen was D & T food. As Richard could cook we thought possibly he might stand a chance. The teacher was adamant that Richard could not cope with the GCSE coursework which is largely written work, analysis, marketing, etc. They don't do much cooking!

I was getting hysterical by this stage. It was like being in a Mike Leigh play!

Finally we went to see the PE teacher (Richard is obsessed with sports). As we sat down the teacher asked us if we knew that PE GCSE was 40 per cent theory. He felt that Richard would struggle but said that he could have a go.

Out of the four options ticked he was only going to be allowed to take one! We asked the school what he was supposed to do all day, then heard from them subsequently that he would, after all, be taking history and D & T food as well as PE.

We may be wrong but it seemed to us at the time that the teachers had been 'leaned on' so that it looked as though Richard was able to cope. What else could we think? They had been insistent at the parents' evening that he was not going to be doing those subjects.

In the event Richard was extremely unhappy and begged to be disapplied from history. This was granted and he spent more time in the SN 'unit'. Later he requested that he drop D & T and PE too. This request was not granted.

Tribunal date granted

We were told by SENDIST that we had been granted a tribunal hearing in May and that we had until a date in March to lodge our evidence. The rules have now changed so I won't go into this process in detail, but will cover it more thoroughly when I'm talking about the second tribunal.

I do remember the time I spent poring over documents, reading the COP, endlessly talking to people. I won't lie to you. It was a lot of hard work gathering together what we thought was a very credible case but we felt passionately that our son was worth it.

We understood that we were allowed to include video and audio evidence for the Panel and so left a tape recorder running in the kitchen during mealtimes. The children were totally unaware of what we were doing. It was powerful stuff, we thought. The LEA were arguing that Richard was a happy boy and yet on the tapes you could hear Richard ranting and raving continually like a stuck record.

We interviewed him with a borrowed video camera. He came across as being quite sweet but very immature and odd.

We gathered up all our precious evidence which entailed hours of hard work collating, writing, photocopying. We sent it off to SENDIST by the required date.

The Bundle

Two weeks prior to the tribunal SENDIST sent the Bundle to us and the LEA (see Chapter 6). At the same time this was sent to the tribunal Panel so that they could examine the evidence and have time to consider what they'd read prior to the tribunal.

Unfortunately, it was at this time that I discovered that SENDIST had only included one piece of paper as our evidence, as I described in Chapter 6. I was distraught but had to rush around collecting all the attachments together and dash off to our nearest town to photocopy them all *again*. We then had all these documents sent by motorbike courier to SENDIST in London. We didn't have a copy of the video and we did take a copy of the audio tape, but decided eventually not to use it as the Panel wouldn't have time to listen to it properly.

A solicitor is appointed

Through the NAS tribunal support service we were fortunate to have been accepted to be amongst the first to be granted the services of a large firm of London solicitors – *pro bono*. We deliberated about whether it was better to have a solicitor or whether to just represent ourselves at the hearing but when we heard that the LEA had engaged a barrister we felt we had no choice but to have legal representation.

The solicitor and her assistant who handled our case were sympathetic and professional. However, the arrangement with the NAS was in its infancy and we weren't able to meet them until shortly before the tribunal hearing; and, as I wrote earlier, neither we nor they had been to a tribunal hearing before. They did their best and we are very grateful to the NAS for trying to help us as we would have been completely alone otherwise.

First tribunal hearing

This hearing was a very difficult experience and I will admit I was very frightened. So much rested on the outcome I felt overwhelmed.

A large part of the argument on the day was over whether Richard was autistic or not. We said he was, following the diagnosis from our independent psychologist. The LEA said he wasn't. Their argument was that our man wasn't qualified to diagnose ASD. This was later refuted by the independent psychologist but by then the damage had been done. The independent psychologist couldn't attend the hearing (in retrospect we should have asked for a different date so he could). The tribunal believed the LEA.

We did so much wrong. We took a box containing all our files into the tribunal hearing with us. This was disastrous as I hadn't appreciated just how difficult it was going to be to make notes, listen and think all at the same time.

The first time I was asked to produce a document to prove a point I couldn't find it as I was so stressed. It was ghastly. I still feel sick just thinking about it. All the points had to be addressed to the Chair. We felt intimidated and out of our depth.

The Panel must have thought we were quite mad as we had taken one of Richard's toy monkeys with us as a mascot. Richard had always been fond of these stuffed toys but as he became more stressed they had become an obsession. By this time he was communicating through the monkeys with us. For example: 'Monkey's hungry.' 'Monkey loves you. Do you love monkey?'

Unfortunately, at one point in these serious, legal proceedings I leaned against the toy. It let out a prolonged monkey cry. It was very embarrassing and we never did get the chance to explain what the monkey was doing there in the first place!

We were like cats on a hot tin roof afterwards. You are supposed to receive the decision within ten days but for some reason the decision was delayed. We lost. We were devastated.

A review?

We asked SENDIST to 'review' the decision. You can only do this if you believe that the tribunal hearing was flawed through a point of law. We believed that the fact that all our independent psychologist's evidence had been set aside because the LEA PEP had alleged that the independent psychologist wasn't qualified to diagnose had a large bearing on the tribunal decision and we enclosed evidence to show that he *was* qualified.

In spite of this evidence we were refused a review.

At that time the only course left open to us would have been appealing to the High Court, for which we would have required legal aid. We were so exhausted and dejected we just didn't have the mental energy to apply.

So what did we do?

My husband and I were both very depressed. We did have some options but they meant a lot more hard work. We both felt deflated and Richard was degenerating. Things were very tense at home and the strain was definitely telling on our marriage. My lovely husband, my best friend for over twenty-five years, could barely talk to me. I don't blame him in the slightest.

I must have looked a wreck, my health was dreadful and I was heading for one of the worst bouts of asthma in my life. I wasn't a bundle of laughs to live with.

I remember one long, lonely drive to London with him. I was driving. The journey takes approximately 4 ½ hours and we didn't exchange one word the entire time. Bizarrely I wept all the way but only out of one eye, the one nearest the door, so I don't know if my husband was even aware. It was a wretched time and all my pain was just leaking out of my eye.

I've never felt so insecure. We've always been a cuddly couple with the same daft sense of humour. We became two people just co-existing in the same house – dreadful.

I couldn't talk about this. I couldn't blame my husband and it would have felt disloyal to talk to anyone else, so I felt even more isolated. I still loved my husband. I prayed that we were going to be able to work this out somehow. I felt enormous loyalty to him and didn't want it to seem that I was complaining because I wasn't. I understood how he felt. I just didn't know how to put it right.

Appealing to the High Court – was this a course of action?

In the early summer I spoke to one of the educational advisers at IPSEA. He told us about special needs solicitors. We didn't know such people existed. We made an appointment. The solicitor outlined a possible course of action.

We could appeal to the High Court, but it could cost anything up to £40,000! Legal aid was a possibility but by this stage we were both so deflated that sorting out all the myriad forms was a Herculean task.

The forms aren't as complicated as they seemed at the time. Basically you have to prove two things:

1.   that you have a case to answer

2.   that your income falls below a certain amount (the criteria have changed recently). This was complicated for us as we are self-employed.

Social Services close Richard's file

Just after the tribunal we received a letter from the social worker who had been visiting Richard. Social Services hadn't at that time actually done anything to help but we were alarmed to see that this man had written 'no further action/case closed' on the bottom of his assessment.

We wrote immediately to the Head of the Children and Families Team, who were dealing with Richard's case (incorrectly as we later found out; he should have been a client of the Children with Disabilities Team). This was very worrying as it had taken us years to get any social worker to become involved at all.

Later in the year we managed to get Richard a social worker allocated to him as part of the Learning Disabilities 'satellite' and it was arranged for Richard to receive two hours' respite per week with a Family Aide worker.

Statistics

Richard had received a peculiar SATs result for English. He received 'U' for unclassified. The SENCO telephoned and told us that he was 'devastated' that Richard had scored such a low mark that the examiners were unable to record a level. The SENCO had worked very hard with Richard to try to help him under difficult conditions. The school asked for a re-count and he was then awarded a '3'. Apparently a re-count always picks up a mark or two and there is no 1 or 2 category for this stage so he went straight to a level 3.

We were left feeling bemused and rather angry by this strange marking system, as it made it look as though Richard was doing fine at school, but perhaps we were a little over-sensitive by then.

The post-tribunal Statement arrives

In June we received the new Statement. We were deeply unhappy with it. It 'named' the wrong school but also, in spite of our evidence, all mention of ASD/Asperger's had been removed from the Statement. Teachers using this as a guideline would therefore not have this vital piece of information.

The only light on the horizon was the fact that Richard had been referred for another assessment by a different professor in psychology. Unfortunately, we had to wait until September for the assessment.

This referral came from the local adolescent and child psychiatrist who did not feel, at that time, that she was sufficiently qualified in Asperger's to diagnose. I hoped that things would be different this time as I had filled in copious forms, sent off Richard's reports and had an hour-long 'screening questionnaire'/interview conducted by the assisting doctor prior to the assessment.

Richard's state

At the beginning of the summer holiday I took the children for their dental check-up. The dentist, normally sanguine and cheerful, was extremely concerned for Richard. He told me that Richard had been repeatedly biting through his lower mouth leaving scar tissue. The dentist was sufficiently alarmed to write to Richard's psychiatrist and said that the only time he had seen anything like that was with 'very disturbed people who would be banging their heads on the wall'.

The psychiatrist also saw this as an internalized sign of tremendous stress.

Definitive diagnosis at last

Another five-hour assessment with the professor in psychology gave us the definitive ASD diagnosis.

The professor stated that, while she could not place Richard exactly in one part of the 'spectrum', he most definitely *was* ASD and I should read up on, and treat him as, Asperger's. She believed that there was a genetic cause for his autism. She didn't buy into the 'early years' deprivation' theory which had often been levelled at us so that no action had to be taken. She said that when autistic-type tendencies occur, such as in some of the children who emerged from the dreadful Romanian orphanages, these tendencies faded when the children were placed in a stable environment. Richard had by then been with us for eleven years and he was getting worse.

It was a very stressful, yet moving, experience. Richard was so good. He hid behind his fingers for the whole of the assessment but he was calm and patient, even submitting to blood tests (to check to see if he was Fragile X). I was very proud of him. He must have been very frightened and confused but he trusted me when I told him that this should enable him to get help. I treated him to a snack in a local supermarket (we had a long drive home) and told him I would buy him a present for being so good. We set off up the aisles. Richard darted ahead then rushed back to drag me over to show me what he'd found.

It was the cutest 'mummy' gorilla with a baby attached to her chest.

So we drove the many miles home with Richard waving the gorilla's furry paw at passing motorists. He sat her on his knee, talked to her and kissed and stroked the soft fur. It was very sweet. He was like a five-year-old. But he was nearly fifteen! How could the tribunal Panel

have believed he behaved normally for his age? It was a surreal experience. As I drove home I was repeating a mantra to myself: 'I wasn't
making it up. I'm not mad or hysterical. We were right.'

A different tack?

Neither my husband nor I had the heart for another fight so soon after
the tribunal and I was treading on eggshells with my lovely man, so it
was all very tricky.

We thought we had run out of time to appeal to the High Court until
a chance remark from the clerk at SENDIST. I had telephoned her to ask
a question and she told me that this information would have been
contained in the letter that the LEA had sent following the tribunal. I
denied all knowledge and she made me read out the LEA letter out to
her.

'Well there you are then,' she said, 'the clock hasn't started ticking yet
as they forgot to tell you that you had the right to appeal!' This was not
the first time this had happened.

I was trying to be realistic and had almost given up on Richard
getting to SN school and had started looking at special needs colleges
(there is a long lead-in time for this sort of establishment).

My long-suffering husband had managed to get our finances into
shape to present to the legal aid board. We did fit the criteria financially –
a mixed blessing. We were worse off than we thought!

A review?

The SN solicitor suggested that instead of taking this course of action we
ask the LEA for an urgent meeting to 'review' Richard's Statement.

This was just after the definitive diagnosis of ASD and, as Richard's
circumstances had changed, the new LEA EP said that of course he
should have a review. Clause 9:44 (p.129 of the *Special Educational Needs
Code of Practice for Wales*: National Assembly for Wales 2002) seems to
imply that you can ask for an 'interim review' in this sort of case.

Richard starts to refuse to go to school

The pressure of school work was getting to Richard. He had commenced the GCSE coursework and he was increasingly distressed and very difficult.

We did everything to get him into the car so we could take him to the school bus. We cajoled, bribed, wheedled, shouted, insisted. Looking back I feel ashamed. We thought we were doing the right thing and felt trapped in the situation.

He was still biting the inside of his mouth and his face was often very swollen. Sometimes he had dried blood sticking to his face on his return from school. Such was his distress that he would rather endure the pain from the inside of his mouth than the torment of mainstream school.

Understanding dawns

In October we endured another morning scene. Richard was shouting and crying and ran away into the fields. I couldn't catch him and had to get Jack to the school bus, but as I drove away my stomach was a pit of fear. It was a wonder I didn't crash on the seven-mile drive home as I was so scared that I was going to find Richard hanging from a beam on my return.

Thank God, he wasn't, but he was nowhere to be found. I had just resolved to call the police when he reappeared. I looked at my son and he just looked at me and understanding flooded through me. What were we doing to him?

He had clearly been weeping as his eyes were red rimmed. He was soaking wet as it was raining and he was shivering with cold and probably fear.

Not fear of me, but fear of life and of those confusing, frightening people who were 'out there'. He reminded me of a startled fawn and I knew one false move from me and he'd run off into the fields and woods again.

'I think you should have a hot shower while I make you a cup of tea, don't you?' I said gently.

He nodded and we went into the house together. That was the last time we tried to force him into school. I wrote to his head teacher, 'I could not live with a tragedy on my conscience, could you?'

The 'black pit'

We were concerned about Richard's mental health and were convinced that he was suffering from depression. I suggested this to the psychiatrist. She said not to bother to take him to the GP as he would only be referred back to her, but I couldn't get her to commit to anything and therefore no help was forthcoming.

Richard missed over half of this autumn term in all. He would go into school for one or two days and then have to take three or four days off at home. He was in a bad way. There were some days when he would get up and get into his school uniform and then get back into bed, draw the curtains and stay under his duvet all day – fully dressed down to his shoes. He wasn't sleeping – he was hiding.

The Truant Officer came to see us who, of course, didn't have a clue about autism. He talked to us as though Richard was your usual type of truant 'bunking off down the high street with his friends'. This was non-sensical as:

1. Richard wasn't bunking off to go anywhere as he was too frightened to leave home and

2. Richard didn't have any friends.

Extraordinary as it seems now we were still trying to maintain some sort of feeling of loyalty to his school at this time and, while we were no longer forcing him to go to school, we insisted that if he didn't feel able to go then he had to do some small chores to help at home. We also, rightly or wrongly, did not allow the television to be switched on during what should have been school time. We were firm but gentle and it definitely calmed him.

Of course, these absences made his problems worse as he fell further behind with the GCSE coursework, which meant even more pressure when he was in school – in spite of the LSA 'glued' on.

The DoE at the LEA agrees to a meeting

In the January following the review meeting the DoE agreed to meet with us. The children's retired primary headmaster, who is a good man and was very concerned about Richard, set the meeting up and came with us.

We put the case to the DoE. Our son was disaffected, distressed, depressed and refusing to attend school. We were receiving no help; no alternative schooling had been proposed to help him. We still hadn't seen the new draft Statement which had been agreed to in November. He promised to come back to us by the February half term so that if Richard were to change schools he could begin straight after half term.

Half term came. We didn't hear anything. I telephoned and we were told that no decision had yet been made as the Statementing Panel had to meet.

We waited. They turned us down.

We were managing to get Richard into school a little more frequently but it was a delicate and difficult situation. He was being bullied and this continued unabated. Richard would now get off the school bus and go straight into the SENCO's room. At break time he hid out in the SENCO's room. At lunchtime he would dash to the canteen (he had been given an early lunch pass as he couldn't cope with the noise), then disappear into the SENCO's room for the rest of the lunch break. The SENCO kept Richard safe but this could hardly be called inclusive schooling.

In February we received a telephone call from the school stating that Richard was hysterical and they could do nothing to calm him. Unfortunately we were at the other end of the country attending a review meeting for Alice so could do nothing about it. All we could do was send our love to our disturbed son.

In early March we received a call from the SENCO to say that Richard had run out of a class and the SENCO had to run around the school trying to find him. The school pacified Richard by saying that he no longer had to take part in practical PE – he could just observe!

The SENCO stated that Richard was quite unco-operative, unpleasant to some members of his social group, very tearful and generally very unhappy and that he wouldn't talk to the teachers. Another teacher telephoned to complain that Richard had been truculent, argumentative and rude.

Still no action was taken by the LEA. No new Statement was issued and no help given. We questioned how the LEA could still consider this an 'appropriate' educational placement.

The Green Mile

At Easter we decided we all needed a break and booked a family holiday to the Canary Islands. Richard looked terrible, sort of pasty, yellow (as he hardly set foot outdoors at that point), and we thought some sunshine would do him, and the rest of us, a lot of good.

We worked out a daily routine for him (and the others – another delicate situation) and for the first three days things went relatively smoothly. Then, for no reason we could fathom – except for the fact that the wind changed direction – Richard became very difficult.

He threw a noisy, violent tantrum. He stamped so hard on my big toe that it swelled and later the nail fell off. My husband had to restrain him and we had to lock him into the apartment as we were scared he would hurt himself.

This was a very frightening experience. We were miles from home in an apartment building, where someone might reasonably summon the police following the noisy disturbance, with a very tall young man who was out of control. We managed to calm him down as the day wore on but we were all very edgy.

We had hired a video to watch with the children in the evening – *The Green Mile*, by Stephen King. It was fortunate that we watched with the lights off as I silently wept throughout. I looked at the central figure in the story – John Coffey, an innocent man accused of murder – and saw our son Richard. The expression of anxious bewilderment in his eyes, the acceptance that he had done something wrong, even though he didn't know what – was Richard. Was this what his life was going to be like because he didn't understand the world?

The children went off to bed (Richard had not left his room but had eaten and drunk) and I hit rock bottom. My husband and I talked all night – between sobs. I knew we couldn't go on any longer without any support. This young man was becoming seriously disturbed. This was way beyond our qualifications and resources. We loved him but we actually talked about asking Social Services to take him into care so that he might get proper psychiatric help. We didn't want to but were at our wits' end.

It was a dreadful night.

We dozed fitfully as the sun rose. I was not looking forward to the day. I felt overwhelmed. Just after nine o'clock Robin's mobile phone rang (we had diverted the calls from home as we run a business).

'You wrote to me in November,' a voice said. 'Do you still need help?'

An answer to prayer?

This is making me cry as I write this. The timing was incredible. I had written thirty letters in November. They were letters begging for help. We were so desperate I'd lost my pride. Any sort of help was welcomed, be it information, practical help or financial help.

'But you didn't reply,' I said.

This lovely lady, Chris, is quite simply our angel. She works for a philanthropic trust who sometimes give financial grants to adopted children who are going through a difficult time. She told me that she received 150 letters a week and that she only kept the most compelling.

I told her that we most certainly did still need help and explained the situation. We had received two very kind offers of help but they were very small grants towards the full amount needed to fund Richard's place at SN school. I thanked her but said that we needed much, much more and I couldn't see how we could raise all that was required.

Nonetheless, she told me to write when we returned home, which I did at length.

Things got worse but the police were magnificent

On day two of the new term I went to pick Richard up from a Christian youth group (the only thing he would go to – I suppose he felt safe there with much younger children) which occurred straight after school in the village where the bus dropped them.

It transpired that there had been another incident on the school bus. Richard was in a very sorry state. It was fortunate that the leader of the group is a teacher at a special needs school and a mother herself, so she had tended to him.

Richard had been attacked on the school bus by a group of boys (this was not the first time). They had punched him in the head, spat upon him so that spittle dripped down his face and shirt and taunted him with 'Jew, Jew, Jew' and 'Paki'. He is neither – but that is incidental. Their spite was terrifying.

Richard was very upset. So was I. My husband was away on business. I sent a fax to the DoE at 1 am and copied in the school. I told him all about the incident. I took Richard straight to the GP next morning where she found the bruising to both sides of his head. Where the louts hit him on the side of his head his face rebounded off the bus window. When I described the condition Richard had been in for the previous few months she also diagnosed clinical depression.

At last the LEA respond – no change to Part 4 of the Statement

The DoE did not respond to this fax, but the day after the assault on the bus the LEA wrote to say they had decided not to change Part 4 in the Amended Statement they were about to issue for Richard.

I had heard nothing from the school at nearly three o'clock in response to this very serious letter. I telephoned them and the deputy head said he would look into it and call me back.

Just before end of school another teacher telephoned me. He said that he had only just been told about the incident and was shocked and saddened. He said that it was too late to do anything about it that day but he would make full investigations the following day. He also said that if Richard had been his son he would have called the police.

So that is what I did. I telephoned the local station and said that we had a problem and I didn't know whether they were able to do anything about it but could I tell them hypothetically. I explained the situation about the repeated bullying and the most recent incident. The police were magnificent. They said that they took this type of assault very seriously and drove out to take a statement from Richard. They were very gentle with him, which we really appreciated. He was in a very shocked state which, added to his existing condition, was a huge concern.

They took a statement from me and Robin (who had returned) as well and asked for details from the friend who had met Richard from the bus on the night in question. She said that Richard had looked like a 'whipped dog as he tried to clean the slobber from his face and shirt'. Jack had been sitting with him comforting him and trying to help. Bravely, one of the schoolgirls on the bus also offered to give evidence. She said that she thought it was 'disgusting' the way the boys had treated Richard.

The school were very quiet about it all. They said they would look into it, then tried to implicate Jack, which we thought was a bit rich under the circumstances. Richard would not go to school and we certainly weren't going to force him.

The five boys involved were punished. Their punishment was that they were warned and were to be banned from the school bus for five days! We were disgusted. This hardly seemed much of a punishment for these boys and Richard couldn't go to school for two weeks after the attack.

The police took all five down to the police station individually to be interviewed. We then discovered that a video of this bus journey existed. We have seen this video and the behaviour sickened us. The video was handed to the police who used it in their case. We also later showed it to the tribunal Panel to refute the LEA's testimony that Richard was a happy and successful child!

The letters flew between the LEA and my keyboard. Still they wouldn't act to help our son. Still they wouldn't issue the Amended Statement so we couldn't appeal against it. We had seen them in November to discuss this: it was now April.

We wrote to the Children's Commissioner for Wales following the assault and he wrote a letter expressing his concern to the LEA. I won't tell you about the letters between us and the LEA in case this page self-combusts.

We were extremely concerned for both our younger sons by this stage. Jack was still going into school. The school said that they felt that they had resolved the matter 'satisfactorily'. That wasn't the way we felt. The school were sheltering behind their 'anti-bullying policy' that all incidents should be reported to the deputy head. I'd said on a previous occasion to Jack that he should report the latest incident.

'What's the point?' he said. 'Nothing changes. Nothing happens.'

Richard returns to school – briefly

We managed to get Richard back to school at the end of April. Before he had even returned home on that first day I had a telephone call from the careers officer to say that he had just interviewed him about work experience.

I told him that I really wished he hadn't. Richard was terrified by the prospect and we had told the school as much. The careers officer didn't know Richard and nobody had told him that Richard was autistic.

'I worked out he wasn't the full shilling,' he commented!

Richard didn't go back into school again for another three days after this. (Bizarrely this was the incident which led to us finding another piece of Alex's jigsaw puzzle as detailed in Chapter 9.)

In early May the draft Amended Statement was finally issued by the LEA with Part 4 unchanged. We immediately asked them to issue the Final Statement (so that we could commence our appeal).

The miracle!

On 22 May the 'miracle' occurred. The 'angel' who had telephoned me when we were away with Richard at Easter called again to say that the trustees of her organization had met and that they would pay the balance on Richard's fees so that he could go to SN school – immediately – while we battled with the LEA!

On the 27 May we formally withdrew Richard from the school. The relief was enormous.

A new beginning – peace at last

Richard started at his new school in early June straight after half term. We hadn't told him that we were still fighting to get him there – we couldn't unsettle him further. Robin just said to him one morning, 'It's OK, you don't have to wear your uniform today.'

Richard looked at him and whooped with joy. 'Am I going to Cruckton?'

Robin didn't even have to reply.

'I'm going to Cruckton.' He ran around the house calling to his brothers.

He was so happy the day we took him to join the new school. From the very first minute he was relaxed. It has been a success. It has all been worth it. I just wish that having been offered the place at the age of thirteen he hadn't been made to wait until he was 15 ½ to get there.

There have been rocky days, but only a very few and all related to the dreaded GCSEs. The difference was that his new school totally understood his fears and were able to skilfully support him through the exams. They had to undo a lot of his anxiety. His self-esteem was non-existent.

He passed five GCSEs – hoorah!

More important, he is, for the most part, calm and happy and he has a 'life'.

Chapter 12

Tribunal II:
The Mummy's Revenge!

Under the terms of the grant from the educational trust it was still necessary to fight the second tribunal. Quite apart from their terms we knew that having a decision against us would count against us when we applied for funding for SN colleges for Richard later in his life. It was an important day therefore.

I have described the preparations for this tribunal in Chapter 7 and so will not repeat them here. We arrived at the hotel at about 9.30 am – approximately an hour prior to our hearing. Our representative, Janet, had stayed the night with us. We met our expert witnesses, the professor and the headmaster, in the hotel lounge. I caught sight of the LEA EP and the Head of Social Services (the LEA expert witness). They were talking to a lady whom I presumed to be their barrister.

My heart was hammering. I felt scared. I'm not telling you this to put you off but I want you to know if that is how you feel you are not alone. However, be of good courage. I had a very nice experience while getting a grip on my emotions in the ladies' loo. I bumped into a lovely lady, who knew me and the children. She was being trained for ordination and she was there for a clerical conference.

I explained briefly what we were doing at the hotel (I'm not sure she totally understood but she was very kind). I asked her to pray for us to give us strength to get through the day. Now don't scoff: we all have different beliefs and that's mine, OK? It did make me feel a little better to feel a whole room full of clerics would be putting in a good word for me with 'Him upstairs' and it was lovely to see her kind and friendly face.

There was a delay as there was a legal issue which needed sorting out. We were asked to go and discuss 'late evidence'. Janet went to meet with the LEA barrister and certain points were agreed. We had asked the President of SENDIST if we might enter some late evidence the day prior to the tribunal. We were fortunate. He agreed to it. We had some very important late evidence from the police, etc.

Don't rely on this. Try to get your evidence in on time. The President may not allow it and then it cannot be entered in your case.

The Clerk to the Tribunal came to talk with us. It transpired that we had the same Chair as for the previous tribunal. Did we want to continue or did we want to ask for an adjournment? We felt at this stage we had to continue and to trust in his professionalism. We agreed that we would go ahead.

All of this had caused a considerable delay in the commencement of the proceedings. I think some of our gang were awash with coffee and I had probably consumed about half a bottle of Rescue Remedy. Eventually the Clerk told us that it was time to go through and for the hearing to begin.

The chairs were drawn up in a straight line across a wide table from the Panel who were already seated when we came in. I am very uncomfortable sitting in a straight line so I deliberately moved my chair back about a foot so that at least I could see the faces of the LEA representatives and ours without craning around. Still, I have absolutely no recollection whatsoever as to what the LEA barrister looked like: my brain has blotted it out.

We all sat down opposite the Panel and began arranging papers, pens, files, etc. on the table. We all poured a glass of water. I had Janet on one side (my right-hand 'man') and my husband (who was looking a little pale around the gills) on the other (my other 'right-hand man'). The headmaster sat next to him and the professor was on the end.

The professor had attended several tribunal hearings as an expert witness, which was useful as he seemed very much at his ease – in direct contrast to us.

I have had to ask my husband for his recollections of the events as mine, whilst I have total recall of some of the previous meetings, seem 'patchy'.

The Chair introduced himself and his Panel (two men this time). And so we began. The Chair explained that the LEA would give their evidence first.

The LEA's evidence

The LEA presented their case. I remember thinking 'here we go again' as it sounded like such legalistic jargon. I'm sorry. I don't want to alarm you but this book will be of no use to you unless I tell you the truth. This is why you need to use *everything* in your power to get help and make sure that you have *experienced* legal representation on the day.

You have to listen, digest, make notes, think, remember, not get angry, write questions – all at the same time. You must not interrupt. This is very difficult, I discovered. Every time something contentious was said we would make notes for later. Janet was serenely magnificent during those hours in the tribunal.

A couple of times something was said and I turned to her with a protest in my eyes. She just very patiently laid a reassuring hand on my arm. She was like a loyal terrier: circling the attacker, watching them carefully and knowing when to bite them on the bottom – metaphorically speaking! She really was incredible. She has such knowledge of the system, both professionally and personally, that it is difficult to pull the wool over her eyes.

I was encouraged because I realized, as I listened to the Panel's questions to the LEA, that clearly they had read our Case Statement. One of the Panel referred to specific pages in our evidence.

The LEA EP looked very uncomfortable. He came across as decent and seemed to care about the child in question, but the Panel were firing a barrage of very incisive questions at him and he didn't seem prepared for the intensity of their probing. Suddenly he said he had to leave the room. Even the LEA barrister looked surprised, and it was turned into a general 'comfort break' for the rest of the us. It was a surreal experience and we are probably not the only parents to feel that.

After a break we all returned to the hearing room. The Panel continued to question the LEA representatives and then their expert witness.

One of the bones of contention in our case was that Richard was being asked to return to his old school (where you will recall he had been clinically depressed, refused school, self-harmed, been bullied and failed academically). This was being justified by the fact that they were about to install a special 'Asperger's unit' in the school. As I wrote in Chapter 7, we believed this to be inadequate. We had tried, and failed, to get answers from the school and the LEA to basic questions such as:

- Who was the teacher that was being appointed?

- What were his or her qualifications?

- Where had he or she been based previously?

- What were the ages of the pupils going into the unit?

We felt it was reasonable to expect answers to these questions. Fortunately, so did the Chairman and the Panel.

One of the Panel members said that he was puzzled as to how a teacher could be in place in the January when it was now November (the interviews had just taken place) and teachers have to give one term's notice to leave another placement. It transpired that the new teacher had been doing 'supply'. Under more rigorous questioning it then transpired that the person appointed didn't actually have the qualifications to teach in this country at all but was a psychologist training for her Masters.

Our expert witness, the professor, then spoke up and commented that the new 'teacher' would not have much experience of autism in that case. He told the hearing that he was familiar with the course the new 'teacher' was following and that students received one half-day lecture on autism during the whole course.

'It isn't a bad lecture though,' he said. 'I give it!'

We pointed out that the other children going into the unit were small boys from Year Eight. Our son was in Year Ten and man-sized. This did not seem a very good idea, bearing in mind the state that some of the children – including Richard – could be in. It certainly meant he would be set apart even more and wouldn't be given the chance to be integrated with his peers.

My husband tells me that he remembers being slightly encouraged by the fact that one of the Panel didn't seem very impressed with the proposed provision. I don't remember that. I think I was catatonic by then.

The Panel then turned their attention to the head of Social Services to talk about their report. A quote from this report states that 'Richard does not receive respite care away from home, but efforts will be made to try and locate respite care to support his family with a foster carer or similar provision. The aim of the placement would be to give Mr and Mrs ... [us] regular respite to support [Richard's] IEP at ... [the mainstream school]'.

The Panel asked who would provide the respite and the head of Social Services stated that they liked to place children with people fully trained in working with autism.

However, when pressed for a clear answer by the Panel as to 'exactly who' would provide this respite, the head of Social Services had to admit they didn't have *anyone at all* – let alone someone fully trained in working with autism! (We actually already knew this as we had gleaned this information by a throwaway remark from another social worker whose job it is to try to provide respite care. 'There isn't any at all. We can't find anyone,' we had been told shortly before the tribunal.)

Clearly a mistake had been made by the head of Social Services. Or perhaps she had misunderstood information she had been given?

Our evidence

The Chair announced at the end of the LEA's evidence that we would break for lunch.

Janet took this opportunity to look at what I'd painstakingly written in preparation for the tribunal. I had drawn up, in large font, a chronological time line of key events.

'You'll be fine,' she said. 'Just keep to these points.' She didn't want me wandering off at a tangent as we only had the afternoon to put a lot of information across. I remember feebly muttering something about 'having a bit of a problem'. We were invited back into the hearing.

My husband spoke. I believe he was quite eloquent: I'm afraid I've no idea what he said.

Then the Panel all looked directly at me. 'Please, could you tell us about your son?'

The Chair was kind. The other Panel members smiled encouragingly. The problem really manifested itself then.

Something had happened to my brain and I couldn't read.

I looked at them.

They looked at me.

An expectant hush fell upon the hearing.

'I don't know where to start,' I heard myself say. 'So I won't.'

My startled husband nudged me and pointed to my papers. 'It's all written there,' he whispered. 'Just read that out.'

I was stricken.

I have no idea what happened. I knew that there were words in front of me – 'but', 'and', 'the'. I just couldn't make any sense of them. I was petrified.

Eventually, I did say something. Quite a lot of something. I don't know that it made much sense and I don't know whether it bore much relation to the impassioned, informed speech that I'd written.

Thank goodness, one of the Panel then asked me a direct question about a particular incident. I managed to answer that and I was then a little more coherent.

Our expert witnesses then spoke and answered questions.

The headmaster of the SN school was fantastic. He spoke with such clarity, conviction and passion about Richard and the other young lives in his care.

The professor was also wonderful. He gave his evidence calmly and with authority.

Suddenly our part was over and we were allowed another 'comfort break' before the conclusion. Our party stood outside the hearing, Janet, still magnificent, gathering us, making sure that we were all ready for the last 'push'.

Quite suddenly I was overwhelmed. I felt wretched. We were fighting for Richard's life. We'd all been working night and day to gather the evidence to prove the case to help our son. I'd just blown the whole thing and let everyone down by behaving so ineffectually. It was too much. I couldn't hold back the tears any longer.

Janet, bless her, was our strength again. She was there with a tissue and a big hug and words of comfort and support for me. I will never be able to adequately express my gratitude to her for helping us through this day.

The headmaster rubbed my back sympathetically. My husband was a tower of strength as usual and held my hand as we were then invited back into the hearing.

The LEA barrister summed up their case.

Janet summed up our case.

She then invited my husband to make his closing statement which he did. I was so proud of him. He spoke with love and concern about our troubled boy. Janet then took a risk and asked me to speak.

I had been advised by Janet that we needed to say something to 'sum up' at the end of the tribunal. I knew that I would be pretty drained by then so had written it the day before. You must write what is in your heart. This was what was in mine which was pretty mangled at the time.

I managed to get this out – just – although the last bit came out one word at a time and in a squeak.

> I've heard Richard described in many different ways in this last year – often negatively by his old school. You will have seen words such as 'difficult', 'truculent', 'argumentative', 'selfish', 're-lentless', 'manipulative', and his 'behaviour can be challenging'.

> I would like people to realize Richard's behaviour is distressed rather than difficult, troubled rather than truculent, afraid rather than argumentative. I would like Richard to be thought of as a human being first although his perception may be different, the world itself is as much his as it is ours and he deserves an appropriate place to finish his school days with dignity so that he can step out into the world without fear…thank you for listening and I hope you agree with our case.

(I offer my thanks to the wonderful Phoebe Caldwell who set me off in the right direction to write this.)

The Chair thanked us for attending, for showing faith in him and for allowing the Hearing to take place. We appreciated this act of common courtesy and kindness. We packed up all our notes and files of papers and left.

We all went to the bar. I think we were waiting for a piece of paper or something from the Clerk. I don't drink but I really wished I could have had a brandy!

Eventually, we were out in the cold November evening saying goodbye to our 'team'. This had been one of the most intense days of my life but without the resolution – we'd have to wait for that.

As we drove away the floodgates opened and I didn't stop crying for several hours. You know those cartoon cars that go through a flood and when the doors open the person inside is washed out by the rush of water with a fish in their ear? Yep, you get the picture. That was my husband.

I was inconsolable. I'd ruined our whole case.

The decision

This time there was no delay. Within two weeks we had the decision.

Part 2, Part 3 and the vital Part 4 had been changed. The special needs school was named. The Special Educational Needs and Disability Tribunal ordered the LEA to change the Statement of Special Educational Needs to reflect this decision. *We'd done it – we'd won!*

A brighter future

Now we are hoping that Richard will go on to continue his life at a special needs college. This would have been impossible had he been made to stay in mainstream school. He would have probably ended up in a psychiatric unit like others I know who did not receive help.

Chapter 13
Jack's story

Jack's chapter is going to be the 'unfinished symphony' of this book. Well, I suppose all the children's chapters are to an extent, but we have just had an extraordinary week and I'm still reeling. If I wait for the denouement this book will never be finished. Perhaps I'll have to tell you the next thrilling instalment on the website? A bit like *The Archers!*

Jack probably wouldn't like me saying this, as he's a teenager and it may not sound very 'cool', but he's a very nice person. This is just as well as his has not been an easy lot. Now he is fifteen and we have discovered that Jack has far more problems than we thought.

Jack has grown up in a household where, until not so long ago, his older siblings had constant tantrums. They shouted and screamed and threw things all the time if they didn't get their own way. Daily life was a war zone. It was very difficult for Jack to invite friends home as he risked losing them once they'd experienced one of his siblings' tantrums.

This is pretty difficult whatever your position in the family but as the youngest this must have been particularly hard. Often he had to have the understanding and maturity of the oldest child.

All four children always wanted the same two flavours from the selection of four yoghurts, so we used to devise little puzzles and quizzes to (a) exercise their minds and (b) try to be as fair as possible. In retrospect this didn't work, although the children enjoyed the questions and would join in usually with enthusiasm especially if it was about a times table. However, autistic people find it difficult to empathize with another person's point of view. So if the yoghurt they wanted went to the victor, fairly, they had another tantrum.

From an early age Jack would offer to hand over the yoghurt if he had won, if that would stop the tantrum. We didn't ask him to do this: he took stock of the situation and decided that any pleasure would be severely diminished if his sibling was shouting and 'carrying on'. This was very mature behaviour from a young boy and we are very proud of him for this.

Difficult role models

We all know that as children we learn so much from copying our family (parents, siblings). This was very difficult for Jack as so much of what he saw was very odd.

We did get a little time alone with Jack, when the others had gone off either to school or play school, and he was a delight. He was a very cheerful child and would even wake up smiling from afternoon naps. Walking down the street in the local town with him was always an adventure: he wanted to explore everything and his sunny nature seemed to draw people to him like a magnet. Folk would stop us on the pavement for a chat and to compliment him on his dimples.

He was curious about everything and seemed to soak up knowledge like a sponge. He was fascinated by the world of nature and once the other children had gone off to school would potter around the garden lifting rocks, watching beetles or intrigued by some special flower or insect.

Jack adored listening to the schools programmes on the radio. He would sit, thumb in mouth, rapt. Then he would come trotting into the kitchen to find me to talk about what he'd been listening to. He was a bright, inquisitive, happy and sociable little boy who was a joy to have around and never any trouble at all.

We didn't think he'd have any problems making friends. He had to go into hospital when he was four and I stayed with him. He happily played with the children before the operation, went off to theatre and then slept solidly for seven hours! I had a constant stream of little dabs appearing by the bedside whispering 'Can Jack come to play now?' He eventually woke up, wolfed down sausage, chips and beans, got back on the tricycle and pedalled off down the ward to the other children.

He loved books and was happy in his own company turning the pages and studying the pictures. He appreciated rhythm and rhyme and we used to make up poems as we walked the lanes around our home together. Most memorable of these was the poem which began:

Munch, munch, munch,
Crunch, crunch, crunch.

This was inspired by our walk when we were chomping an apple and scuffling through the crispy golden leaves. OK, it might not sound like much but he was only three at the time and we had fun adding things on the end.

But dyslexics can't read – can they?

Jack loved being read to and appeared to be 'reading' with us at a very early age. When he was three I can distinctly remember reading him a story one night (about a bear and the moonlight). The next night we looked through it together and he 'read' it to me – word perfect – including the inflections I'd used!

We couldn't quite work out how he was doing this but he seemed to have a wonderful memory for the words of poems and songs. He learned Wordsworth's 'Daffodils' off by heart at a very young age – long before he went to school, just for fun, and seemed to love it.

Writing was another matter entirely. Although he could hold a pencil and we gently chugged our way through Key Stage workbooks to help handwriting, etc., it remained one of his least favourite pastimes. I didn't push it at the time as he was so keen in other areas and was so obviously learning because he was always able to discuss new knowledge and then relate it correctly to another situation. Knowledge appeared to be 'going in' and being digested.

I didn't want to 'switch off' his enthusiasm by insisting he did something he really didn't enjoy when there were so many other things that he definitely attacked with enthusiasm – and he was still very young. I still don't really know whether I should have done this differently.

We encouraged him to do all sorts of things with pencils and crayons including joining the dots and practising letters – all the things parents would normally do. We had no idea that he had a Specific Learning Disability until many years later. Yes, Jack is dyslexic, but it was only when he was thirteen years old that the diagnosis was confirmed.

Home-schooling

Jack didn't begin school until he was six years old because, just as he approached school age, all his siblings came back to be home-schooled after their disastrous primary school experiences.

We had watched the other children having a very miserable time at the local school but not been able to understand fully why. We couldn't bear the same thing to happen to this keen little boy so Jack was home-schooled too.

We taught our little class of four (aged nine, seven, six and four) at the same level. We had to go back to basics with the others and start again at the beginning with literacy and numeracy, so it seemed logical.

Alphabets, numbers, times tables filled our waking hours. Although the other children did create problems some of the time we had inadvertently created a very secure framework for their lives and they were therefore fairly peaceful. Certainly this period was calmer than we'd known when they were still struggling in their first primary school.

We had no help from the LEA – well it had been our decision to withdraw them – although we didn't realize at the time that the children should have all been receiving either masses more help or specialist education in different placements. We personally taught them everything except science: we paid a friend who was a retired science teacher to come in for a couple of hours a week.

We really concentrated on getting the basics right as a solid foundation. The older three all eventually became very good at times tables (which harmed them when we were searching for the right diagnosis as it muddied the waters). Learning by rote wasn't so difficult for them – understanding a concept was.

However, Jack still doesn't know his times tables at the age of fifteen. He will work his way through them all to get to an answer. He does understand the concept behind them but just cannot remember them even though we tried teaching them to him as songs and rhymes.

We did an awful lot during this period as well as 'the three Rs'. We were concerned by the older children's lack of friends and we didn't want them to become further isolated, so all the children were taken to swimming lessons, ballet (to straighten out the knees, remember?), where Jack passed his primary exam as he was a nice little mover, gymnastics, drama (Jack played a wonderful cat in a sweet production of *Papa Panov* – his heartfelt meow was much acclaimed!), museums, castles, art and craft days, wildlife days. We also did a lot of cooking which they all enjoyed. Jack's speciality was shortcrust pastry. Strangely Jack doesn't seem to be able to cook now although the others still enjoy it.

The kitchen table became a 'cafeteria' and they all 'bought' their meals with toy money (even at nine years old money had been a mystery to Alice). We even had a real till with a ting! The children thought this was great but they were warned that they had to check their change as sometimes the lady in charge of the till (*moi*) made mistakes and if they didn't have enough money left out of their kitty at the end of the week they would have to have dry crackers for lunch – sounds cruel but it certainly focused their minds! It only happened once, by the way, and Alex having dolefully munched his crackers *always* checked his change thereafter!

Their lives certainly weren't dull.

One by one we introduced the others to the new primary school; Alice after nine months of home school, Alex after approximately sixteen months and Richard a couple of months after that. Jack stayed at home with me for another couple of months and then we took him to the school too.

I can remember sitting outside the head teacher's office with young Jack on my knee. He had picked out a book from the library and we were looking through it together.

Although I can remember feeling sad, as it was the end of an era, I felt peaceful that at last I was delivering a child to school who wouldn't have any problems. Hollow laughter stage left!

How wrong can you be?

Jack's writing was awful and I felt very guilty, blaming myself for not trying harder to make him write. The first teacher commented that she thought he had 'hyper-mobile' joints (Alex also had this problem only more so) and she had to sit him on a table on his own as he spread himself all over the place. Jack was seen by the physiotherapist who confirmed the teacher's suspicions. He was given exercises to do to try to correct this which did help.

I think the teachers genuinely liked Jack but they found he had a bit of a 'butterfly' mind which doesn't sit well with the National Curriculum.

His Year Four teacher said she thought he had a photographic memory which was weird as he always loses everything. It became a tradition that on the last day of term I would trawl all the school corridors and cloakrooms gathering up all Jack's clothing. His head teacher commented that half the lost property in the school was Jack's! It probably still is!

At his Year Six parents' evening Jack's teacher smiled and said 'Well – he's Jack'. What was that supposed to mean? We were puzzled by his lack of success in tests and his SATS didn't seem to reflect his ability – an opinion with which the teachers concurred. He was obviously much brighter than his siblings – we couldn't understand it. However, there was a lot of very urgent work being done with his sister which rather took precedence.

Jack continued to have a way with words (spoken, of course). One night, when Jack was seven years old, Robin came home from work and asked where the absent Alice was.

Jack took his thumb out of his mouth. 'She's dining with God,' he replied.

Alice was often either storming off to her bedroom, smashing up things as she went, or had been sent to her room when things became too 'hot to handle' with the rest of the children around.

On another occasion Jack and I were lucky enough to witness the Northern Lights.

'Wow!' he cried. 'God's having a disco!' Nice image, Jack.

A difficult set of footsteps to follow

There is no doubt that, in spite of all our best endeavours, Jack has not had an easy time. This lovely sunny child has grown into an anxious adolescent, which is very sad.

When Jack followed his siblings into primary school we had no idea what this was going to mean to him. In hindsight (I *hate* hindsight) it would have been easier, dyslexia aside, had Jack attended a different school to the others. The primary school that they attended was in a small town twenty miles away (*ergo* a forty-mile round trip). This might sound outrageous but we live in a very rural area with very little choice. Our nearest proper shop is the same distance away. It is a half hour journey each way and is expensive on petrol but is accepted as the norm around here.

We were drawn to this particular school because the headmaster had been much praised as a decent, kind, caring man – which he is.

Jack's problems really mushroomed as his siblings got older. Things really started going *badly* pear-shaped when he reached high school. There were all sorts of funny little incidents with Jack at primary school but at the time the oldest two children were the ones we were most concerned about.

Cowardly bullies!

All of the older children were bullied on the school bus, particularly when they got to high school. I didn't really realize the extent of it until then. As the children moved up through the school the bullying escalated in frequency and aggression. I have now come to the conclusion that the bus journey was twenty minutes of unsupervised bedlam.

The children do not use the seatbelts provided. Instead, the trouble-makers roam up and down the bus picking on the more vulnerable children. I feel sorry for the bus company who are liable but impotent.

There were so many instances of bullying that I've erased half of them from my memory. It impacted very badly on Jack as he seemed to be piggy in the middle and things got worse after Alex left school. Jack was then left on the school bus with the other children and Richard.

I gave Jack the book *Lord of the Flies* to read. 'It's just like the school bus,' he commented. And he was right.

Richard is very particular about where he wants to sit on the bus. The other children realized this and refused to let him sit where he wanted to. We explained to Richard that he had no more right to sit in a particular place than anyone else. However, by the same token he also had as much right as the others to sit where he wanted.

Richard and Jack would often get off the school bus white-faced and shaken having endured another hellish time. Favourite possessions would be taken and thrown out of the school bus window, blows would be exchanged, and one boy was trying extortion with menaces to get money out of Richard at one point. On this occasion my husband got onto the school bus, approached the revolting child involved and told him to 'pick on someone his own size'. The boy just smirked. He knew we couldn't do anything about it except complain to the school, which we did *ad nauseum*, but they seemed to be able to do very little about it.

The other children on the bus spent their time smoking, spitting and picking on the vulnerable passengers. It was ghastly.

Jack tried to protect his older brother but as the younger, smaller boy it was difficult. It was also problematical as it seemed to get Jack into trouble with the school as well. They seemed to have a policy of 'it takes two to tango', so if two boys were found fighting then both were punished regardless of who started it! Poor Jack found himself in detention several times because he had waded in to try to stop the bullies picking on Richard. In the end he gave up protesting. It was most unfair. Don't get me wrong – he's no angel, but…!

Things all came to head when Richard was so nastily assaulted on the school bus that we had to involve the police (see Chapter 10).

Not long after this incident a young boy was killed following an accident involving a school bus in south Wales. The report mentioned 'horse-play'. My husband and I looked at each other as we had heard this term used when Richard had been punched in the head. Not quite our interpretation of 'horse play'.

I can hear you all shouting at me: 'Why didn't you take them all to school if they were having such a difficult time?' Well, it wasn't that easy. It would have meant an extra 400 miles on the clock each week for me to do two round trips each day to take these children and I did have to work as well! With everything else that was going on in our lives by then this was just a 'bridge too far'. The school had an 'anti-bullying policy'. We kept hoping that it would be effectively implemented – to no avail. Our sons were bullied up to the day they left the school. The school seemed impotent.

We're proud of Jack for standing up to the tormentors on his brothers' behalf but wish that he hadn't had to.

More problems

Jack must have witnessed some pretty bizarre behaviour from his siblings and I'm sure wished himself anywhere else but at the school or on that bus. I know how cruel kids can be when confronted by children who are in any way different. Ours were and paid the price. It really isn't cool to have an older brother shouting, screaming and crying.

When Jack arrived at the high school in the wake of the others teachers were by then realizing that the other two boys (Alice had left by then) were, shall we say, a little unusual. Now Jack was experiencing educational difficulties too. He has always presented as a bright little spark but it was becoming apparent that there were problems which were holding him back.

However, they were different problems.

Alex, for example, seems to be able to write about subjects without actually understanding them at all. Although his writing isn't good he can copy passages from books. Jack finds it extremely difficult to write about subjects even if he appears to have understood them and can talk intelligently about them. Even when copying from the board or from text his spelling is all over the place which *really* hacks off teachers as they think he is being careless and lazy.

Richard would come home from school and experience problems with homework.

'What was the teacher talking to you about?' I'd ask, trying to help him to remember.

Richard would look blank. He really didn't seem to know what had been going on at school. In stark contrast Jack used to come home and tell us, almost verbatim, what they'd been learning; yet when it came to exams or the dreaded SATS he scored extremely poorly and he was always losing his homework and being put in detention for not doing it! I'd seen it so I knew he'd done it but I'm sure the teachers thought I was making it up.

Dyslexia?

We knew something about dyslexia. I have a dyslexic nephew. What we didn't appreciate early on was that it can take several forms. My nephew, another bright boy, is very obviously dyslexic. It took him years to learn to read and even now he has to work twice as hard as everyone else.

Jack, by contrast, was always an avid reader. As I've said, he loves words, poetry and song. This proved misleading and it took us a long time to work out what was going on (and even longer to get him diagnosed and helped), for when you ask him to write down his knowledge he struggles terribly.

We were baffled by his problems but were asking for help to no avail. We'd even been to a dyslexia school but been too blinkered to see. We took Jack with us when we dropped Richard off for his week at the dyslexia summer camp. The children were taken off for a tour whilst the parents were given a talk. We watched and listened with interest – it was a good talk.

'It sounds more like Jack,' we said of their description!

Jack came back from the kid's tour. 'It's great being dyslexic,' he said.

Still, we didn't get it. But, as I say, at that time we had hugely pressing problems with both Richard and Alice and they had to be our priorities. I did try to book Jack in to the camp the following year but sadly that school was closing.

Dysgraphia

Jack has 'dysgraphia' (which is another type of language disorder – an impairment of the written language) as well as dyslexia. He can read (although he doesn't read as well as I thought he did – his intelligence seems to help him to guess what it says) and can understand what he has read. He can verbally answer questions. But somehow the brain scrambles the messages when information needs to travel from his brain to his hand to write. Weird and very frustrating for sufferers. Even working on a keyboard Jack has difficulties arranging his thoughts. This a bit of a drawback in the modern world. We hope that he will learn coping skills as he matures.

An LEA assessment – hope at last?

We finally managed to get Jack assessed. After his assessment the PEP talked to me. Clearly thinking I was just being a fussy mother, *again*, his report regarding Jack was really quite dismissive.

I can remember being very depressed and thinking 'Is it just me?' The trouble is that I may be a daft old bat but Jack's assessment just didn't add up, it wasn't logical and I said as much, very politely, to the PEP. To illustrate what I meant about Jack I told the PEP about an incident in the car when Jack was eleven years old.

I had been driving with Jack in the back seat. He was reading a book (he was always reading) as I was mentally ruminating about yet another problem we were having with Alice.

'Hmm, it's a dichotomy,' I thought aloud.

'Mm,' said a voice from the back seat.

'You don't know what a dichotomy is,' I said.

'Is it when you have a door marked "damned if you do" and a door marked "damned if you don't"?'

I was flabbergasted!

'How on earth do you know that?' I asked him.

Apparently some time before this conversation he had been reading the 'Far Side' cartoons and there was one entitled 'The Dichotomy of Hell'. Somehow, this 'not very bright' ten- or eleven-year-old had:

- understood what it meant
- worked out how to pronounce dichotomy
- and remembered this and been able to use it in context.

All by himself! Well, I'm sorry, but I think that's pretty darn clever – don't you?

When I recounted this anecdote to the PEP, he just looked at me. The whole tone of his assessment was: 'he's not very bright, what do you expect – his siblings aren't very bright either. However, he isn't so unintelligent as to warrant much help and doesn't meet criteria for a statutory assessment. Go away and stop bothering me.' I didn't find it very helpful.

I talked to some good friends of ours who are very experienced retired teachers who know the family and Jack well. I asked them if they thought that Jack just wasn't very bright. They didn't agree.

Following the receipt of Jack's Year Seven report I wrote a letter to the high school pointing out that we might all have missed something. I had by then started reading up on dyslexia and SN generally. Jack's report was almost 'textbook'. In every subject the teachers commented that he was 'keen' and 'expressed himself well vocally/orally' in class. However, they pointed out that he hadn't revised well as he had done badly in just about every exam – some spectacularly so! I think he achieved 23 per cent for English that year in his exam. This is a ridiculous mark for someone with a good vocabulary, who is such a keen reader, who seems to understand what he is reading, and who can discuss what he has read or make it relevant to something else that is going on.

Specific Learning Difficulty!

During the summer holidays we had arranged for Alex and Jack to be assessed by the same independent psychologist who had first indicated that he thought that Richard might have Asperger's syndrome. The assessment revealed that Alex had an IQ of 67 and that Jack had an IQ of 108! He also mentioned that Jack had a Specific Learning Difficulty.

Please try to resist kicking this book across the room but I didn't know that a Specific Learning Difficulty meant dyslexia!! Another eighteen months was to elapse before a definitive diagnosis was made.

I beg you not to judge us but to remember what else we were going through at the same time with the others and to understand just how many 'balls' were juggling in the air at that time.

OK, so we dropped a few.

The slippery slope

Jack was moved down to the bottom English set and his behaviour then started to deteriorate. This was Year Eight and I think he was becoming so fed up that he had clearly thought he might just as well be hung for a sheep as a lamb.

He was bored witless by the work that the English class were doing. I am not condoning naughty behaviour but it must have seemed like a very long day to Jack with the added bonus of trying to stop his brother being bullied on the way in and out of school daily.

In the 'remedial' English class the work was well within Jack's capabilities but he was not able to shine as he is very bad at spelling and writing. In his previous class they had been studying literature which he enjoyed. In the remedial class they weren't studying any literature. I clearly remember saying to him that if he just worked hard he would be able to get back up into a more interesting class.

I was wrong again but this time I realized it very quickly. I did apologize to Jack. I worked out, as he did, that there was no way on earth that he was going to get out of that class by hard work. It was just the wrong sort of class. Jack and the teacher were at loggerheads.

I wrote to the school again pointing out where I thought things were going wrong and the fact that this had now developed into something of a personality clash with the teacher.

The teacher telephoned me and told me that Jack hadn't improved at all from being in her class (which sadly didn't surprise me). She said he didn't 'deserve' to go up a group and if he did he would be taking the place of other children who perhaps 'deserved it more'.

Now had she said that to me a few years earlier I would have meekly backed down. In fact I had done just that under very similar circumstances, when someone used a similar phrase much earlier referring to Alice. I may be stupid but I'm not that stupid! I politely but firmly disagreed with the teacher. The school put Jack up a set in English and he was a little more cheerful. He still wasn't doing very well but at least his interest was recaptured a bit as the class were studying Shakespeare and poetry.

And so Jack's high school life chugged on, not terribly happily for the most part. He did manage to make a few 'friends', unlike his siblings, but because he is easily led, unaware of time (he still has problems telling the time even now) and constantly losing everything (a very dyslexic problem) he was often in trouble. He has a highly developed sense of 'honour' and would always own up if he'd done something wrong (sometimes, we've been told he will even own up when he hasn't done anything wrong!).

His life was a struggle. He had to spend hours and hours completing homework that probably should have been done in twenty minutes. Then, to compound his misery, he would lose the work and be kept in detention for not doing it! I would tell the school that he had done the homework. I don't lie; I had seen the completed work, but I spoke in vain. It must have been extremely disheartening for Jack.

Jack was then suspended from school for a day for hiding a pair of trainers. He was a clot – fair enough. When asked, he said he had done it to cheer himself up! While we always tried to support and respect the school's discipline policy we were a little sceptical about the justice of this decision, bearing in mind the bullying we knew had been going on for years without proper reparation.

The final straw came when a teacher who knew and liked Jack (as he was working with the Duke of Edinburgh Award with him) telephoned to say that he was incandescent with Jack as he had 'deliberately failed his maths exam'. He came bottom of the whole year! I explained that I didn't think Jack would do that as he really wanted to succeed. The teacher said there was no other explanation as he had been receiving grade As for his homework in the run-up to the exam and this was the same work they were being examined upon.

It later transpired that Jack had only completed about half the paper as his writing and thinking are so slow that he'd run out of time. No wonder he'd done so badly. We felt so frustrated for him.

Definitive diagnosis at last!

We decided after this debacle that things were getting desperate. I telephoned the Dyslexia Institute in Bangor to make an appointment for Jack to be assessed. We did have to pay for this (although you might be referred through your psychologist if you are lucky) but I was still getting nowhere with the LEA and knew that while they wasted time another of our children was watching his school days slip through his hands – so God bless the bank manager again!

The staff at the institute are very kind and understanding. I had made an appointment for Jack and then one of the psychologists telephoned me to discuss his visit and get a better picture of Jack by running through some questions.

I mentioned to the institute that we had paid for an independent assessment previously. The psychologist asked me what the 'conclusion' said. I read it out including the part about the 'Specific Learning Difficulty'.

'There you are,' she cried. 'They've already said it. SLD. Jack is dyslexic!'

Yes, I know that I should be sent to stand in the corner with a dunce's cap on my head for not knowing better but in my defence I also have to point out I'm not a trained professional. The high school had been in possession of the report for nearly eighteen months as well and nobody there had pointed out that was what SLD meant and had gone on arguing the toss every time I mentioned that we thought he might be dyslexic.

Only a couple of months before I'd been to Jack's parents' evening. I had mentioned to Jack's English teacher (he'd been moved down again) that we thought it was highly likely that he was dyslexic.

'That's interesting,' she'd commented conversationally.

Further injustice

Jack was very miserable and my heart was breaking watching my sunny, funny, loving, keen child going down the plughole! He was increasingly frustrated and upset. This was compounded by the fact that he was watching Richard becoming very disturbed and manic. The atmosphere at home was tense and unhappy.

One of the measures the high school took was to tell Richard that he didn't have to do homework – it avoided the inevitable tantrum in class. This didn't really help Richard much as it meant that he was slipping further behind with his work, which meant more pressure. The pressure left him unable to cope and then he would refuse to go into school.

At the same time that Richard was being told he didn't have to do homework Jack was being put into detention for not having done homework even if he had done it but lost it! Jack, quite rightly, thought this was a tad unfair!

We did protest but to no avail. By this stage Richard was in such a state that the relationship with the school became very strained. Something different had to be done.

A school for dyslexics?

I telephoned the British Dyslexia Association to try to find a dyslexia summer school which might help Jack to understand what was going on in his life and help him during the summer holidays.

I started trawling around the suggested schools (there weren't many). I spoke to an independent fee-paying boarding school in North Wales where the headmaster's very helpful secretary told me that unfortunately they didn't do a summer camp but the more she described the school the more I thought it sounded like dyslexic heaven (or should that be hevean!). Two thirds of the pupils are dyslexic and the whole ethos of the school is geared to restoring their confidence and teaching them to 'accentuate the positive' and learn coping skills to help them through their lives.

Jack didn't have a Statement. We didn't have the strength to fight for a Statement for him. We were still involved in a bitter struggle with the LEA regarding the wholly inadequate Statement for Richard (whose clinical depression had long since been diagnosed and whose stress was sending the stress levels of the whole family soaring).

It was around this time that, as I described in Chapter 10, our miracle happened and we were generously given the funding for Richard to get to his new school (immediately). The same organization wanted to give the family a gift because they were disgusted with the way our children had been treated.

The gift was enough to cover the expected deficit for Jack's fees!!

Yes, we were stunned too. It *exactly* met the need.

A new beginning – hope at last

Jack started at his new school the following week after a hastily arranged interview with the headmaster where Jack was so nervous we could feel the sofa shaking under us!

We miss him terribly while he is away, but just over a year on, we feel we've done the right thing for him. It hasn't all been plain sailing as he tries to sort himself out. He is a teenager who is trying to 'find himself' like any other teenager but he has a lot of baggage now about his worth as a person, which is very sad. It was also a shame that he arrived just at the time when he had to really buckle down straight away for GCSE work. Even one year earlier would have helped him to have time to sort himself out a bit before the exams.

The headmaster and staff have been very supportive and we are extremely grateful for all their care and extra efforts to try to help him make up for lost time.

We pay as much as we can towards his school fees and we have been fortunate enough to secure support from a number of philanthropic trusts who together contribute the rest. I won't name them – but God bless them all.

Did you know that, when tested, an alarming percentage of prisoners turn out to be undiagnosed dyslexics! And yet there have been some extremely successful dyslexics in history. Think of Winston Churchill, George Patten, Albert Einstein, Richard Branson, Lynda La Plante, Susan Hampshire, Cher, Leonardo da Vinci, John Lennon and Hans Christian Andersen – just for starters! I prefer to concentrate on this list but keep the previous statistic firmly in mind if I feel my energy flagging when straining my sinews to get help.

Accentuate the positive

Jack's current school really accentuates the positive aspects of dyslexia and I know that some employers actively seek dyslexics.

When we were still doing two jobs to pay for Alice's Steiner school my colleagues in the office where I worked started discussing dyslexia. A lady I worked with commented that in her previous office three of the five men she worked for were dyslexic.

'Was it a firm of architects?' I enquired.

Her jaw dropped. 'How did you know?'

I may not know much but I know that sometimes architects prefer to employ dyslexics as they have the peculiar ability to see the 'whole picture' which is a huge bonus for an architect.

Jack remains to be convinced – but we live in hope. He has experienced some small success at last, and we hope he can build on these new experiences and leave the past behind. However, he still loses lots of things and he is extremely anxious about the impending GCSEs, even though we're not putting pressure on him. We've just said to 'do your best' so that he can feel content, but whatever happens we have the peace of mind that he will definitely have a better springboard into life from his new school than he would have done otherwise.

What is life like as a misunderstood dyslexic?

Life as an undiagnosed, misunderstood dyslexic is very confusing and depressing. If enough people tell you, or imply to you, that you are stupid eventually you begin to believe your own press.

When we went to Jack's interview for his new school the headmaster showed us a sculpture in his study. It was a dramatic modern piece made out of wire. It showed a person rolled into the foetal position surrounded by menacing figures towering over them.

The first girl pupil to enter the school, a dyslexic, had made it and said that this was what she felt like before she arrived there. A powerful image indeed.

Re-building work continues

Jack plays rugby for the school and could be an asset to the cricket team if only he could get organized enough to get to the practices. He has completed his Bronze Duke of Edinburgh Award and he was supposed to be going in for the Silver but we think he is too overwhelmed by GCSE work at present so it will have to wait.

He has worked hard but in fits and starts. There has been rather odd behaviour which has caused problems for him at the school. Not evil but very silly behaviour without any thought for the consequences. As the headmaster said last week 'Jack shows a worrying lack of discernment'. This is particularly worrying as this is one of Alex's main problems. A lot of this odd behaviour seems to stem from his excessive fear of the GCSEs. Worryingly, we have seen Jack display some of the behavioural problems recently which both Alice and Richard displayed at exactly the same stage. Today I was at the school to discuss Jack, and the family history, with the local doctor and he has referred him on to the local psychiatrist for further assessment.

I'm not being a hysterical mother. We had hoped that Jack had escaped with just the dyslexia gene but, as we know that the other siblings share diagnoses of ASD/Asperger's, Attention Deficit Disorder, Learning Difficulty, Attachment Disorder and possibly Pathological Demand Avoidance (PDA), it would seem grossly unfair to let Jack struggle if he suffers from any of these. The SENCO carried out an assessment today (the 'Spadafore Attention Deficit Hyperactivity Disorder Rating Scale' to be exact). There are four subscales. Jack's scores were in the 'Severe' category for two of these and in the 'Moderate' category for the other two! I was stunned!

Jack didn't present as the classic ADHD child. Did he? Well, when I think about it all the things that over the years we have just thought of as rather endearing traits – his scattiness and butterfly mind and inability to stay focused on a task – are all ADHD traits. He was just so darned nice and so undemanding we didn't recognize it!

'How on earth did he get to this age without us knowing?' I asked the SENCO. She replied that he had been using his intelligence to mask his difficulties. She has suggested Ritalin as a possible short-term solution. Robin and I really don't know what to do for the best. On the one hand we really don't want to hand out strong drugs to our son but on the other he is falling apart rather at present and if it would help him to experience some calm to survive the next few months whilst he goes through the dreaded GCSEs (and allows us time to set up diagnostic assessments and appropriate help for him) then we may be doing him a disservice not to allow it. However, Ritalin can only be prescribed at the consultant psychiatrist level so we still have to wait to see when we can get an appointment with him. All very difficult, isn't it?

On a one-to-one basis the Jack we know and love is still there but he has started to refuse to go to certain lessons – he would rather fail himself (been there with Richard) and ask to be disapplied (and there). Matron has said that he seems to be 'going inside himself' (been there too with Richard).

I think the SENCO is probably right. It may just be that because of his higher IQ he has managed to cope, sort of, up to this age but the extra pressure and work of the GCSEs, plus teenage hormones, plus extra stimuli, plus not eating properly/not sleeping properly have exacerbated other, more latent problems.

'I don't like feeling out of control,' he said at Christmas. I misunderstood him and thought he was talking about the teachers and his parents. Now I know that he was talking about himself being out of control.

We think we are going to ask for a Statement (I know, I know, but what can you do?). It is a bit late in the educational system but it would probably be of value and we have to find out the full picture in any case so that we know what help he is going to need for the future.

Today I took Jack to the homeopath which was very interesting and following a battery of tests he has given us some medicine to help Jack feel a little better.

Yesterday I took Jack to the cranial osteopath for another treatment (his fourth I think). Jack has a very tight skull apparently so the osteopath is working on this. This branch of osteopathy claims to help with special needs and the osteopath is very good, so we feel it is worthwhile.

Next month we are taking Jack to the Institute for Neuro-Physiological Psychology for an assessment (www.inpp.org.uk). The homeopath feels that Jack would be a good candidate for this. At the institute they assess whether there are 'retained reflexes' from infancy. These affect the development of the brain and the way the two halves of the brain 'talk' to each other, thus impeding progress. They apparently do a lot of good work with adopted children so we feel this is another avenue worth pursuing. (Go to my website for the latest information.)

We are enormously proud of Jack (and I'm not just saying that because out of all the children he is the only one likely to read and understand this book). He is a remarkable young man who has had to overcome an awful lot in his short life. He has a lot of things going for him and has the attributes of a decent human being – empathy, kindness, warmth – and at the end of the day that is what counts, not what exams you pass. We hope he will grow in confidence. We feel privileged to have been chosen to be his parents.

Chapter 14

Frequently asked questions

Because I've now joined various groups I meet lots of parents of children with SN. This is one of the most important aspects of actually getting out there and meeting people – the sharing of priceless information over a 'cuppa'.

In some groups my children are older than those of the other parents. Whilst I envy the fact that they have achieved a diagnosis for their child at a much earlier age than we managed, I am aware that I have gone through the system which some of them are only just entering. I sometimes feel like the 'old village woman' but I'm happy to share information if I have it. Of course, if I am with the parents of older 'children' then it is my turn to sit at their feet.

The following are some of the genuine questions I've been asked recently. Maybe one of them might be relevant to your situation:

Q. *'My child doesn't have a social worker. He isn't "at risk" from us, so surely Social Services won't be interested?'*

A. Make sure that you contact the Children with Disabilities Team. This is the department you need. We floundered around with the Children and Families Team, who have a completely different role and who didn't know what to do with us, and this wasted a lot of time. It is important for you and your child that you have the support of a social worker because, apart from being able to offer you services (if their budget allows), they will have access to information and facilities that you haven't. You will need a social worker in your corner when accessing funding.

Q. *'My child is very demanding and challenging. I'm not sure I can carry on without a break. Can I get any respite care?'*

A.   It depends very much on the area in which you live and the budget constraints on Social Services. We have not been given any respite care but we did have a Family Aide until family commitments took him away from us. Although we only had him for a short time he did a good job and Richard looked forward to going out with him.

Since writing this above paragraph we have now been offered, out of the blue, a Family Aide for six hours per week for four weeks of the summer holiday. This is very good news. Richard has met his new Aide, a lady this time, and seems very relaxed with her. She is going to take him out bowling and to the cinema. Simple things, but it makes a difference, as he is now nearly seventeen and is painfully aware that he is of an age where he shouldn't need to go out with his 'Mummy and Daddy' but has no friends of his own and is not able enough to go on his own. This will give him something to look forward to during the long summer holiday and will give us all respite.

You could possibly access residential respite but it may be, as ours is here, that it is a very long way away (one hundred and fifty miles' round trip!). However, we have never used it or even been offered it. Ask the Social Services CDT. It depends on the availability of suitably 'qualified' people and accommodation.

Q.   *'Help! I am having to ask for a Statement. It seems very complicated and I don't know where to begin. Is there anyone out there who can help me?'*

A.   There are organizations out there who will either be able to help you themselves or point you in the right direction for educational advocacy advice. Contact any or all of the following:

>   IPSEA
>   ACE
>   OASIS
>   The National Autistic Society – educational advice and advocacy.

Check Appendix 1 for contact details.

Q. *'I'm certain my three-year-old is ASD and has Asperger's syndrome. The psychologist I had seen said he agreed having heard the description I gave of him. However, following an assessment where my son, uncharacteristically, behaved like an angel the psychologist changed his mind and said he just had "behavioural difficulties". I am very worried that now that this is going into the Statement that is being prepared he won't get the help he needs. Is it possible that the psychologist is wrong? Also, is it possible that the psychologist has been lent upon by the LEA when they came to look at their budgets?'*

A. Generally speaking the diagnosis of autism is regarded as a medical matter. A consultant psychiatrist, consultant paediatrician or consultant psychologist should be able to diagnose. You could try asking your GP to refer you to one of several diagnostic centres around the country if you're in doubt. I suggest you contact the NAS for details or contact the following:

> The Centre for Communication Disorders
> Elliot House
> 13 Mason's Hill
> Bromley
> Kent BR2 9HT
> Tel: 020 8466 0098

You could try the Maudsley Centre for Behavioural Disorders (Tel: 020 8776 4256), or Dr Baron-Cohen, Consultant Clinical Psychologist, who runs a diagnostic service for adults (18 and over) at:

> Lifespan Asperger Syndrome Services
> Brookside Child and Family Consultation Clinic
> 18d Douglas House
> Trumpington Road
> Cambridge CB2 2AH
> Tel: 01223 746001

Adults (I am aware that your 'child' may be over 18 years old) who want to be assessed need to be referred by their GP or social worker. OAASIS or the NAS may be able to help you find a centre or consultant near to you (check Appendix 1 for their contact details).

To help your case you could also try to get an independent assessment.

Q.   *'I would like my child to be seen by an independent psychologist but I simply don't have the money. Is there anybody who might be able to help me please?'*

A.   Look in your telephone directory, or ask your local Citizens' Advice Bureau, and see if there is any 'carers' support' available locally. Our branch is run by a wonderfully understanding woman. She has accessed a fund which gives grants to carers to help the people they are caring for either with respite holidays or in other ways. I know that recently she helped find funding for a mother desperate to try to get her child independently assessed. It's worth a try.

Q.   *'My child hasn't had an annual review of her Statement. Her circumstances have changed. Should I contact the LEA and ask for a review or should I just wait for them to sort it out?'*

A.   Don't wait. The LEA has statutory duty to review Statements on an annual basis. Write a letter straight away to the LEA, copying in your child's school, and urgently requesting an annual review. It is the responsibility of the LEA to bring together all the people and Advices required to set up the annual review.

Q.   *'My child hasn't had his transitional review. He is fifteen years old now. It seems like a lot of work. Should I bother?'*

A.   Yes, this is important. It is your child's right by law to have a transitional review. They start in Year Nine. A transition plan should be drawn up. You should be working with an organization called Connexions, and the Children with Disabilities Team of Social Services. They need to be involved in the forward planning for your child's future.

At sixteen your child's review will be led by Children's Services with Adult Services in support. At seventeen the review will be led by Adult Services with Children's Services in support. At eighteen Adult Services should take full responsibility for your child (all being well!). It is imperative that you work with these people. Social Services aim for a 'seamless transition to adulthood'!

Check the *Special Educational Needs Code of Practice* 9:45–9:64 for further information about transitional reviews.

Q. *'Can I home-educate my child if she can no longer cope with mainstream schooling?'*

A. Yes, you can home educate your child. You are allowed to 'educate your child otherwise' under section 7 of the 1996 Education Act, or the Scotland Act of 1980, section 30. This applies to all children including those with SEN.

You just need to write to the school and LEA and inform them of your decision. You will need to keep proof of the fact that you are actually giving your children an education and you might have a visit from someone at the LEA.

There are some excellent organizations set up by people who either are home-schooling or have home-schooled. They organize get-togethers so that your children can work together on projects and socialize with other home-schoolers. They also organize trips to museums and theatres, etc. There is no need for your home-schooled child to be bored with outside input, energy, enthusiasm and imagination. They can still attend the usual round of out of school activities too so don't need to feel left out. See Appendix 1 for addresses of helpful organizations.

Q. *'If I am home-schooling do I need to follow the National Curriculum?'*

A. No. You can however buy Key Stage books on the core subjects from any good bookshop. We do know people who have home-educated through to GCSE level.

Q. *'Do I need to be a qualified teacher to home-educate?'*

A. No. Check out an excellent organization called Education Otherwise on www.education-otherwise.org for information. But I'd say that you do need to be extremely committed to your children and have an interest in learning.

Q. *'Are there any holidays especially for children with Special Educational Needs? Holiday times are very difficult for us especially when my child is at home with his siblings. My child could not cope with a normal holiday for children.'*

A. Yes, there are holidays that specifically cater for children and adults with SEN. Contact Mencap, the National Autistic Society and Holiday Care (see Appendix 1). They will send you lists of holiday providers.

Alice went off to the Lake District on an adult SN adventure holiday for a week with Chrysalis Holidays. She had a wonderful time and has asked to go again next year which is a good sign.

Alex is enjoying an adult SN canal boat holiday, with Options Holidays, at the time of writing and is having a wonderful time.

Richard sets off on a children's SN activity holiday next week, at Red Ridge Centre in Cefn Coch, Mid Wales, which we think he is going to love.

These holidays make the long summer break from their routine more bearable for them and give our children a chance to have fun with people of their own age in a safe setting while imparting a sense of independence to them which would be impossible without this structure. I wish I'd known about them years ago.

Q. *'I cannot afford the prices. Is there any financial assistance available for respite/holidays for my child?'*

A. Yes. Ask your social worker or Mencap, your local branch of the Carers' Association (they should have information that will help and sometimes there is a carer's grant available which could be used towards the cost of a special needs holiday), NAS and Holiday Care for names of organizations who can be approached for possible assistance. See Appendix 1.

Q. *'I think my child might need to attend a special needs residential college. What should I do?'*

A. Contact your local Special Educational Needs Careers Advisor (SENCA). He will be able to advise you and make suggestions using the Association of National Specialist Colleges (NATSPEC) brochure (or email natspec.org.uk or look on the Web at www.natspec.org.uk). However, do bear in mind that LEAs do not like to send people 'out of county'. There may not be any residential SEN colleges in your county so the onus will then be on you to prove your child's needs and build a case for her attendance at a particular college. The SENCA is very important as *all* applications funding for SEN colleges *have* to be processed through him.

Be prepared to make time to dig for information to see which is going to be the best place for your child. You may need to write to colleges, talk on the telephone to prospective colleges (even Camphill colleges differ subtly so you may need to speak to several), arrange visits and fill in application forms. Don't rely on the SENCA to find this information for you. I have found every single one of our children's SN placements by myself purely by being a 'bloodhound'! Having investigated their set-up I then spoke to the SENCA and Social Services regarding funding. You will need to show that your local further education college cannot provide for your child's needs.

Q. *'Does the Statement continue after my child has gone to SN college?'*

A. No. The Statement ceases as soon as your child leaves school. However, your child having a Statement can be an important tool in securing a place and funding at an SEN college. Having said that, neither of our two children currently attending SN colleges has a Statement. It is therefore not impossible to get them there without one but we have had to fight, fight, fight for funding.

Q. *'So who funds a place at SEN college?'*

A. My children are part funded by ELWA (which was the Welsh Funding Council – it will be different in your area but your SENCA will be able to tell you) and part funded by Social Services. This is why it is so important for your child to have 'met criteria' for Adult Services. Some children will be part funded by 'Health'.

Q. *'Would my child qualify for any benefits? I'm really struggling with all the extra expense incurred because of his disability.'*

A. Yes, quite possibly. Talk to your Benefits Office and ask them for details. It could be that your child could qualify for Disability Living Allowance (DLA) at the very least and possibly others. The benefit system is changing all the time so you will need to ask for advice on the current status. Mencap also employ people to advise you regarding benefit rights (see addresses in Appendix 1).

Q. *'Can I qualify for any benefits?'*

A. Yes, if you earn less than a certain amount per week and are caring for someone for more than 35 hours per week there is a Carer's Allowance. Ask the Disability Living Allowance people for information. I didn't know about this and we would have qualified; it would have helped us a lot.

Q. *'I really struggle to complete forms. Is there anywhere I can go to ask for help with these?'*

A. Yes. Telephone your local Citizens Advice Bureau. Tell them what you need help with and ask for an appointment. Most bureaux have someone who specializes in helping with these forms. They can be complicated and you should ask for help or you may complete them incorrectly and your child will miss out on benefits to which she is entitled.

We didn't know anything at all about DLA until our eldest was nearly seventeen. Initially, I felt really embarrassed. Don't. Children with Special Educational Needs tend to require 'extras' and the money for this has to be found from somewhere. Alice has been granted DLA and this extra amount of money has been extremely useful. We have spent at least £1200, in total, on having the three boys independently assessed, for example.

Nobody told us about DLA and I feel a bit sick as had our children been properly diagnosed when they were younger we could have been legitimately claiming this incredibly useful extra financial help years ago, so possibly I wouldn't have had to make myself ill doing two jobs as well as trying to care for our mob!

Q. *'I've heard about "person-centred assessments". Is this important for my child?'*

A. Yes. You will need to talk to your social worker. The first time I had to do anything like this for my children they were eighteen and seventeen respectively. The person-centred assessment is prepared by the Adults with Disabilities Team social worker. It is another blueprint for your child as she enters adult life and should clearly state needs and requirements to meet those needs. I suppose it is like a grown-up's Statement.

Q. *'My fifteen-year-old child has at last been diagnosed with Attention Deficit Hyperactivity Disorder. I think there could be other problems as well and I don't have a clue as to what his IQ is. The LEA educational psychologist doesn't seem to be too bothered but I am worried. Should I try to get him a firmer, clearer diagnosis with an independent psychologist?'*

A. Yes. Get on the phone now, today, and find an independent psychologist. Find the money if you possibly can; it will make such a difference (see earlier advice about grants).

   A clearer diagnosis can only help people to understand your child (and it will help your child understand himself and take away some of the confusion in his head). Also, when it comes to accessing Adults with Disability Services, IQ can still be a very important factor. To access help later, both practically and with funding, it can be very important for your child to be a client of the Adults with Disabilities Team (ADT). The criteria for accessing help can often be an IQ cut off at 70. Although I believe there are plans to change this I don't think it can hurt to have as much information as possible.

   It can be important to get an independent assessment rather than just using an LEA educational psychologist's findings. In our daughter's case the LEA EP miscounted one of her subtests. This led to an erroneous total IQ score which took her over the magic '70' mark. This meant that Social Services, who were part funding her college place, wanted to remove her from college on her eighteenth birthday as they said she 'didn't meet criteria'.

She was reassessed as I described in Chapter 8, and her IQ was found to be 68. She does therefore qualify for help. We wouldn't have known this had she not been re-tested.

So if you think that an assessment may be wrong because it flies in the face of everything you live with, daily keep trying until you get the diagnosis that fits.

Chapter 15

A bit about us

Well, I expect you've been wondering about Robin and me so I guess it is only fair to share a brief picture of our history with you all.

I'm married to a wonderful man who has been my best friend for over thirty years. Now don't reach for the brown paper bags. It hasn't all been a bed of roses – far from it in many ways – but somehow we're still 'clinging to the wreckage'. In fact the relationship nearly foundered on the rocks two years ago because of the horrendous pressure we were under as we desperately sought a solution for Richard.

Why did we adopt?

After two ectopic pregnancies and six painful (this was in the days when you had to have four blood tests daily as well as the barrage of injections), emotionally draining, financially crippling IVF attempts, we decided that something had to change and shyly we enquired about adoption.

We live in the middle of nowhere. We somehow couldn't picture a single child living here on their own so said we might consider two children. I was thirty-five by then and my husband thirty-six years old; too decrepit to be considered for a baby – but a toddler, possibly.

We contacted Social Services and spent six months being vetted and having police checks. Vetting finished in January. In February we went away for a week on holiday. We took with us the Parent to Parent (now Adoption UK) details of children waiting for adoption. It broke our hearts and many tears were shed as we viewed these scrubbed bairns clutching their teddies and gazing imploringly at the camera.

We turned a page and there was a sibling group of four. How we laughed.

'You'd have to be mad to adopt four,' we said.

'You have to live in the south of England,' we said.

'We've only got one bedroom,' we said.

Of course we made the phone call when we got home. We were approved as adoptive parents in general in April. Passed as adoptive parents for the four in May. Met them in June, fell in love of course, and brought them all home in July.

'It's an answer to prayer,' we said.

'It must be. It's happened so fast,' we said.

Don't think us cynical if we feel as though possibly the social workers did everything in their power to rush the paperwork through to get the children here before we could change our minds! Frankly, I don't blame them. These kids deserved a home and probably weren't very easy to place.

We were allowed a brief look at some files. It was all very cloak and dagger and frankly most of it could have been written in a foreign language for all the sense it made then (now would be different). We were told that:

- Alice could be a little moody
- Alex had a hearing problem that was being sorted out with grommets and a speech impediment that should improve as he had recently had his tonsils and adenoids removed
- Richard got a little high on Smarties
- and Jack was 'as bright as a button'.

Yes, well!

About adopted children

As an adoptive mother I wanted to devote a chapter to adoption but there isn't space. With more people leaving parenthood until later in their lives, adoption is much more common. There are statistics now (Maudsley Hospital findings) that show that many adopted children suffer educationally because a large proportion are adopted as older children – there are very few babies available for adoption.

We were part of the Maudsley Hospital research which was carried out over a long period of time – nine years I think. We agreed that they could follow Alice's progress and they visited us three times, interviewed me very thoroughly on each occasion and then used the results of these interviews along with the comments of other adoptive parents in their findings. The final results made depressing reading.

Adoption is considered an option for children these days for very different reasons. Often these children are available for adoption as a result of early years' neglect or abuse and because of this have emotional and educational 'baggage'. Often they have been shunted around in the foster care system before they are adopted. This can cause problems, such as Attachment Disorder, which can have life-long consequences.

Our older children had been in at least five different foster placements, interspersed with time back at their home with their birth mother, before they came to us. Their birth mother, each time, would be unable to cope and the children would go into another foster placement. Imagine how this constant shunting around would affect any small children. Then imagine how much worse it would be for children who are autistic, bearing in mind that autists require order, hate change and need a strong framework to try to make sense of their world. Then add on the trauma of a new adoptive home and family at the age of six, or five, or three. It is unimaginable really. We have been assured that our children's autistic problems are genetic in origin but their early years' experiences must have compounded them.

A social worker commented to me that most prospective adoptive parents are decent, caring people who wish to give a home to a child. They have no idea what they are getting into – we certainly didn't. I think we give a whole new meaning to the word naïve.

The Maudsley Hospital study showed that, tragically, quite a number of adoptions do eventually break down under the strain and the children find they are back in the over-burdened care system and further damaged by their experience of rejection. If the adoptive parents had been receiving adequate help and support this tragedy might be averted.

If you are considering adoption, or are an adoptive parent already, I urge you to join Adoption UK (see Appendix 1) for support and advice both nationally and locally. We have belonged to a local group for just a year now and I feel incredibly close to all these courageous people who have experienced similar traumas to us – or worse. In spite of it all we generally end up laughing – sometimes a tad hysterically – when we get together. They are my heroes and I take my hat off to them all.

What about the strains on you and your partner?

Don't be ashamed to admit you are overwhelmed. It is hardly surprising and you are doing your best. You are very important people trying to do a difficult job. You may not feel like it, but you are.

All children need their parents but you don't need me to tell you that children with SEN need their parents even more.

I visualize myself as a 'path sweeper' frantically dashing along in front of the children trying to clear the path of obstacles that will be dangerous for them or too confrontational or just too plain scary! This isn't because I am overprotective but we have learned, to our cost, that our children are very vulnerable young people who are more at risk from some sectors of society than others might be.

The pace of the twenty-first century really isn't suited to a lot of people with SEN and some simply do not cope with life at all. The statistics for prison sentences and suicide for people with SEN are frighteningly high and these tragic figures have been one of the driving forces keeping me going as I've tried to help them through the years.

I was so ashamed that we weren't the cornflake advertisement family. I felt such a failure as a mother that for a long time I tried to hide our problems from our friends and families. This situation couldn't go on for ever though.

It was the day before Christmas Eve about four years ago that I simply fell apart. Things were so grim and the prospect of Christmas with the four children, who were all in such a state because we couldn't get any help, was so bleak. I was sitting in a black pit of despair and was hiding from Alice, praying that she would sleep for a while longer to delay the inevitable daily dose of vitriol and horrendous tantrums which started from the moment she woke up and continued virtually non-stop until she went to bed. I couldn't see any way out of the pit as we still couldn't get the LEA or social services to help.

It was at a time when I had still been unable to achieve a Statement for Alice even though I had finally got the LEA EP to assess her. The LEA EP had concluded that indeed our daughter did have some sort of learning difficulty and her reading comprehension was that of an 8 ½-year-old. As she was now almost sixteen and in a group studying for GCSEs it was hardly surprising that she was struggling.

Thoughts were whirling around my head:

She can't stay here.

But where can she go?

We cannot cope with her.

She cannot cope with us and the world.

What is wrong with her?

If nothing is wrong with her, as some people have said, then what is wrong with me?

At that point my sister-in-law telephoned and said something nice to me, trying to be encouraging, bless her. That did it – I started crying and simply could not stop. She insisted I ring the doctor. As luck would have it our GP was off duty and I drove, still sobbing, to see the total stranger who was our locum.

I think I used a whole box of tissues while in his office. It was as though somebody had taken the stopper out of a bottle. I had been so strong for so long but at the end of the day I'm only human.

To his credit the GP did not patronize me, did not try to minimize our situation and genuinely seemed to understand. He told me that his brother's son had special needs so he had witnessed first hand the sort of stresses and strains we were going through.

I remember at one point saying to him 'but I'm such a cheery soul really,' (which I am), as I practically washed him out of the door on the flood of tears. He smiled sympathetically at me.

He was amazed to find that I wasn't already on any anti-depressants. He gave me some Prozac which he strongly recommended I take but warned that it could be some weeks before I saw any improvement. I was shattered. I used to be so irritatingly optimistic – how had I sunk so low?

Meanwhile he gave me three tablets and suggested I take one when I returned home. Later I discovered that these were Valium but never having had anything like this before I didn't realize what they were.

I drove home swollen eyed but feeling slightly calmer. On my return my daughter threw a full-scale tantrum. My heart started to pound again and I burst into tears. I hadn't even had time to take my coat off. I went to my bedroom and took just one of the tablets.

This was how my husband found me some time later slumped on the floor at the foot of the bed like an abandoned rag doll, still in my coat and clutching the packet of tablets.

The tablet had worked almost instantly. As I've mentioned I don't drink and am allergic to lots of medication so my body tends to react quickly to anything new. My husband put me to bed and I slept for hours and was floating from that single tablet for two days. I have no recollection of that Christmas or how I prepared a meal, I just remember sitting in a chair feeling totally detached.

I will admit now that I felt ashamed that I'd had to resort to Prozac but 'putting my brain in a sling', which was how I came to think of it, did have a good effect and I felt more human.

Unfortunately, however, I coughed solidly for the next year until I realized that it was the Prozac that was affecting my chest. I stopped the Prozac and for a while the cough stopped too. I now take a daily St John's Wort tablet to boost me. I am almost certain that I am over the worst now that the children are all in the appropriate placements, but there are some days when the enormity of the responsibility for their lives still feels as though it will overwhelm me. On those days I try to just tackle the simple stuff of life and leave conquering the world for my 'strong' days.

During the next year my husband was also put on Prozac as he was diagnosed with clinical depression. He couldn't go to work for three months. We now know that this is not uncommon as we know other couples where either one or the other partner has had some sort of mental breakdown due to the stress of accessing help for their SN child.

We are both a lot better now but I don't know that I will ever be quite the same as I was. Maybe we are still recovering from the strain of the last few years and I will improve more. I told you I was the eternal optimist so I live in hope – for us all.

I am telling you this not to elicit a sympathy vote but to share my experience with you and perhaps encourage you to seek help if you are feeling similarly desperate. Other parents of SN children can be a wonderful support as you don't have to explain to them or feel embarrassed. I have made some dear friends this way and, even if I don't manage to see them often, we help prop each other up on dark days with an empathetic 'shoulder' on the end of the telephone or an email. Thank you all if you're reading this by the way.

I keep in my mind the poor soul who jumped off a bridge in Gateshead with her autistic son because she had failed to access help and could no longer go on. I totally understand now the depths of her despair, but what a tragic waste of two lives. I've been to that 'black place' in my mind which I think could be described as 'hell on earth'.

Chapter 16

Special needs children who are officially adults

Pity the budget-makers for they shall inherit the undiagnosed!

I heard something quite extraordinary recently. I was waiting for the ladies' loo at an All Wales Forum 'do' and someone 'high up' in Adult Services was also in the queue. She was saying how often she thinks she has her budget sorted out and then out of the blue she'll get a nineteen-year-old land on her desk (well the file anyway) and she has never heard of him before. Suddenly she has to find £20,000–£40,000 per annum to fund a place for him and her budget is a mess.

I presume this is because the LEA are so reluctant to Statement and without a Statement it is so difficult to get help from Social Services. They therefore aren't part of the CDT.

So it is only when a young person goes completely to pieces that the adult services team are *forced* to do something by the police or another agency. I wonder if she was talking about Alex as he wasn't a client of children's services and he must have 'suddenly landed on her desk'!

Special needs colleges

There will always be a difference of opinion regarding what is right for your child. I am not going to be so presumptuous as to try to tell you what is best for you and your family. All I've done is to tell you what has worked for us and hope that you will extract something from that which will be of use to you.

Some families are strongly of the opinion that having others care for their child is absolutely out of the question and that they want to keep the child at home with them into adulthood no matter what.

While some might argue against special needs placements we can only say from our experience that our children suffered, in varying degrees, in mainstream education. When in mainstream they may have been 'included' in the broadest sense but in reality they were 'isolated'. Now they are totally included in the smaller communities they inhabit while being able to access the wider community as much as they are able and with support.

As I have shown you in other chapters there were different paths that we had to tread with each of our children. It is strange as on paper they would appear to be almost identical. However, and this is something that some professionals have a problem with, they all have different personalities and had experienced different situations, therefore different solutions were called for as we reached this stage with each child.

I have told you about the different children and the colleges they attend in their chapters and contacts for the colleges can be found in Appendix 1.

How do you get funding for special needs colleges?

- Try to get a clear-cut diagnosis for your child. This may sound insulting but it is true. There is still a 'glass ceiling'. If your child has an IQ over 70 you may find it very difficult to access funding for your child. However, even if this is the case do not give up – ever. Legislation is supposed to be changing so battle on.

- Talk to the local Special Needs Careers Advisor (SENCA). You should be able to find out who this is through your local branch of the careers service. Alternatively, you could ask the school or the LEA where he or she is based. All applications have to be processed through this person so it is important that you establish a connection as quickly as you can. He or she will have information regarding all the residential colleges in the UK. You can also access information regarding special needs colleges through Natspec, the Association of National Specialist Colleges (for contact details see Appendix 1).

- Natspec publishes a list of special needs colleges both in hard copy and online. The colleges all have different remits; some cater for a mixture of disabilities, some specialize in a particular disability. They should specify whether they are for people with mild, moderate or severe learning difficulties. To give you some idea Alex and Alice are both considered to have moderate learning difficulties.

- Be warned. You may be lucky or you may be faced with a similar situation to ours. Social Services do not like funding placements 'out of county'. However, where we live there is nothing 'in county'! This will make no difference: they still won't like it – so roll up your sleeves again!

- The onus will be on you to *prove* that your child's needs cannot be met by the local FE college. Your case will be greatly helped, of course, if your child's Statement already mentions a waking-hours or 24-hour curriculum, as this has established the 'Need'. You will need to visit the local FE college to discuss this with their special needs department. Telephone the college and make an appointment to discuss this. If possible take along any psychological or other assessments your child may have had as proof that their provision will not be adequate. *Be prepared for a fight!*

- Funding for residential special needs colleges is usually shared between the relevant funding council and Social Services and/or Health. For example, Alex is joint funded by Education and Learning Wales (ELWa) and Social Services while Alice was joint funded but now is funded entirely by Social Services. There are different funding councils in each of the countries in the UK.

- *You need a social worker.* If you don't have one ask your GP to refer your child to the Children with Disabilities Team.

- Do try to form a good relationship with your social worker. It should help him to help you. Things can be difficult and it will be beneficial if he understands where you are 'coming from' so he can help fight your corner when it comes to persuading his manager to part with her budget.

- There is no shame in having a social worker attached to your child. It is a necessary part of this process.

- Request, in writing, a person-centred care assessment (PCCA) from your social worker. Your child is entitled to one of these – by law. The PCCA is a blueprint for the 'care' that your child has been identified as needing. It is very important that this is done and also very important that it is done *correctly*, identifying all the needs and risks (to and from the community, for example). Make sure that you are allowed your input. I wrote a letter in which I explained all my fears and concerns and backed this up with all the evidence I could muster to support my worries. This was tacked on the end of the PCCA. For example, when things became desperate with Alex, I was at least able to quote the PCCA back to the social worker when Social Services were refusing to support our funding claim. They had identified that 'Alex was at risk to and from the community'. If something further had happened to him and they had refused to act in spite of what they had noted in the PCCA they might have left themselves open to claims of negligence.

- Some social workers have been extremely kind and helpful. I don't envy them. Their job must be very stressful sometimes – but not as stressful as ours!

Communities

Alice is possibly coming towards the end of her time at the wonderful Camphill college. We are now looking at Camphill communities for Alice's future where she will be able to work in the smaller or wider community as much as she can but, as a vulnerable person, will be able to live in a safe, emotionally supported, fulfilling environment and be happy. We think she'll have far more freedom and choice and we hope the transition should be relatively smooth. She's been assessed by Delrow College and we have visited the four suggested communities. Following a successful interview we are now waiting for her to go for a two-week visit.

It is a good life. They work hard but also have a full social and cultural life with as much dignity and independence as they are able to access. We see this as a far more 'normal' route than Alice returning home to us when her time at college is finished. Where we live there are no job prospects and her social life would be small to nil.

If she is accepted by this community her funding will change again as she will become a 'tenant' and should then be eligible to access Housing Benefit with 'top up' from Social Services – all being well (see Appendix 1 for contacts).

Health provision for people with special needs/ learning disability

If you are experiencing problems write to the chief executive of your local NHS trust. Apparently, by law, the chief executive must respond to your letter within ten days. I was told this by a very senior man in the NHS the other day and filed this away in my brain under 'useful information I might need'!

I also heard recently of dentists who specialize in treating people with SN. This might sound daft but autists, for example, feel pain in different ways. It might therefore be crucial to have someone who understands this when treating your child. Ask your local NHS trust for information or go directly to an organization like the NAS.

What will happen to our special needs 'children' when we die?

We have had to address the question of our own mortality. We are all going to 'drop off our twigs' some day. It is very important that you make appropriate provision for your children after you've gone. Do not be dispirited – there are people out there who can help you.

Obviously, if your child is a client of Social Services that is helpful. If you have managed to get them to complete a person-centred community care assessment this will address all your child's risks and requirements of which they must be mindful, even after you're gone.

However, it is *very important that you consult a solicitor who specializes in wills and trusts for people with special needs.*

This is a very specialized area of law. I strongly urge you to talk to Mencap (see Appendix 1 for contact address). They have a wills department and they can also send you a list of solicitors, in your area, who can handle your will for you. I found this extremely helpful. Because we have four special needs children and run a business, making our will felt very complicated. The solicitor we saw was very kind, understanding and knowledgeable. He appreciated our concerns and has drawn up a document which at this moment just needs checking and signing (I do hope I don't 'pop my clogs' in the meantime!).

It is very important that you organize your affairs. Well, it is important for anyone to organize their affairs but even more so in our situation. If you die and you leave all your money to your children it could mean that all the benefits that you fought so hard for during your lifetime will be withdrawn from your children until all the money you've left is used up. Then someone will have to start all over again.

In your 'expression of wishes' you can ask that Cousin Flo keeps an eye on the child (do ask Cousin Flo first). Your solicitor will advise you that he needs to set up a 'discretionary trust' and you will need to ask perhaps three people, a friend, family member or accountant/solicitor, to be a trustee.

The discretionary trust will not affect your children's benefits but would mean that if they need anything specific – a new washing machine, a holiday, an expensive piece of clothing, for example – then the trust could make discretionary payments to cover the cost. But this will *not* affect:

- DLA
- Income support
- Housing Benefit
- Incapacity Benefit.

This is obviously very important. We, the parents of special needs children, are not trying to defraud the country but are trying to assist our children even after we've 'shuffled off'.

Once you have made your will you then have the peace of mind that your offspring can live their lives decently and if they need some little 'extras' the money you leave will mean that they will not go without.

Direct Payments?

So, I've made the beds, filled the washing machine, cleaned up the kitchen. Now it's my time and I'm going to treat myself by rushing off...to an all-day conference entitled: 'Everything you wanted to know about Direct Payments but were afraid to ask!'

This girl knows how to have fun!

However, in this confusing world of special needs I've learned that knowledge is power. Before we managed to achieve diagnoses for all the children I bumbled around desperately seeking solutions and sometimes, through sheer luck, found out things that helped. Now we know what we are up against I know that I must be more vigilant and keep abreast of new funding/benefits changes so that I don't slip back into the mire of confusion.

I now belong to several organizations and am on mailing lists for local events. I belong to both the national association of the excellent NAS and two local-ish branches, as well as the All Wales Forum. It is AWF who are hosting the 'Direct Payments' day. The local events are invaluable. Not only do you get to meet other parents who are in a similar situation – which is very helpful and has made me feel far less isolated – but it is also extremely useful to hear from these people about how national initiatives work in our area.

I'm attending today's meeting because I've heard very mixed reports about Direct Payments and it does seem to be a bit of a postcode lottery currently. Now that we have two children who are 'adults', one of whom (we hope) is about to move into a community where her funding will be handled differently, this is now an issue in sharp focus for us.

I have now returned from the meeting. The gist of the system regarding Direct Payments is:

- This is money given to your child by Social Services for his or her care support. In reality, unless your child is very able, he or she will need your help and support and if no parent was willing or able then an advocate would have to handle the running of the scheme.

- You cannot get Direct Payments unless you have a community care assessment and you need to contact your social worker to avail yourself of them.

- Direct Payments do not affect benefits.

- You can spend Direct Payments on: respite care, day centre provision, work or training opportunities.

- The legislation for this has been in place since 1997 (I'd not heard about it until recently). In England you have the right to be assessed for Direct Payments. They have to offer it to

218 SURVIVING THE SPECIAL EDUCATIONAL NEEDS SYSTEM

you (in Wales it isn't mandatory) but they do not have to give it to you.

- You can access Direct Payments for children under eighteen following legislation in 2001, so they are now available for people from birth to old age. The person who will be receiving Direct Payments must agree.

- If it improves the independence of your child then you *should* get the service.

There are associations, such as the Shaw Trust, who will assist you in running the Direct Payment scheme and will help with payroll, etc.

If it doesn't work out then you can go back to direct service provision from Social Services.

It was suggested that an Independent Living Trust (ILP) be set up for the child or person for whom you care so that a number of people are responsible for the arrangements for spending the money. This is apparently a good long-term solution (particularly if you are an elderly or otherwise disadvantaged parent/carer).

I could see that there may be some real value in 'drawing down' some Direct Payments if you can access them. It depends as to whether your county is up and running with Direct Payments. If they aren't it could be very problematical.

One lady at the meeting had managed to go through the system and has been awarded Direct Payment to pay for a personal assistant for three days per month respite care for her son. However, she started the process in April 2002 and was finally awarded the payment in July 2003! She had also had to instigate a complaints procedure against Social Services to get things shifting. So clearly the motto is 'don't hold your breath'!

A father asked whether, if enough people opt out of the day centre that his severely disabled daughter attends, the centre will close. She has no other option. This is obviously a valid point and there may be a sticky transition if more and more people move over to Direct Payments.

If the person for whom you care demands Direct Payments then it could create problems for you as the carer. This is not so relevant in the case of our children as I don't think they are able enough intellectually to demand it. But if you had a fairly physically disabled person in your care who was able enough to demand these payments but not able enough to handle the scheme you might find yourself in the situation of having the scheme and the work involved foisted on to you *whatever* you think about it, which doesn't seem quite fair.

Unless you receive support from Social Services or someone like the Shaw Trust it is very difficult to make the Direct Payments scheme work. Interestingly enough, we were told it actually costs Social Services more to implement for people with a learning disability but it saves a lot with people with physical disabilities.

We actually had three people from the Children with Disabilities Team attending.

When asked directly how much training they had received in this area (bearing in mind this has been legislation for children for two years and for adults for six years) one replied 'well, we're here today'!

I felt sorry for them. It must be quite difficult for them to handle enquiries when they haven't received adequate training or information.

Another social worker divulged that our 'county is reluctant to supply Direct Payments for children unless asked'!

I'm not sure where I would be able to find sufficient people to set up an Independent Living Trust (ILT). I don't know whether they are paid for their time as they are trustees with a legal entity or whether they would be expected to give up their time for nothing. If the former it would be a further drain on the Direct Payment amount and if the latter I would find it awkward.

The Shaw Trust (see Appendix 1 for contact) is a national organization; however, for some peculiar reason they are not active in *our* county!! They would be worth contacting for further up-to-date advice on this as I think this scheme will evolve.

I also learned about something called the Independent Living Fund. You may be able to access the ILF during the holidays to 'draw down' some funds for your child if they are receiving £200 per week from Social Services during term time. You could say you are interested in accessing the ILF and see what they say.

Of course, it depends on your individual circumstances, but I suppose that if you are not happy with the services that are being provided at present and think you could do better for your child by 'contracting out' then Direct Payments could be for you. I hope this is helpful.

Chapter 17

And in conclusion

Being honest, there have been some days when I just wanted to run away. Perhaps some of you have felt like that over the months and years that you have been trying to help your children.

Some people do actually run away. I can't condemn them but my heart goes out to those who are left behind still trying to sort it all out. It mainly seems to be the fathers who find they can't go on and leave. I know quite a few single mothers who struggle daily, financially and emotionally. I expect I'll get letters from fathers now who have held on in there against all the odds – I apologize. Well done all of you parents still hanging on in there, still loving fit to bust, you really do deserve a medal.

There have been times quite recently when our children have all been happy, safe and well, thank God, but I have still felt overwhelmed by the enormity of being responsible for their lives. Every single post brings more paperwork it seems. More decisions to make. More juggling acts with our time and energy. Some of our children are now adults, under law, but emotionally they are still nine- or ten-year-olds, incapable of handling 'grown-up' decisions. We then have to be diplomats as we try to help them make decisions whilst respecting their position as adults. Truthfully, I sometimes find this wearying. It's emotionally exhausting constantly trying to smooth the path for your children. Sometimes it would be very nice if someone would do that for you.

If I've offended anyone in the writing of this book (if you work for the LEA you may be feeling a little sensitive) please forgive me, but this has been my perception of what it has been like going through the system. I feel very sad that this system 'stole' my children's childhoods and damaged us all in various ways from which we are still trying to recover. I was rocked to my foundations by some of these events, which were a personal attack against me and everything I've believed in, and I don't think mentally I've recovered even now.

What a sad liturgy this is of wasted lives. We can't give these children back their childhood and I find that hard to forgive. I just hope we can help them to have the most peaceful and rewarding lives as adults.

I'm very proud of our children. What they have overcome in their short lives is monumental. They are polite, kind, decent people – but people who have difficulties. We now pray that they will go on to have happy, fulfilled lives – living as independently as they are able, being useful citizens and contributing to society in their own ways.

I do hope that this book assists in some way to help you to overcome some of the many obstacles out there and help you and your family to lead happier, less stressful lives. I'd like to think that if I've done nothing else I've given you hope. If we could succeed after getting so much wrong there really should be a chance for you.

My dear friend Gizzie is an inspiration. Gizzie is a six-times survivor of cancer but uses her passion to run a 'wish' foundation to help fulfil wishes for other cancer sufferers. It was she who christened me the 'velvet bulldozer'. She said: 'I've been given lemons in my life. Now I'm making lemonade!'

I hope that I've made your 'lemonade' a little sweeter. So good luck and God bless you all.

Appendix 1

Useful contacts
and other information

It's taken years for me to find the information in order to help my children and compile this list. Obviously my main area of interest has been in autism and dyslexia, but many of the following organizations cover a wider remit.

Depending on the particular difficulty of your child you will find others. Let the Internet be your friend. You can sometimes quickly access information through this medium – if you know what you are looking for.

This was my difficulty. I had to trawl through so much to find precisely what I was looking for. Another problem was that I didn't really know *what* it was that I was looking for. It may seem glaringly simple. Professionals sometimes assume that you know what is out there to help you – but if you are anything like we were you don't.

I hope these contacts set you off on a useful 'trail' which will end in success for you and a happier life for your child.

Most important! Where to get your free copy of the *Special Educational Needs Code of Practice*
In England contact:

> The Publications Department
> The Department of Education
> PO Box 5050
> Sherwood Park
> Annesley
> Nottingham NG15 0DJ
> Tel: 0845 6022260

Since devolution there are different *Codes of Practice* in Scotland and Wales.

In Scotland contact:

> The Scottish Executive
> Victoria Quay
> Edinburgh EH6 3QQ
> Tel: 0131 556 8400

In Wales contact:

> The Education Department
> National Assembly for Wales
> Cathays Park
> Cardiff CF10 3NQ
> Tel: 029 2082 6078

Their Pupil Support department was very helpful. They sent me one of their own copies of the COP as I obviously sounded so desperate and they had run out. It was a bit dog-eared and dusty but I was very grateful.

Department for Education and Skills

DfES publish a useful booklet entitled *Special Educational Needs (SEN): A Guide for Parents and Carers.* Contact:

> DfES Publications Centre
> PO Box 5050
> Sherwood Park
> Annersley
> Nottingham NG15 0DJ
> Tel: 0845 6022260
> Email: dfes@prolog.uk.com
> Website: www.dfes.gov.uk/sen

Children's Commissioner for Wales

> Mr Peter Clark
> Children's Commissioner for Wales
> Oystermouth House
> Swansea Enterprise Park
> Llansamlet
> Swansea SA7 9FS
> Tel: 01792 765600

The All Wales Forum

This organization is for parents and informal carers of people with learning disabilities and is very worthwhile. It reports back to the National Assembly on issues which affect our daily lives, and it was the source of invaluable information and support during our tribunal battle.

You can access training, funded by AWF, to help you cope better with your particular problems. Subjects include:

- Dealing with Difficult and Aggressive Behaviour (similar to the one we attended two years ago which was extremely useful in helping us to understand *why* our children sometimes behaved as they did)

- workshops and support available for disabled people wanting to start up a business
- BT and Carers Wales – offering help and support online
- Life Options Project SCOVO – practical approaches which enable young disabled people to think about and choose their life options
- Sexuality and Personal Relationships
- Inappropriate Sexual Behaviours: Children and Young People with Learning Difficulties

and a host of other events which will help you help those for whom you are caring. I wouldn't have known about any of these had I not attended the AWF meeting. It informs carers and gives carers a voice, so I feel it is worth sparing a couple of hours occasionally. Contact:

> All Wales Forum of Parents and Carers
> 35 Plymouth Road
> Penarth CF64 3DA
> Tel: 02020 015027
> Email: travers@charityfutures.com
> Website: www.allwalesforum.com

Sadly, there is no equivalent to the AWF in England but you may find parents' groups through Mencap (see below).

Scottish Consortium for Learning Disability
In Scotland parents' groups are connected to the Scottish Consortium for Learning Disability. Contact:

> Scottish Consortium for Learning Disability
> Adelphi Centre
> Room 16
> 12 Commercial Road
> Glasgow G5 0PQ
> Tel: 0141 418 5420
> Website: www.scld.org.uk

The Rowan Organization
The Rowan Organization work with disabled users in various parts of the country. Contact:

> Rowan House
> Lime Tree Courtyard
> Main Road
> Ratcliffe Culey CV9 3PD
> Tel: 01827 718972

Email: info@therowan.org
Website: www.therowan.org

Direct Payment assistance

As mentioned in Chapter 16, Direct Payments can be wonderful. However, they can also appear complicated. You will need help to deal successfully with Direct Payments. The following are very helpful organizations.

The National Centre for Independent Living

The National Centre for Independent Living focus mainly on England and Scotland but they'd be able to point you to your most local contact. They have contact details for all support schemes.

National Centre for Independent Living
250 Kennington Lane
London SE11 5RD
Tel: 020 7587 1663

The Shaw Trust

The Shaw Trust can help with sorting out the Direct Payment scheme. They are also a good resource centre for finding local day projects for disabled people and can help with job 'brokering'. Good people to know.

Shaw House
Epsom Square
Whitehorse Business Park
Trowbridge
Wiltshire BA14 0XJ
Tel: 01225 716300
Website: www.shaw-trust.org.uk

In Wales:

The Shaw Trust
Disability Action Centre
The Courtyard
Llandarcy
Neath SA10 6EJ
Tel: 01792 325307 or 01792 325306
Email: ian.folks@shaw-trust.org.uk

The National Autistic Society

The NAS can help you in many ways including providing advice, specialist publications, support and an educational advocacy service.

The National Autistic Society
393 City Road
London EC1V 1NG
Tel: 020 7833 2299
Website: www.autism.org.uk
Autism Helpline: 0845 070 4004
Advocacy for Education Service: 0845 070 4002

The NAS produce a card which states: 'This young person has autism [or Asperger Syndrome]... Please help us by being understanding and showing tolerance.' This can cut down any anxiety you may have about trying to explain what the problem is or about your child having to explain as he or she gets older. People may not totally understand what autism entails and this card might help your child access assistance.

All three of our autistic children have these cards in their wallets and we have encouraged them to use them. We have explained to them that they shouldn't be ashamed of being autistic.

Autism West Midlands

I don't live that close to the West Midlands but I am a member of this society and have found them very helpful. Several times, when faced with a brick wall, I have telephoned one of their representatives and been given good advice which has helped us. They hold all sorts of activities for parents, children and siblings and often host courses and workshops. Autism West Midlands has also set up Coddington Court School – a school for autistic children. Contact:

Autism West Midlands
18 Highfield Road
Edgbaston
Birmingham B15 3DU
Tel: 0121 450 7582
Information/helpline tel: 0121 450 7575

Resources for Autism

This is the organization that helped us win the second tribunal and provided a national advice and expert witness service. Their remit is changing but it would probably still be worthwhile to contact them.

Resources for Autism
858 Finchley Road
Temple Fortune
London NW11 6AB
Tel: 020 8458 3259
Website: www.resourcesforautism.org.uk linked to
www.autismconnect.org

Autism London

A friend who also has an autistic daughter has just sent me the website of Autism London, which apparently has lots of information. Included in their site is a fact sheet of holiday centres which might be worth checking out. They also offer advocacy and support. I can vouch for neither but always feel it is worth investigating as that is how I've found some of the most amazingly helpful stuff.

> Autism London
> 1 Floral Place
> London N1 2FS
> Tel: 020 7359 6070
> Website: www.autismlondon.org.uk

The Challenging Behaviour Foundation

The CBF provides and accesses support, advice and information in addition to raising awareness of challenging behaviour.

> The Challenging Behaviour Foundation
> 32 Twydall Lane
> Gillingham
> Kent ME8 6HX
> Tel: 01634 302207
> Website: www.thecbf.org.uk

The Early Years Centre

I found the people at the Early Years Centre to be very kind and helpful. They would have been invaluable had we found them when the children were young.

> Professor Elizabeth Newson
> The Early Years Centre
> Ravenshead
> Nottingham NG15 9AH
> Tel: 01623 490879

The British Psychological Society

The BPS hold a list of all independent educational psychologists. I dearly wish we had found out about independent educational psychologists when our children were young. Contact:

> The British Psychological Society
> St Andrews House
> 48 Princess Road East
> Leicester LE1 7DR
> Tel: 0116 254 9568
> Fax: 0116 247 0787

Email: enquiry@bps.org.uk
Website: www.bps.org.uk

This website will help you look through lists of independent psychologists and also tells you how to make a complaint if you feel it is necessary (and if you have the strength!). There is also a section on expert witnesses. You will need an expert witness to make a convincing case at any tribunal. Although personal recommendation is the best way, this site should help you find one if nobody can make any useful suggestions.

Eagle House

I have recently taken Jack for an assessment at Eagle House, which I highly recommend. Eagle House provide invaluable psychological, speech and language, and occupational therapy assessments. Contact:

Eagle House School and Assessment Clinic
224 London Road
Mitcham
Surrey
CR4 3HD
Tel: 020 8687 7050
Fax: 020 8687 7055
Email: admin@eaglehouseschool.co.uk

The British Dyslexia Association

The British Dyslexia Association should be able to give you details of competent independent diagnosticians.

The British Dyslexia Association
98 London Road
Reading
Berkshire RG1 5AU
Tel: 0118 966 8271

The Dyslexia Institute, Bangor University

Contact:

Dyslexia Unit
University of Wales
Bangor
Gwynedd LL57 2DG
Tel: 01248 382203

Funding

If you are looking for help with funding your child at a school independently then for first point of reference contact *The Educational Grants Service* (formerly known as the Independent Schools Council – ISC) through:

> Mrs Julie Burns
> c/o Jet
> 6 Lovat Lane
> London EC3 8DT
> Tel: 020 7626 4583

Write to Mrs Burns or telephone explaining your particular difficulties and circumstances. She will be able to give a list of the most appropriate trusts to contact depending on those circumstances. All the trusts have a different remit. Some, for example, are set up specifically to help children of single parents, or adopted children or children already in an educational establishment and where the parents' financial circumstances suddenly change, through bereavement or redundancy. It would therefore be pointless wasting your time and theirs if you do not 'fit' their specifications. We found this organization to be a lifeline and because of it we could rescue Richard while we continued the fight with the LEA.

Free education law advice and representation

The *Children's Legal Centre*, based in Colchester, is a unique, independent, national charity concerned with law and policy affecting children and young people.

The centre operates the Education Law and Advocacy Unit. Their solicitors and barristers provide free legal advice on all issues of education law including:

- special educational needs
- bullying
- exclusions
- local authority duties
- disability in schools
- obtaining a school place
- school transport
- discipline issues
- human rights
- work experience and child employment.

Contact:

> The Children's Legal Centre
> University of Essex
> Wivenhoe Park
> Colchester CO4 3FQ

Lawyers can be contacted on 0845 120 2966. All calls are charged at local rate and the line is open 10.00 am to 1.00 pm.

I didn't find out about this centre until our tribunal battle had been won – but I wish I had known of it as I think they could have been extremely helpful in our mega fight with authority.

SENDIST

See Chapter 6 for more details regarding SENDIST's role in legal appeals and tribunals. Contact:

> Procession House
> 55 Ludgate Hill
> London EC4M 7JW
> Tel: 020 7029 9726
> Website: www.sendist.gov.uk
> SEN helpline: 0870 241 2555
> Discrimination helpline: 0870 606 5750

Mencap

Mencap have a very wide and varied remit and can advise on anything from benefit entitlement to holidays for children and adults with special educational needs. Contact:

> Mencap National Centre
> 123 Golden Lane
> London C1Y 0RT
> Tel: 020 7454 0454
> National helpline number: 0808 8000 300
> Email: webmaster@mencap.org.uk
> Website: www.mencap.org.uk

Mencap have a very good department who deal with helping families with welfare benefits advice. They will help to make sure that the person for whom you are caring is receiving all the benefits to which he or she is entitled. They are very friendly and helpful.

Help to find schools and colleges

The NAS publish a booklet of schools, units and classes for children with autism. Contact NAS (see above).

The Association of National Specialist Colleges

Natspec publishes a list of special needs colleges both in hard copy and online. This will be an invaluable tool if it is decided that your child requires a special needs college when they finish at school. Contact:

Janice Biggs
NATSPEC Administrative Officer
36 Gresham Road
East Ham
London E6 6DS
Tel and fax: 020 8471 3284
Email: janicefaldo.natspec@btinternet.com
Website: www.natspec.org.uk

Camphill

Camphill run schools, colleges and communities. Our daughter Alice is at a wonderful Camphill college in Wales. It has changed her life. Contact:

The Camphill Advisory Service
19 South Road
Stourbridge
West Midlands DY8 3YA
Tel: 01384 441505
Website: (England and Wales) www.camphill.org.uk
(Scotland) www.camphillscotland.org.uk
(Northern Ireland) www.camphill.org.uk

Coleg Elidyr

A very special peaceful place set in a magical Welsh valley.

Coleg Elidyr
Rhandirmwyn
Nr Llandovery
Carmarthenshire SA20 0NL
Tel: 01550 760400

Derwen College

Derwen is another college for your consideration (with more bustle than Coleg Elidyr) which accepts children with a range of disabilities and is very wheelchair friendly (able students are encouraged to play wheelchair basketball!).

> Derwen College
> Oswestry
> Shropshire SY11 3JA
> Tel: 01691 661234
> Website: www.derwen.org.uk

Ruskin Mill

Ruskin Mill is another college which we can recommend but probably is more for higher functioning and more able-bodied students (as it is set in a beautiful, but steep-sided valley). Its philosophy is based on the teachings of Rudolf Steiner.

> Ruskin Mill Further Education Centre
> Millbottom
> Nailsworth
> Gloucestershire GL6 0LA
> Tel: 01453 837500
> Website: www.ruskin-mill.org.uk

Cruckton Hall School

Cruckton Hall is a wonderful school for autistic boys we can highly recommend.

> Cruckton Hall School
> Cruckton
> Shrewsbury
> Shropshire SY5 8PR
> Tel: 01743 860206
> Website: www.youngoptions.co.uk

St David's College

St David's is an excellent day/boarding school for dyslexic children we can highly recommend.

> St David's College
> Llandudno
> North Wales L30 1RD
> Tel: 01492 875974
> Website: www.stdavidscollege.co.uk

Contact a Family

Contact a Family is a national support group for the families of those with special needs. Not only have we found them a useful source of information but we have also attended a couple of their special information days. One of these discussed coping with 'difficult behaviours' and the possible reasons why these behaviours are displayed. This was a doubly useful time. We were able to see what Richard was getting out of his. It really opened our eyes and helped us to see the children's behaviours in a different light. We felt that we were able to help them better after attending this course. Not only did it help us understand the reasons why Richard was self-harming, it also brought us into contact with other parents similarly suffering and trying to help their children. We were able to listen to other people's stories and to chat over the buffet lunch provided. I persuaded my husband to make time to come to this two-day course and we both felt it was a very worthwhile experience. Contact:

> Contact a Family
> 209–211 City Road
> London EC1V 1JN
> Tel: 020 7608 8700
> Freephone helpline: 0808 808 3555
> Email: info@cafamily.org.uk
> Website: www.cafamily.org.uk

Adoption UK

Adoption UK is a very helpful organization to support adoptive parents 'before, during and after adoption'. I now belong to Adoption UK and attend a local get-together every couple of months with other adoptive parents. I don't want to be negative but out of the seven of us with adopted children all but one mum have at least one adopted child with SN. Some of them have had a very difficult time indeed and continue to do so. The government needs to address this problem urgently. Contact:

> Adoption UK
> Manor Farm
> Appletree Road
> Chipping Warden
> Banbury
> Oxfordshire OX17 1LH
> Tel: 01295 660121
> Helpline: 0870 7700 450

For further educational advocacy advice

IPSEA offers free and independent advice on local education authorities' legal duties to assess and provide for children with special educational needs. These include children with physical disabilities, sensory impairment, emotional and behavioural difficulties, and general and specific learning difficulties (including those arising from specific conditions such as Down's syndrome, autism and dyslexia). Their website is another excellent site and well worth visiting. Contact:

> Independent Panel for Special Education Advice (IPSEA)
> 6 Carlow Mews
> Woodbridge
> Suffolk IP12 1EA
> Advice line: (England and Wales) 0800 018 4016
> (Scotland) 0131 454 0082
> (Northern Ireland) 01232 705654
> Website: www.ipsea.org.uk

I received very good advice and support from IPSEA. I would urge you to investigate IPSEA to strengthen your chances of success. The website is regularly updated so changes in legislation can be taken into account.

The website also discusses landmark cases of negligence brought against LEAs. Visit the site even if it means going to your local library. Ask the librarian to help you find the site if you aren't very computer literate. I have found librarians very helpful and sympathetic. Once into the site it is very user-friendly and full of good advice.

ACE

ACE offers advice and guidance on all aspects of state education.

> Advisory Centre for Education (ACE)
> 1c Aberdeen Studios
> 22–24 Highbury Grove
> London N5 2DQ
> Helpline: 0808 800 5793
> Website: www.ace-ed.org.uk

OAASIS (Office for Advice, Assistance, Support and Information on special needs)

OAASIS produces very useful leaflets and are a very worthwhile organization as they can offer good advice to people going through the 'system'. It took me a while to find OAASIS but I was glad I did. They have an excellent and informative website with good links to associated sites. Contact:

> OAASIS
> Brock House
> Grigg Lane
> Brockenhurst
> Hampshire SO47 7RE

Tel: 09068 633201
Website: www.oaasis.co.uk

Education Otherwise

Education Otherwise is a UK-based membership organization you should contact if you want to home-school your child. They provide support and information for families whose children are being educated outside school, and for those who wish to uphold the freedom of families to take proper responsibility for the education of their children. We became members and found it very helpful in many ways. It has an excellent and informative site. Contact:

Education Otherwise
PO Box 7420
London N9 9SG (enclose an A5 SAE)
Tel: (England) 0870 7653510 (Scotland) 0870 7653580 (Ireland) 0870 7653610 (Wales) 0870 7653620
Website: www.education-otherwise.org

Further reading

You should be able to order these books through your local library. Alternatively contact the NAS for their publications list. You should be able to check this out on their website.

Jessica Kingsley Publishers (www.jkp.com) have a strong interest in autism and special needs publications.

Autism

Archer, C. and Adoption UK (1999) *Next Steps in Parenting the Child who Hurts: Tykes and Teens.* London: Jessica Kingsley Publishers.

Attwood, T. (1998) *Asperger's Sydrome: A Guide for Parents and Professionals.* London: Jessica Kingsley Publishers.

Baron-Cohen, S. (1998) *Teaching Children with Autism to Mind-Read: A Practical Guide for Teachers and Parents.* Chichester: John Wiley.

Haddon, M. (2003) *The Curious Incident of the Dog in the Night-Time.* London: Jonathan Cape.

Nye, A. (ed) (2000) *The Autism Handbook.* London: National Autistic Society.

Wing, L. (1996) *The Autistic Spectrum: A Guide for Parents and Professionals.* London: Constable & Robinson.

I have just read the Mark Haddon book, which is a work of fiction seen through the eyes of a fifteen-year-old boy with Asperger's syndrome. It made me laugh. It made me cry. I recognized some of the situations. I would highly recommend it as an insight into the 'Aspie' mind.

I went to a wonderful workshop called 'Speaking the Language', by Phoebe Caldwell. This remarkable woman looks at things from a different perspective. She has developed a system for reaching people who would appear to be unreachable. I went to one of her workshops and she gave us the example of a lady who was blind, deaf and autistic! Ms Caldwell found a way to communicate by watching the way she banged on her table, copying the rhythm, and thus changed her life. Fascinating.

You Don't Know What it's Like by Phoebe Caldwell with Dr Matt Hoghton published by Pavillion Publishing (Brighton) Ltd:

> The Ironworks
> Cheapside
> Brighton
> East Sussex BN1 4GD
> Tel: 01273 625526
> Website: www.pavpub.com

Adoption

If you have an interest in adopted children then books on Attachment Disorder by Caroline Archer may be of help. I also found some helpful information regarding Attachment Disorder on the Internet just by typing 'Attachment Disorder' into the search engine.

Conciliation

Resolving Disagreement in Special Educational Needs: A Practical Guide to Conciliation and Mediation, by Irvine and Adam Gersch, examines conciliation and the law (published by RoutledgeFalmer, London).

Books for 'reluctant readers'

I had a heck of a job finding books for my children, particularly the autistic boys, once they hit adolescence. It was difficult trying to keep their interest when the books they were capable of reading were aimed at a much younger audience.

I can recommend the series of books in Stanley Thornes' 'Spirals' range. Some are non-fiction and some are fiction. They deal with more typically teenage topics but are written in a style, short sentences and paragraphs, which is easier for the youngsters to understand. They have titles like *Snow Beast* – a sort of Beast-of-Bodmin-Moor adventure – and *Beware the Morris Minor* – a spooky tale of kinetic connection with a car.

The series also publishes plays, which are great fun. I've one called *Cowboys, Jelly and Custard*: lots of 'pongs' and puns which the kids love. The ones I've read have been written by John Townsend who is himself a SENCO and all-round good egg!

I had a glorious half an hour of peace when I bought four and the children all sat and read and then swapped books – thank you John!

Contact:

Nelson Thornes
Delta Place
27 Bath Road
Cheltenham
Gloucestershire GL53 7TH
Tel: 01242 267100
Website: www.nelsonthornes.com

Disabled travel assistance

I have only discovered during the last twelve months that the railway network, for all its faults, has a fairly reliable disabled assistance system. So far it has always worked and when I have put one of my young people on a train the staff have been helpful and kind. There has always been someone to meet the children and help them find their connecting train which is a boon. It gives the children a feeling of independence while being relatively safe.

For disabled assistance telephone 08457 484950 and ask for the revelevant telephone number for the network you are using. (In Wales I telephone 0845 3003005.)

Disabled person's railcard

If your child is in receipt of DLA they can apply for a disabled person's railcard. It cost £14 this year and entitles the cardholder to a 33 per cent reduction in fare. Also, very usefully, it entitles the person travelling with the cardholder to the same discount. I think this will be a worthwhile investment. We have already saved more than the card cost us.

Special needs holidays

I only discovered recently that such holidays exist for people with special needs and I now have experience with trying to sort out both children's and adults' holidays. A word of advice – *book early* to avoid disappointment. Mencap publish a good all-round guide and will also make suggestions for places to go to ask for help with funding holidays (see above for contact details). The NAS also publish a list of special needs holiday providers (see above for contact details).

Holiday Care will advise on assistance with travel in the UK or if going abroad:

Holiday Care
7th Floor, Sunley House
4 Bedford Park
Croydon CR0 2AP
Tel: 0845 1249971
Website: www.holidaycare.org.uk

This year our children have enjoyed special needs holidays with the following organizations:

Christian Camps in Wales (CCIW)
Mr M. Carson
Red House
Plealey
Shrewsbury
Shropshire SY5 0XA
Tel: 01743 790470
Email: cciw@cciw.co.uk
Website: www.cciw.co.uk

Options Holidays
Barnsley
Cirencester GL7 5EF
Tel: 0700 079 0348

Chrysalis Holidays
13 Winwick Lane
Lowton
Warrington
Cheshire WA3 1LR
Tel: 01942 671581

Red Ridge Centre
Cefn Coch
Welshpool
Powys SY21 0AZ
Tel: 01938 810821

Trevanion House
Trevanion Road
Wadebridge
Cornwall PL27 7PA
Tel: 01208 8114903

I met the owner of Clynfyw Countryside Centre at an All Wales Forum meeting and he impressed me greatly. Unfortunately, by the time I found him he was fully booked, but I hope to use him next year. Contact:

Clynfyw Countryside Centre
Abercych
Boncath
Pembrokeshire SA37 0HF
Tel: 01239 841236
Website: www.clynfyw.co.uk

Possible sources of funding for special needs holidays

I didn't know until very recently that it was possible to access funding for our children's holidays. When all the children are at home together life is very difficult for them and us. As we have three autistic people living under the same roof there can be dreadful friction. Part of the problem with autism is that there is no natural spirit of compromise. People who don't understand the problem have said to us in the past that this is a natural occurrence with all children. If they saw our children in action they would change their minds.

We therefore learned a long time ago (long before we knew they were autistic) that we had to split them up for chunks of the holiday otherwise the house was broken up around us as they took out their frustrations on us and the home. We saw this as a necessary, if large, expense and scraped together the money somehow each year.

This year, because I found out about possible grants, I applied for and was successful in receiving three grants towards helping with respite care and with a special needs holiday for Alex and Richard. This was a real God-send. My advice to you would be to initially contact Mencap (see above), 3H and The Family Fund Trust for current advice.

> 3H Fund (Help the Handicapped Holiday Fund)
> 147a Camden Road
> Tunbridge Wells TN1 3RA
> Tel: 01892 547474
> Website: ww.3hfund.org.uk

> The Family Fund Trust (for families with severely disabled children)
> PO Box 50
> York YO1 9ZX
> Tel: 01904 62115
> Email: info@familyfundtrust.org.uk
> Website: www.fhaonline.org.uk

Also check out your local branch of the Carers' Association. Try calling the Citizens' Advice Bureau if you cannot immediately find their contact details. They should be able to help. It may be called something slightly different in your area but carers now have rights too and there should be someone in your area to support you.

I was lucky enough to be able to access a carer's grant which helped towards the cost of respite and a holiday for Richard. They are there to assist you so *ASK FOR HELP!* It took me a long time to learn that, which is why I'm shouting at you here.

Appendix 2

Extract from a letter to a psychiatrist to help with the diagnostic process

Thank you for making time for us the other day. You will no doubt by now have added to Alex's file a report from the SALT. If you haven't received this please let me know. We would agree with her that his speech has definitely deteriorated over the last year. Please God he gets the funding from the funding council for Derwen and he will then receive regular speech therapy as part of the curriculum. We think he has regressed in other ways behaviourally in the last year.

I apologize as I was a little below par health-wise during the appointment, and in pain, so it was difficult to think straight. We had also just seen the report the head of Social Services has sent in for Richard's tribunal, the inference of which is upsetting to say the least. Although I understand that it is all about money and budgets and that the report is not echoing the views of the social workers who actually know the children and with whom I work, it is hard to swallow. I hope that we shall be seen to be vindicated. If not, we shall just have to somehow hold our heads high as we know the efforts and love we have lavished upon all these children, in spite of all their problems, and the wonderful experiences they have had with us.

I apologize for the delay in sending this to you. However, I have been considering your questions over the last few days. Such a lot has happened to us with all the children over a long period of time, as you know, so it isn't easy to dredge through it all. Memories kept cropping up which I've added on over the days. I therefore hope the following ruminations are of some use to you.

I was quite shocked, while watching a television programme late one night about a family with an autistic young son, by just how much we did without really realizing what we were doing which has helped.

This family on the television, who had a team of helpers coming in and out of their house and helping with their single autistic child, was following a programme which was intended to help in both a behavioural and educational way. The helpers worked with him one to one. They brought back his eye contact when it was lost, gently reinforcing successes with treats. They played games, sang to him, talked to him, read to him, did exercises, enforced the child's awareness of his place in the room/world.

We did *all* of this. The difference was we did nearly all of it by ourselves. Somehow by instinct we did these things. We knew nothing of autism at all. We knew nothing of special programmes. We just saw a child whom we loved who couldn't do *anything* and somehow worked at ways to make him 'connect' with the rest of the world. And we were working with the other three children at the same time. I won't be made to feel a bad mother any longer. We did a lot of good fo these children.

As you know it has only been in the very recent past that we have received any help from Social Services and then only minimally for Richard, in the form of two hours' respite over a short period of time during last winter (the respite worker sadly had family problems and he hasn't had any respite, apart from one day in August, since February) and a little financially for Alice (but not any practical hands-on help).

We tried from the very early days to give the children a very strong framework for the days, weeks and years. A pattern they could follow to give them a sense of stability and permanence to compensate for their early childhood experiences. We also tried to be as uncomplicated with them as possible so that they would know where they were with us. 'Yes' meant yes and 'no' meant no. A health visitor commented positively on this in the very early days of our parenthood.

But, as the professor said to me regarding Richard, 'it is true that children who have early years deprivation can display autistic tendencies but they get better'. She pointed out that Richard had been with us 'for eleven years in a stable, loving home and had got worse' which is why she felt it was a genetic problem. Alex's behaviour also seems to have become more extreme as he has got older.

I heard a Radio 4 article a few weeks ago where the mother of two autistic boys described one of them as a 'trained autist'. I connected with that description as I think our children certainly fall into that category.

We have done so much with them over the years that some behaviours have been trained into them. Sadly it has been our misfortune, and the children's, that this has muddied the waters somewhat when it came to accessing diagnoses and help.

The day after the appointment with you I had the misfortune to find Alex's pyjama bottoms outside in the garden, under his bedroom window. They were heavily soiled, and stained with urine. I am not talking about a bit of stained clothing here. This is soiling that had to be *scraped* off, then rinsed, then washed. Having dealt with this and put them in the washing machine I then proceeded to Alex's bedroom as there was an unpleasant smell coming from that part of the house. I stripped off his bed as I wasn't sure if his 'accident' had occurred there or elsewhere, and then traced the source of the bad smell to his wastepaper basket. He had put a heavily soiled, encrusted, pair of underpants into this basket. If it weren't for the fact that this has all happened before I would be aghast.

Alice used to put used sanitary towels outside her window instead of disposing of them in the place provided. She had a lot of 'accidents' and would hide soiled underwear behind furniture, only for it to be discovered sometime later when the smell led us to them.

Richard, during stressful periods at high school, soiled and urinated in his clothes then hid the clothes in the middle of his drawers of clean clothes.

Because there have been a lot of 'accidents' over the years I have taken the attitude that if this happens then they should just rinse underwear through and pop them into the washing machine. No more would be said about it. Yet still they do it. It is almost as if it is deliberate. A means of non-verbal communication if you like. I can only surmise that Alex is very anxious having not heard about his funding for Derwen – he has been checking the post daily – and perhaps is anxious about seeing you even though I had explained very gently to him that there was nothing to worry about and that we were seeing you to try to help him further. He could not tell me when I gently asked why he had put his pyjamas out of the window. I did not pursue it and just asked him not to do it again but suggested that perhaps the washing machine would be a better place for them. He calmly agreed.

'Accidents' most often happen when there is an 'occasion': perhaps if we were going out on a family treat or had taken the children to stay with family or in a hotel. It was then very stressful for us as we had to deal with the dirty bedding, etc.

As I have stated before, but wouldn't do so in front of Alex, he is terribly immature and often misunderstands totally what is going on around him. We have been told by his manager at his supported work scheme that 'he doesn't like being asked to do things sometimes, does he?' I can only assume that he has expressed himself inappropriately with some sort of tantrum when faced with something he was unsure of.

I cannot remember whether I told you about the letterbox incident. Forgive me if I did. Alex will talk the hind leg off a donkey (in a very monotonous tone and usually about a subject which is as dull as ditchwater to most of the population – I've seen the most well-intentioned and kindest eyes simply glaze over under the onslaught).

When Alex's supervisor sent him to post a letter it was to give himself a bit of peace from Alex's incessant chatter. When Alex did not return for quite a while his boss began to be concerned. He walked to the end of the road on the industrial estate. No Alex. He made himself a cup of tea and tried not to panic about losing him. Just as he was finishing his tea Alex puffed in, bright red in the face.

He had not posted the letter in the letterbox, which is just at the end of the road (a two-minute walk), but had gone all the way down into the town centre to the post office (probably a two-mile walk)! They were so relieved that he wasn't lost they all had a good laugh about it and took him out and showed him the post box!

A précis of Alex

Alex:

- Is very pedantic. Something has to be exactly as you've described it or he picks you up on it, often aggressively.

- Will argue black is white.

- Used to flap his hands like a penguin.

- Is very literal and doesn't understand a lot of humour unless it is a 'learned' piece of humour that we've taught him. Irony is very difficult for Alex and we have to explain what we mean, otherwise he starts to huff and puff and gets very cross about why something cannot be exactly as we've said.

- Has, over the years, had a succession of strange facial tics and grimaces. For years there seemed to be something new appearing each week. We might manage to help him get rid of one and then another odd behaviour would crop up. We commented to each other that he was like a semi-deflated balloon. You'd squash one bit in and another part would pop out. It was as though he 'needed' to have something twitching: flicking his tongue in and out was one of them, or fiddling with something. With the benefit of hindsight he probably did need them, but we didn't know.

- Used to rock when little. We distracted him out of this eventually.

- Was hopeless at climbing. Jack, by contrast, climbed everything.

- Was hopeless at team games at school. Was just tolerated really.

- Used to chew on anything; including his bedhead, clothing (holes were regularly chewed in cuffs), tissues, dried glue, plasticine, paper, books, toys – this was mentioned in his first primary school report. I'm funny about people chewing paper, it makes me gag, so I remember this particular one well.

- Used to disappear into school with barely a backward glance, even from early days when other children were grizzling and holding on to their mothers. I used to naïvely believe that this showed a bit of independence and confidence in us. I now think that actually it was more a case of 'out of sight, out of mind'.

- Is very 'Forrest Gump'ish. The way he goes to work is a prime example of this.

- Often misunderstands and flies off the handle. I went to a workshop organized through the NAS given by Phoebe Caldwell. She talked of people who hear the first word and the last word of the sentence. I think this is what Alex does, as often we've said something which was explained in the middle part of the sentence but he has flown off the handle at some imagined slight. We think this could land Alex in very difficult situations if he were with people who didn't understand him. So it is perhaps a blessing that at present he doesn't go out into more 'grown-up' environments by himself.

- Is very formal in his language and has very old-fashioned manners (quite endearing to people but strange).

- Learned to be 'friendly' when taught by us but has no 'friends' as he doesn't know what to do really with a friend. Never invites anyone over or to anywhere else and has *never* been invited to anyone else's house or to socialize.

- Would come on to your lap when little but only for the briefest moment before struggling free and running off to somewhere else.

- Had *no* imaginative play whatsoever. Not a clue. I would make dens for the children (my favourite pastime as a child – I was great at mud pies and making houses in the hollow of a tree). They would sit under the table/tree with me but blankly, and once I left they would follow and have no interest in staying.

- Behaves very immaturely. His care manager (Alex tells me off if I call her his 'social worker') commented on his balling his fists into his eyes during our time with her 'like a mole' (he was 17 ½ years old then). Alex was still appearing, quite voluntarily, in the improvised Nativity play put on by the church during the carol service on Christmas Eve last year. It didn't faze him that he was now probably three feet taller than the other Wise Men (from the lower primary school years). Again quite endearing and gives him pleasure so we didn't dissuade him and the lay minister knows our children and regards them with affection, fortunately. Also, there can't be many sixteen-year-olds who excitedly tell their parents that *Little Mermaid II* is coming out soon on video!

- Reads but really doesn't understand what he's read. Similarly, he will watch a TV programme but cannot explain the plot. The other day I asked if I could just turn over to check the news. He said 'but I'm watching this side'. When I asked conversationally not confrontationally, 'What's it about?' as if I were joining him, he looked at me blankly and said 'I don't know'. It was some sort of thriller like *Silent Witness*. When he was little, in the foster mother's home, we observed him with the television on. He was not engaging at all with the content of any of the brightly coloured programmes but just fought with Richard over the remote control and then flicked from channel to channel (maybe he liked the lights flickering by – I don't know). He still does that if left to his own devices.

- Handles stress in an almost identical fashion to Alice and Richard, i.e. usually with an extreme reaction. This is despite our attempts to simplify the children's lives and make them as stress-free as possible.

- Used to make a huge fuss if someone just 'touched' him saying 'Ow-er' very dramatically. We used to josh him and tell him to stop making a fuss as no-one had hit him. In retrospect, maybe it really *was* hurting him.

- Would, if given a new drinking flask, drink until he wet himself. At other times he wouldn't drink enough.

- Was terrified of fireworks. It has only been in the last few years that we have been able to persuade him to a firework display and even then he still has reservations and puts his fingers in his ears.

- Seems to be able to do things some days but is incapable of repeating the task the next, no matter how many times you teach him.

- Will often 'jump' when you appear even if you have approached normally and none too quietly. It is as though he isn't tuned in or aware you are coming towards him.

- Doesn't know how to dress appropriately. We have to kit him out with the right weight of clothes or he'll be muffled up in the summer and in his summer clothes when it is snowing. Then, when we finally get him into the correct clothes, he won't change to the next season's appropriate clothing until I remind him, usually several times.

- Finds learning things and applying them difficult. We have been teaching him certain things for years but the knowledge doesn't seem to go anywhere.

- Instantly butted in with 'I did that too' when, the other day, Alice mentioned that she is learning first aid at college and said she'd put Daddy into the recovery position. We said would he like to show us how to do this on Daddy then. He looked totally blankly at us and then said 'I did it at college'. He couldn't do it now. The concept of applying something he had learned was simply too much for him. Similarly, he used to spout bits of health and safety regulations at us while he was studying at college. However, he used to leave pan handles sticking out on the cooker and come to supper with hands that reeked of faeces. It would appear that he can write about some of these things if given sufficient help – but simply cannot apply it.

- Is very superficial.

- Likes things his own way.

- Is quite 'disconnected'.

- Was very late achieving all his childhood milestones – sitting up, walking, talking.

- Appears to learn something, only to immediately regress to the previous stage of development – shoelaces and buttons took forever as did riding a bike (a whole year of blood, sweat and tears). He would just stand and wait for someone to do things for him. Getting all four children out of the house in the winter (into coats with buttons or zips, hats, gloves and boots) took ages and was frankly a nightmare.

- Baffled his primary school. He seemed to be able to read one day and then not the next. They found him very difficult to teach as he was so easily distracted and wouldn't sit still. It was unfortunate that the first three school years were taught together in the same large classroom (it is a small village school) and the teachers would constantly find that Alex had wandered away from what he was supposed to be doing and would have his hands in the sand pit or in the water with the much younger children. He used to take 'snacks' from the other children's bags and eat them. All of this caused a lot of friction. There would be an 'incident' virtually every single day.

- Was very much in his own world. We worked and worked with him to draw him in to our world. He will still on occasion gaze, slack-jawed, into middle distance and appear as if nobody were home just as he did when he was five years old.

- Is clumsy. He has broken two washing machines – not deliberately.

- Is socially very awkward with his peers who would be classed as 'normal'. He is much more comfortable with adults who presumably don't make the same demands on him or perhaps make more allowances.

- Was hyperactive when young and had no attention span. He still channel-hops if left alone, making no connection with what he is watching.

- Was, and still is, easily distracted.

- Sometimes used to run around with the boys or play with a ball but really only when my husband or I were there. If left to their own devices the game would break down almost immediately.

- Did not play with his toys – he broke them all.

- Talks *at* people and takes no notice of their reaction to what he is saying. You could die of boredom and he would still keep on. The speech he uses is 'reported'. We could all be watching the same football match or TV programme, for example, and he will tell us what is happening as though we hadn't just seen it for ourselves. We have tried many times to help him to rephrase things but he just doesn't 'get it'.

- Gets very cross if interrupted, cannot pick up where he left off, and will go right back to the start of what he was telling you, several times if interrupted several times!

- Can get quite miffed if someone else wants to say something.

- Does not understand other people's personal space, never has, and will stand right on top of people, much too close for comfort. I have seen people step back and have had to explain to him many times that some people find this intimidating, as he is now nearly six feet tall!

- Has little or no empathy for others.

- Even now doesn't exchange eye contact properly and sometimes I actually have to tell him to rearrange his facial expression. I know that sounds cruel but when he is out in the world I want to try to help him to be accepted.

- Can appear very 'gauche' and naïve. I suppose this is more noticeable now he is so tall and grown-up looking.

- Can be over-affectionate with strangers. I think his care manager was quite surprised when he kissed her when he met her for the second time! This was when we were going through the community care assessment in her office with her, so it could hardly be confused with a social visit! He will also do this with men (we had a painter redecorating our house and he received a smacker!). This has also become a little alarming since he is now man-sized.

- Is very gullible and therefore very vulnerable. When in Year Six of primary school he attended a fete and was walking around on his own. A girl came up to him and asked for money. Alex gave her £5. This was all his money for the day and had been saving his pocket money for months. He was very upset when he realized it had all gone. He never saw it again, of course. This is what his adult life could be like.

- Was persuaded, while at college, to go down to a pub during college hours with a boy he doesn't know very well. He then drew out £10 at a time from his savings account at the building society, until he had spent £50 in a morning on playing pool and buying drinks for the boy. He doesn't go to pubs and has never expressed any interest before or since. Alex is not the sort to bunk off – it's against the rules isn't it? It was a lot of money for him and someone had obviously thought, here's a nice, gullible, easy touch. We handle all his money for him now with his agreement and he has savings for 'college' or for special treats in his account.

- Had terrible problems, and still does sometimes, in unscrambling the words of a sentence so that it is in the right order. This seemed impossible when he was younger and it has taken us years of practice and gentle correction to get his level of communication to the point it is at now. By contrast I cannot remember a time when Jack did not speak in sentences that were in the right order and perfectly tensed. Tense was a mystery to Alex which took, literally, years to sort out. Alex now appears to have quite a large vocabulary but sometimes will use a long or grown-up word and if asked doesn't know what it actually means but has obviously heard someone else using it.

- Usually speaks in a very monotonous voice which the speech therapists don't think is due to a physiological cause.

- Often speaks too loudly.

- Is outraged if anyone breaks 'the rules'.

- Used to receive comments from teachers on how polite and helpful he was. Well primed, I'm afraid. Because conversation was such a problem for them all we would rehearse in the car on the way to school: 'Hello Miss... Did you have a nice weekend/holiday? Can I help?' We were told that he was the most 'diligent register monitor' the high school had ever had! Also, because of their lack of play and therefore lack of ability to amuse themselves, we have always involved the children in helping around the house (with appropriate incentives). They are therefore well used to helping with washing up, peeling potatoes, etc. We felt this also helped them to make the connection that this was 'their' house and that they weren't just visitors. They had spent so much of their formative years being dragged in and out of a series of foster homes we thought this was very important.

- Finds noise distressing and will stick his hands over his ears if it is all getting too much, or too complicated, for him in a conversation. If it is still too much he will run off. It's as if he is emotionally 'overloaded'.

- During a school trip to see Roald Dahl's *The BFG* at the theatre, when in high school, had run out through the emergency exit in the middle of the production, obviously frightened by what was happening on stage, and the teachers had to chase him down the street. Someone 'forgot' to tell us about that incident and we only learnt about it last year!

- Has taken 12 ½ years of us reminding him to 'learn' how to 'feel' that his nose needs blowing. He would get to the stage where he would actually have mucus running down his upper lip until very recently (aged 17 ½) but he did not seem to feel it nor the need to blow his nose. Even at a meeting at his mainstream further education college his tutor had to tell him to blow his nose. This is not something she probably has to do for many of her students!

- Was terrible at writing stories at school and has no imagination.

- Will watch the same videos time after time. Was watching *The Lion King* for the umpteenth time only last Saturday.

- Likes the routine of church.

- Has been, and still is, attention seeking with adults.

- Has always been completely unfazed by other people's disabilities. It is as though he can't see any difference. While in some ways this is admirable it makes one wonder how he 'sees' the rest of the world. The first time we visited Alice at her college for people with moderate learning difficulties, Alex had a great time hanging around with the other students (on a very superficial level because that is how they also operate) and actually wept when we left. He was fifteen then. Is definitely more relaxed with LD people. Perhaps because they make fewer demands on him. He met some LD students whilst he was at mainstream college, although he wasn't on the same course we were told that he gravitated to them during all break times.

- Can only do one thing at a time. He will get very aggressive if, for example, we ask him to take his clean clothes to his room and fetch something while he is there. 'I can only do one thing at a time. Stop asking me to do all these things,' would be his angry response.

- Likes his routines – which we give him. I think we've had virtually the same thing for Sunday tea for the last 12 ½ years: he gets most upset if we haven't any crumpets! And he likes it to be at the same time.

- Gets very anxious when we are about to set off somewhere and will nag me about the time.

- Will wear the same clothes day after day unless otherwise directed.

- Would get, still gets, upset if we give him the wrong cup, not his cup.

- Is surprisingly good with statistics for football and cricket.

- Can pick out simple tunes on the piano. I taught him the basics (as that is all I know). He gets pleasure from this. If he is angry he will often go and play a tune. At a recent function we attended with him there were a cellist and violinist playing. During a break he went to talk to the men. He told me that he'd told them that he played the piano. Then they'd asked him if he had any ambitions. He said, without any trace of embarrassment, that he'd told them 'Yes, to play with both hands!' They must have cracked up! We are hoping if he goes to Derwen that he will learn to play with both hands.

- Relies on us far more than other seventeen-year-olds rely on their parents.

- Needs to have virtually everything organized for him. We believe this was one of the reasons why his stress levels rose and his behaviour deteriorated at home when he was in mainstream further education college. They like to treat their students like young men and women. This was too loose a structure for Alex.

I suppose I could go on and on and perhaps you already think I have. I am trying to give you a sketch of this young man and information that you couldn't possibly glean from an interview with him when he is on 'best behaviour'. If there is anything else we can help you with that will enable you to give Alex a 'label', which I think will be a relief as much to him as us, please let us know.

References

Department for Education (1994) *Code of Practice on the Identification and Assessment of Special Educational Needs.* Crown Copyright 1994. ISBN 0 85522 444 4.

Department for Education and Skills (2001) *Special Educational Needs (SEN): A guide for parents and carers.*

National Assembly for Wales (2002) *Special Educational Needs Code of Practice for Wales.* Crown Copyright 2002. ISBN 0 7504 2757 4.

Williams, M. (undated) *Sendist Challenge or Opportunity?* Peach report, executive summary. www.peach.org.uk

Wing, L. (1996) *The Autistic Spectrum: A Guide for Parents and Professionals.* London: Constable & Robinson.

Index